A CULTURAL HISTORY OF MONEY

VOLUME 3

A Cultural History of Money
General Editor: Bill Maurer

Volume 1
A Cultural History of Money in Antiquity
Edited by Stefan Krmnicek

Volume 2
A Cultural History of Money in the Medieval Age
Edited by Rory Naismith

Volume 3
A Cultural History of Money in the Renaissance
Edited by Stephen Deng

Volume 4
A Cultural History of Money in the Age of Enlightenment
Edited by Christine Desan

Volume 5
A Cultural History of Money in the Age of Empire
Edited by Federico Neiburg and Nigel Dodd

Volume 6
A Cultural History of Money in the Modern Age
Edited by Taylor C. Nelms and David Pedersen

A CULTURAL HISTORY OF MONEY

IN THE RENAISSANCE

Edited by Stephen Deng

BLOOMSBURY ACADEMIC
LONDON • NEW YORK • OXFORD • NEW DELHI • SYDNEY

BLOOMSBURY ACADEMIC
Bloomsbury Publishing Plc
50 Bedford Square, London, WC1B 3DP, UK
1385 Broadway, New York, NY 10018, USA
29 Earlsfort Terrace, Dublin 2, Ireland

BLOOMSBURY, BLOOMSBURY ACADEMIC and the Diana logo are trademarks of
Bloomsbury Publishing Plc

First published in Great Britain 2019
Paperback edition published in 2023

Copyright © Bloomsbury Publishing, 2019

Stephen Deng has asserted his right under the Copyright, Designs and Patents Act, 1988, to be identified as Author of this work.

Series design: Raven Design.
Cover image: *The Master of the Mint*, woodcut by Jost Amman, from *Eigentliche Beschreibung aller Staende*, 1568 (© INTERFOTO/Alamy Stock Photo)

All rights reserved. No part of this publication may be reproduced or transmitted in any form or by any means, electronic or mechanical, including photocopying, recording, or any information storage or retrieval system, without prior permission in writing from the publishers.

Bloomsbury Publishing Plc does not have any control over, or responsibility for, any third-party websites referred to or in this book. All internet addresses given in this book were correct at the time of going to press. The author and publisher regret any inconvenience caused if addresses have changed or sites have ceased to exist, but can accept no responsibility for any such changes.

A catalogue record for this book is available from the British Library.

A catalog record for this book is available from the Library of Congress.

ISBN: PB Set: 978-1-3503-6718-0
HB: 978-1-4742-3709-3
PB: 978-1-3503-6548-3
ePDF: 978-1-3502-5349-0
eBook: 978-1-3-5025-350-6

Series: The Cultural Histories Series

Typeset by RefineCatch Limited, Bungay, Suffolk
Printed and bound in Great Britain

To find out more about our authors and books visit www.bloomsbury.com and sign up for our newsletters..

CONTENTS

LIST OF ILLUSTRATIONS vii
NOTES ON CONTRIBUTORS xi
SERIES PREFACE xiii

Introduction 1
Stephen Deng

1 Money and its Technologies: Mining, Metallurgy, Minting, and
 Non-Metallic Monetary Forms 15
 Arturo Giráldéz

2 Money and its Ideas: Justice, Sovereignty, and the Idea of
 Money as Commodity 39
 Bradley D. Ryner

3 Money, Ritual, and Religion: God's Stamp and the
 Problem of Usury 59
 Stephen Deng

4 Money and the Everyday: Reputation, History, and Symbolism
 on the Eastern African Coast 79
 Stephanie Wynne-Jones

5 Money, Art, and Representation: Text, Image, and Message 99
 Barrie Cook

6 Money and its Interpretation: Two Early Modern Transactions   127
   David J. Baker

7 Money and the Issues of the Age: Coinage, Sovereignty, and the
   Liquidity of Imagination   149
   Brian Sheerin

NOTES   171
BIBLIOGRAPHY   177
INDEX   191

LIST OF ILLUSTRATIONS

FIGURES

CHAPTER 1

1.1	Gold French ecu of François I.	17
1.2	500 reais gold coin ("cruzado"), King Sebastian of Portugal (1557–78).	18
1.3	Transylvania 1681 25 ducat.	19
1.4	Engraving from *De re metallica* di Georg Agricola, Basilea, 1556.	20
1.5	Joachimsthaler, 1525.	21
1.6	Drawing from *De la Pirotechnia*, 1558.	22
1.7	Tokugawa coin—Tensho oban.	24
1.8	Piece of Eight—Potosí 1770.	27
1.9	Cowrie shells.	35

CHAPTER 3

3.1	Maerten de Vos, Render unto Caesar, 1602.	60
3.2	Lucas van Doetechum (1530–84), Parable of the Talents etching.	67
3.3	Jan Provoost, *Death and the Miser*, early 1500s.	69
3.4	Anonymous (Hans Holbein?), Jean Calvin, 1550s.	72

CHAPTER 4

4.1	Map of Eastern Africa showing major sites mentioned in the text.	81
4.2	Silver coins from the Mtambwe Mkuu hoard, with Ali ibn al-Hasan coin inset.	83
4.3	Map of Kilwa Archipelago, showing sites of Kilwa Kisiwani and Songo Mnara.	88
4.4	Pierced Kilwa-type coin from excavations at Songo Mnara.	95

CHAPTER 5

5.1	Gold sovereign, James I, First coinage, 1603–4.	100
5.2	Bronze coin, Emperor Xuanzong (1426–35).	102
5.3	Gold coin of Suleiman I.	106
5.4	Gold mohur of Emperor Jahangir, Agra mint, Taurus.	108
5.5	Morocco, Muhammad al-Walid ibn Zaydan al-Nasir, 1631–3.	109
5.6	Silver larin of the Safavid Shah Tahmasp I (1524–76), Shiraz mint.	111
5.7	Thai ring money, 15th–17th century.	111
5.8	Silver ducatone, Emperor Charles V, Milan.	116
5.9	Gold 4-excelentes, Ferdinand and Isabella, Seville mint.	118
5.10	Gold 10-ducats, Hamburg, 1675.	120
5.11	Bermudan hogg coin.	124

CHAPTER 6

6.1	Post-medieval clipped silver coin, probably a shilling of Elizabeth I.	129
6.2	Promissory note for £10 from Robert Pilkington of Limestreet, London, to Charles Rich of the New Exchange.	130
6.3	Fitting out a hull [graphic]/W. Hollar, fecit.	134
6.4	Portrait of a Man, Maarten van Heemskerck, 1529.	135
6.5	7 gold coins.	139
6.6	*The Shomakers Holiday. Or The Gentle Craft.*	142
6.7	Clipped shilling.	147

CHAPTER 7

7.1	Sixpence of Elizabeth I—struck counterfeit, obverse.	151
7.2	Lead token decorated with six-petalled flower, with casting sprue attached.	153
7.3	Post-medieval trade token: City of Bristol square token.	154
7.4	GLO-160256 James I farthing.	155
7.5	Post-medieval coin, groat of Henry VIII, 3rd coinage.	157

TABLES

CHAPTER 4

4.1	Chronology of major Kilwa-type issues.	84
4.2	Coins at Songo Mnara by context type.	90
4.3	Proportions of sultans/rulers on Kilwa coins.	92

NOTES ON CONTRIBUTORS

David J. Baker is Peter G. Phialas Professor in the Department of English and Comparative Literature at the University of North Carolina at Chapel Hill. He is the author of *Between Nations: Shakespeare, Spenser, Marvell and the Question of Britain* (1997) and *On Demand: Writing for the Market in Early Modern England* (2010). With Willy Maley, he is the co-editor of *British Identity and English Renaissance Literature* (2002).

Barrie Cook has been Curator of Medieval and Early Modern Coinage in the Department of Coins and Medals at the British Museum since 1985 and is currently the department's Senior Curator. He has published widely in his specialist area of numismatics and monetary history in both academic and popular fields. Amongst Cook's publications are: *English Medieval Coin Hoards*, Vol. 1: *Cross and Crosslets, Short Cross and Long Cross Hoards*, with M.M. Archibald (2001); *Coinage and History in the North Sea World c. 500–1250: Essays in Honour of Marion Archibald*, co-edited with Gareth Williams (2006); and *Angels and Ducats: Shakespeare's Money and Medals* (2012).

Stephen Deng is Associate Professor of English at Michigan State University. He is the author of *Coinage and State Formation in Early Modern English Literature* (2011) and co-editor of *Global Traffic: Discourses and Practices of Trade in English Literature and Culture from 1550–1700* (2008). Deng is currently working on a second monograph on *Hamlet* and accountability.

Arturo Giráldez is currently Professor at University of the Pacific (Stockton, California). He has published with Dennis O. Flynn articles on the global economy and precious metals during the modern era. He also has published and edited volumes on the history of the Pacific Ocean, including *The Age of Trade: The Manila Galleons and the Dawn of the Global Economy* (2015) and with Dennis O. Flynn, *China and the Birth of Globalization in the 16th Century* (2010).

Bradley D. Ryner is an Associate Professor of English at Arizona State University. He is the author of *Performing Economic Thought: English Drama and Mercantile Writing 1600–1642* (2014) and a co-editor of *Early Modern Drama in Performance: Essays in Honor of Lois Potter* (2015).

Brian Sheerin is Associate Professor of Renaissance Literature at St. Edward's University in Austin, Texas. He has published on credit economies and patronage culture in early modern England, and currently studies intersections of Renaissance mathematics and Elizabethan literary theory. He is the author of *Desires of Credit in Early Modern Theory and Drama: Commerce, Poesy, and the Profitable Imagination* (2016).

Stephanie Wynne-Jones is Senior Lecturer in the Department of Archaeology at the University of York. She is also a Core Group member of the Center for Urban Network Evolutions, Aarhus University, and an Honorary Research Fellow at the University of South Africa, Pretoria. Her work focuses on objects and spaces in the archaeology of Eastern Africa and she specializes in Swahili coastal culture. Her recent book, *A Material Culture: Consumption and Materiality on the Coast of Precolonial East Africa* (2016), explores the ways we can understand coastal towns through their engagement with the material world.

SERIES PREFACE

When the British Museum decided in 2012 to redesign Room 68, the hall containing objects from its Department of Coins and Medals, its curators made a bold departure from how numismatic material had conventionally been displayed. Rather than cases filled with rows upon rows of gold, silver, and bronze coins of European antiquity, the new gallery design featured all manner of objects, not limited to coin or paper currency, capturing the history of transactional artifacts and infrastructures, from shells to mobile phones. Each case had a theme: cases on one side of the gallery spotlighted money's institutional supports and issuing authorities, while cases on the other underscored all the myriad ways people use money, not just for exchange or payment but for ritual or religious observance, political contestation, adornment, and storytelling.

The intention in preparing these six volumes was to provide readers with a similar experience, inviting them into the wonder-cabinets of money in all its variegation, multiplicity, and complexity. What emerges is money's irreducible plurality, the multiple stories it tells. Money opens windows into plural economic and moral worlds, too, worlds of value and evaluation, wealth and worth. Never merely coin, cash, or credit rendered in strictly economic terms, money is so much more than the old couplet would have it: "Money is a matter of functions four: a medium, a measure, a standard, a store." Instead, money is always also a medium of communication, a set of instruments with which people exchange messages with one another—about price, to be sure, but also about political conviction and authority, fealty, desire, or disdain. And money is a method of memorializing the past so that relations established among people, institutions, the gods, and the ancestors can be carried forward through the present and into near, distant, and imaginary futures.

Money is in this sense both irredeemably "cultural" and "historical," and so it is apt that this six-volume Cultural History of Money should spotlight money's relation to religion, technology, the arts and literature, everyday life, metaphysical interpretation, and a wide variety of issues of the age. While many contributors to the first several volumes are numismatists and archaeologists, trucking in the material evidence of coin and bullion, the volumes also contain contributions from scholars of digital infrastructures, literary and legal historians and science fiction scholars, sociologists and anthropologists, economists and artists.

Archaeologists have long bemoaned the fact that the great majority of ancient coins in museums and private collections today were unearthed without any data having been collected on their surrounding context, rendering much of the ancient and even more recent past a mystery. Even where the context for a particular find is present, its interpretation is always ambiguous. In the contemporary period, money is surrounded by context—cables and wireless signals, data protocols and computer servers, lobbying groups' and legislators' voluminous writings, television soap operas and online social media. Yet, just as with ancient hoards, we have difficulty escaping our own assumptions about what money is, what people do with it, and the style with which they do so.

Take a basic plastic credit card transaction at a physical till. How many users of this everyday payment device would be able to explain how it works? How would a museum curate this technological assemblage? Moving from the simple act of paying to more involved interactions with money, how might an archaeologist of the future deduce, for example, the practice in some Central Asian Muslim immigrant communities known as the "Imam Zamin," which consists of the wrapping of a coin in a piece of cloth tied about the upper arm to protect a traveler? Or the practice from around 2005–9 of what people called "doing tuning"(튜닝하다) to a transit card in Seoul, Korea—dissolving the plastic payment card with acetone so as to remove the radio-frequency identification (RFID) antenna and chip, and creatively stitching it into one's pocketbook, bracelet, or the elbow patches of one's blazer, so you can breeze through the turnstile, with style?

Trapped in our own "coin consciousness," we assume money has to be, or that its value should be found in, a tangible thing, despite the fact that our own interactions with it are increasingly dematerialized in digital networks. We hold on to bullionist conceptions of money's worth, despite our bearing continuous witness to its fluctuations based on prevailing political whims. We think of money as abstract, even as we use it in the most concrete and interpersonal relations. We believe money equilibrates values, rendering goods and services commensurable with one another, measured on one scale of value, even as we use money to demarcate difference—national difference, religious difference, intergenerational difference, differences in class, race, and gender.

The periodization of these volumes is somewhat arbitrary but still Eurocentric. The selection of authors and themes is intended to help disturb this Western-oriented history by globalizing it and insisting on bringing into the frame its political, imperial, and often racial dynamics.

The chapters in these volumes capture money's complexities in both substance and form. In substance, insofar as they attempt a cross-cultural, transhistorical survey of money technologies and cultures that will illuminate its variability and complexity. In form, in that each volume takes up the same thematic areas, but in reading across the volumes one will discover that these themes are themselves complicated by having different eras' understandings of said theme juxtaposed with other eras' often incompatible understandings. Like a ledger book, then—one of the most basic manifestations of money's recordkeeping devices—the volume can be read "down," reading the chapters within one historical period, and "across," reading the affiliated thematic chapters from volume to volume. What emerges is an affirmation that money itself is a cultural history.

Bill Maurer
University of California, Irvine

Introduction

STEPHEN DENG

Conceptions of money in the Renaissance or early modern period,[1] the period roughly between 1400 and 1700, were quite different from those of today. Of course, there was no electronic money, credit cards, bitcoin, etc., but also paper money was just in its infancy[2] and was not in widespread use. Banking systems were relatively small in the period and not typically utilized by the general populace; they were primarily used only by merchants involved in long-distance trade, who themselves sometimes served as "merchant bankers." Although credit was widespread and important, especially for small, local transactions, when most people thought of "money" in the period, they thought of *coinage*, usually either gold- or silver-based tokens that were stamped with insignia of the local authority that produced it (typically, but not always, "the state").[3] Some authorities did use coins made from less precious or base metals, like copper, for small denomination coins. Fernand Braudel refers to copper coins as "black money" (because it blackened quickly with use) employed by "people of small means and the poor" (1981: 458).[4] But coinage in the period primarily consisted of gold and silver in a "bimetallic," virtually worldwide, monetary system.[5]

The stamp was thought to guarantee the quality of the coin, but the coins circulating were generally not uniform, partly because the most common form of money produced by mints all over the world was "hammered coinage," which was relatively cheap to produce but often did not result in high-quality coins. Arturo Giráldez and Barrie Cook note in their chapters in this volume that there were some experiments with trying to produce more uniform coinage—for example, through the use of machinery such as presses and mills—but this technology was often expensive and dangerous, and moneyers, who were concerned about losing their jobs to the machines, resisted their use. In addition to non-uniformity due to the way coins were made, as Cook discusses, we also see mixing of newer coins with older ones, those produced by a previous regime, and even the mixing of various issuers from a given time, sometimes without the permission of the authority in whose realm the outside coin circulated.

So, part of the irregularity in coinage occurred from the circulation of coins by legitimate, or previously legitimate, issuers of coins. However, other causes of non-uniformity involved illegal methods of manipulation. For example, some of the circulating coins would have metal clipped from the edge, with the assumption that the coin could still pass current, while the clipper could obtain some of the precious metal. As Giráldez notes, if the intrinsic value of the coin exceeded its face value, the coin could even be melted down or be taken out of the realm to be used for its metal content, while people would tend to use "cheaper" coins (those whose face value was higher than the intrinsic value of the metal) to pay for taxes and legal obligations. Counterfeiting, the production of coins that look like legitimate coins but have less precious metal content (or none at all), was also common in the period. Some governments would even "debase" the coinage by putting less precious metal content in the coins, in effect mimicking the actions of counterfeiters but from a supposedly legitimate authority.[6] Therefore, while people in the period relied upon coinage as the primary store of value and medium of exchange, sometimes the unreliability of this medium created distrust and uncertainty about the very nature of money. If, for example, a debased, clipped, or counterfeit coin could still pass current, what then was the source of monetary value?

INTRINSIC AND EXTRINSIC THEORIES OF VALUE

This ambiguity about the nature of monetary value, when money primarily consisted of non-uniform coinage, gave rise to two main competing theories of value: the intrinsic and extrinsic theories.[7] According to the *intrinsic* theory of monetary value, a coin was only as valuable as its precious metal content. The stamp on the coin was only supposed to be a guarantee by the issuing authority that the coin contained a certain quantity of this precious metal. The *extrinsic* theory instead held that the stamp itself conferred value on the coin. People would generally believe that the stamp, as a representation of the issuing authority, would allow a coin to pass current at its stated face value regardless of the quality and quantity of the underlying metal. Because the intrinsic theory had a longer established history, there were difficulties in accepting the latter theory when the coinage reached such a poor state—either through clipping, counterfeiting, or debasement—that its users worried whether another party would accept the coin. This was especially true for foreign exchange: if the general quality of coinage from one country deteriorated, the rate of exchange for that country's currency tended to decrease as other countries lost faith in the coinage. As Brian Sheerin discusses in his chapter, an important contribution to the extrinsic theory of monetary value emerged in France in the sixteenth century, with writers such as Charles Dumoulin and François Hotman, who developed the "nominalist" theory, which stated that monetary value was based in the nominal face value of the coin established by authorities rather than by the intrinsic qualities of the coin. But, as Sheerin also notes, this theory remained mostly marginal before the seventeenth century because of the predominance of the belief that coins should have intrinsic worth based on precious metal content.

However, most people using money in the Renaissance were not contemplating the theoretical source of monetary value in everyday exchanges. As with any common practice, theory and praxis were often at odds. The use of copper coins or base tokens in the period—for example, the practice David J. Baker describes in his chapter of local businesses issuing "trade tokens" or "tavern tokens," small change issued at and accepted by certain business establishments such as taverns or even by other establishments in a given neighborhood—seems to fly in the face of the intrinsic theory of monetary value; and, yet, people were still willing to engage in these kinds of transactions. At times, counterfeit coins even replaced "real" coins as the main medium of circulation. Even when people knew a coin was not of its purported value, they believed that others would accept it *as if* the coin were of that value. As long as no one made waves and refused to accept a coin, the entire system could continue to function regardless of the quality of the coins involved. For this reason, while most people probably continued to believe, *in theory*, in intrinsic monetary value, *in practice*, they likely acted as if the extrinsic theory were in effect. Again, however, continued circulation of deteriorating coins could only function on the local level; international money markets would "punish" a country for the general quality of its coinage through shifting international exchange rates. And coins that deteriorated substantially might not even be accepted locally, as was the case for *groats*, lower-valued ostensibly silver coins, that had been debased by Henry VIII (see Baker's chapter on this instance).

At the very center of these competing theories was the nature of the coin's stamp, the key factor differentiating a coin from the mere gold or silver commodity. The question is whether the stamp guaranteed a certain value for the coin based on intrinsic content or itself conferred value on the coin based on social acceptance of the issuing authority as a conferrer of value. Sheerin explains in his chapter that "thinking about the reality of money has everything to do with evaluating the face of the sovereign; to what extent does that face merely verify the coin's value in tale, and to what extent does it *create* that value to begin with?" Interpretation of the stamp would have direct bearing on the power of the issuing authority. For example, paper fiat money, such as modern US dollar bills after going off of the gold standard, relies entirely on extrinsic value because the underlying paper is not worth the designated amount printed on them, and they cannot redeem a certain quantity of gold. This extrinsic value, in turn, depends entirely on faith that the bill will be accepted by another party at the face value. But part of that faith stems from belief that the issuing authority, the US state, will persist and remain financially strong. States in weak financial condition tend to face inflation, or even hyperinflation, because people believe that the value of their bills will continue to decrease due to the financial position of the issuer. Stability of value therefore relies upon faith in the issuing authority. For precious metal coinage, that faith is not necessary as long as one believes that the intrinsic value of the coin is consistent with its face value. On the other hand, if the stamp is seen to confer value on the coin, then we see an expression of faith in the issuing authority's ability to produce value *ex nihilo*. The ambiguity as to the source of monetary value also reflects an ambiguity about general attitudes toward political authorities of the period.

Therefore, the reputation of the issuing authority would affect the populace's attitude toward the coins they are using. Conversely, the quality of the coin—especially its precious metal content—would directly affect the reputation of the issuing authority. Any deterioration in quality would have bearing on the trust people had that the stamp connoted the purported value. The issuing authority's reputation—as well as the country's, for that matter—could be damaged, especially if the authority purposely debased the coinage, that is, issued coins of inferior quality in order to extract from the populace more "seigniorage," the surplus value representing the difference between the face value of coins and the costs of producing the coin, including the "brassage" paid to the mint master for their production, as described by Giráldez. Sheerin explains that debasement could happen in multiple ways: the authority might "cry up" the value of the coins in circulation without any change in the actual circulating coins; it might reduce the coins' weight while keeping the face value constant; it might reduce the precious metal content by mixing base metals with the precious while maintaining current face value; or, it might perform a combination of these practices. One of the most infamous debasements—what came to be known as the Great Debasement—occurred under Henry VIII. The quality of English "sterling" had been mostly maintained for several hundred years. But in the mid-sixteenth century, Henry debased his coinage in order to generate revenue, and English coins quickly lost their reputation in international markets, while becoming subject to many internal jokes. Shakespeare's Hotspur in *1 Henry IV*, for example, refers to the "bloody noses" that must "pass current," a reference to the reddish tint from the copper content and the prominent nose of Henry on his debased testoon.[8] Henry's daughter, Elizabeth I, was quick to restore the quality of the coinage upon taking the throne, but the event had damaged the reputation of English coinage for years to come.

ICONOGRAPHY AND NON-EXCHANGE USES OF COINAGE

Allusions to Henry's stamped face on his debased coins point to another key element of coinage: its visual properties. As a visual representation of the issuing authority, the stamp could perform political and religious work through its iconography, in addition to the economic work through its exchange. As Cook writes in his chapter, the stamp could "reflect the power, the authority, the self-image" of that authority as well as promote religious affiliation and belief systems.[9] Moreover, it might attempt to impress aesthetically by reflecting artistic innovations, culminating in the development of "prestige coins," coins meant as much to be admired for their visual properties as to be used in exchange, and transformation of the coin engraver to the status of esteemed artist. In the Renaissance, Cook notes, one key trend was toward naturalism or realism akin to classical models, which "provided a new conceptual framework for representing personalized authority." However, as "a deeply conservative medium," Cook continues, coins had to connote "trust and familiarity above novelty and variety," and therefore "needed not only to feel right and weigh right, but also to look right." While there was room for some innovation in coin design, any deviations too far from accepted norms might lead to popular distrust of the monetary instrument.

Some coinage traditions, such as Chinese and Islamic coinage, emphasized textual components over visual. Chinese coins, for example, employed minimalist design, with only writing specifying the ruler and sometimes the mint where the coin was produced: no ideological or religious component. Cook asserts that despite the minimalism of this design, "it was evidently viewed as being of political significance, control of coinage being such a fundamental aspect of legitimate government." Islamic coinage, on the other hand, tended to promote religious views by including (though not always) the *shahada* or Profession of Faith: "There is no god but God; Muhammad is the Prophet of God." In her chapter in this volume, Stephanie Wynne-Jones discusses Swahili coins, which, while unique in design, contain Arabic inscriptions invoking Allah and promoting Islamic belief.[10] European and South Asian traditions relied more on a combination of text and image, with iconography representative of the issuing political authority being conveyed through images of royalty or power, like the English sovereign coin, which depicted the ruler aboard one of his ships to convey the sense of naval power.

Because of their visual properties, coins could be used for purposes other than mere exchange. Wynne-Jones discusses how precolonial Swahili Coast money was used "as stores or markers of value; as structured deposits in the foundations of houses; as offerings on tombs; as decorative objects for adornment and display; and as mnemonics for the creation and maintenance of history." The recovery of various coins in sites related to domestic activities, such as near wells or household walls, suggest that these coins were part of everyday practices other than their use in commercial exchange, despite the emphasis on the part these towns played in international trade. In *Coinage and State Formation in Early Modern English Literature* (Deng 2011), I discuss the use of a particular English coin, the angel, in a healing ceremony performed by the monarch to aid patients suffering from the skin disease, scrofula. After the king "touched" subjects, he placed a coin, which was pierced and attached to a ribbon, around their necks and asked them never to part from the coins. Nevertheless, some of these tokens seem to have been passed on to others suffering from scrofula, as if the king's touch had become embodied in these "sacred commodities" (Deng 2011: 137–44). Such examples testify to Wynne-Jones's conclusion that there was "a range of everyday object roles," other than that of economic exchange, "that were . . . fulfilled by coins" for various localized purposes.

WORLD MARKETS AND MERCANTILIST DISCOURSE

And, yet, despite the peculiar local uses of coins, as metallic tokens they maintained value in world commodity markets. As Wynne-Jones notes, "the coins of the Swahili coast fitted within the broader monetary world of Islam, where gold dinars and silver dirhams, as well as lower denominations of copper, set the standard for international measures of value." Regardless of what design was put on the coinage, production relied upon a steady supply of the precious metals used to make them. Giráldez identifies the important European mining districts for silver and copper: Bohemia, Saxony, Tyrol, Hungary, Alsace, and Silesia. But Japan was another important supplier of silver, producing what Ward Barret estimates at around 30 percent of the world's supply of silver in the sixteenth century (1990: 225). And after contact with the Americas, the world's silver production expanded dramatically, leading to the enormous inflation in what has been called the "Price Revolution." Later, as Giráldez notes, metal production would shift towards gold, primarily because the global price of silver declined as production from the Americas continued to increase. During the late seventeenth and early eighteenth centuries, the shift toward gold, whose main beneficiary became Britain, would presage the rise of an international gold standard that would persist into the twentieth century.

Consideration of local monetary dependence on world markets would also influence conceptions of how much power individual states could maintain in the face of global forces, especially when countries experienced significant loss of specie to make coinage. This would give rise to the discourses on how money flows internationally that has come to be known collectively as "mercantilism." As Bradley D. Ryner notes in this volume, early writing on global monetary matters, which were influenced by Aristotle and scholastic thought, would emphasize moral theories of justice in relation to money. This meant that there was a "just value" for any given country's money in relation to the value of other countries' money based on the quantity of specie contained in each coin. A sovereign should therefore maintain and protect the just value of the country's currency against any attempts at manipulating exchange rates. One such proponent, Gerard de Malynes, argued that foreign bankers were purposely keeping the pound sterling low so that foreign countries might steal English specie, the reason for a great outflow of metals observed in the 1620s. In his *Treatise of the Canker of Englands Common Wealth*, Malynes called this exchange manipulation "the very efficient cause" of the trade deficit, "and consequently of the decrease of our wealth, & exportation of our monies" (1601b: sig. B8v). The purposeful undervaluing of English money created an incentive to export it as specie to be used in other countries. Moreover, Malynes argued that the outflow of gold and silver to foreign countries would accelerate increases in foreign prices, forcing English consumers to buy foreign commodities "too dear," and thereby exacerbating the trade deficit by increasing expenditure on foreign products (1601b: sig. B2r, D2r).

But, as Ryner notes, during the seventeenth century, the emphasis shifted away from notions of a just value for money that monarchs should attempt to maintain toward what he describes as "empirical questions of the causes and effects of changes in monetary value," which is thought of "as the result of complex international relationships, subject to political decisions made within the bounds of global economic forces." Thomas Mun, a director of the English East India Company, countered Malynes' explanation by calling the exchange "a mere fallacy of the cause ... a Secondary means," since "it is not the undervaluing of our money in exchange, but the overballancing of our trade that carrieth away our treasure" (1664: sig. H4v, H1r). Mun argued that the balance of trade, the difference between exports and imports, drives balance of payments and not vice versa, since exchange rates are merely "Passive" responses to the "over or under ballance of the several Trades which are Predominant and Active" (1664: sig. I4r).[11] If the English wished to increase their wealth, Mun argued, they "must ever observe this rule; to sell more to strangers yearly than wee consume of theirs in value" (1664: sig. B6r). This suggested that local governments have less control over global forces of commerce; if the monarch's attempt to maintain just monetary value proves futile, it demotes the power of local authorities, who in some theories of monetary value had been thought to be the source of value.

One of the key innovations that permitted global flows of capital without the need to carry large quantities of precious metal was the bill of exchange, or *cambium per lettras* ("exchange through documents"). Bills of exchange, which date back to the period of the Crusades when large amounts of money were required to be transferred to finance campaigns,[12] were contracts for a set amount of money in a given currency to be delivered to a specific party at a set place and time upon receipt of the bill. They were often issued by banks in Italy and France, then eventually in the Low Countries, which were initially established for dealing with foreign exchange transactions (Davies 2002: 154–7). A person who wanted to transport value would purchase a bill of exchange from a banker for a set amount of (usually) local currency. The bill would then stipulate that the person would be able to claim a set amount of (usually) another currency at a specific place and time. It was a way of allowing "money" to circulate long distances without the danger of coinage being lost at sea or stolen. In addition to being a foreign exchange transaction, in the case that the specified currencies differed, it was also a way for bankers to charge interest by taking a premium for the issuing of the bill.

USURY AND CREDIT

Because of this potential for charging implicit interest on transactions, bills of exchange were often used in the medieval period to avoid usury laws. Usury, usually understood to mean any charging of interest on loans that is profitable to the lender, was prohibited in most Christian countries because of biblical passages such as Exodus 22:25 ("If thou shalt geve monie to lone unto my poore people which dwelleth with thee, thou shalt not be instant upon him as an importunate wringer, neither shalt thou oppresse him with usurie") and Deuteronomy 23:20–1 ("Thou shalt not increase monie upon thy brother by usurie, nor corne, nor any other thing: but do that to thine enemy") (quoted in Jones 1989: 7). The latter suggested the possibility of lending at interest to those not considered your "brothers," but generally this was understood to exclude any charging of interest within Christian countries (and similar prohibitions existed in Islamic countries as well). Bills of exchange, however, justified charging interest on the grounds that the profit was uncertain because of fluctuating exchange rates. The bill was not a direct loan because it did not specify a greater quantity of the same currency to be returned to the lender. Rather, repayment would be made in another currency, whose value in relation to the borrower's currency might depreciate by the time of the final delivery. Bills of exchange were therefore a convenient device for establishing an indirect method of charging interest on loans at a time when the practice was generally considered abhorrent.

Usury remained a controversial practice because it implied that money could be used to make more money, especially from motives of greed and at the expense of a "brother." In addition to biblical prohibitions, anti-usury discourse cited Aristotle's discussion of the Greek term for usury, *tokos* or "offspring," which suggested a type of breeding: for Aristotle, an unnatural form of breeding that perverted the concept of natural procreation. Both classical and biblical sources were frequently cited in works such as Thomas Wilson's *A Discourse Vppon Vsurye* (1572), a fictional dialogue ultimately condemning all usury, published around the time of a 1571 statute implicitly permitting the charging of interest up to 10 percent within England. Still, as I note in my chapter in this volume, proponents for allowing a certain maximum permissible rate of interest charged on loans would reinterpret scripture to distinguish between destructive types of usury, denoted by the Hebrew term *neschech* ("biting"), and the more productive types, denoted by the term *tarbit* ("increase"). This differentiation between destructive and productive forms of interest-taking would become transformed into legal rates of interest charging versus "usurious" loans charging excessive amounts. Specific numerical boundaries between regular "interest" and "usury" continue to this day, according, for example, to individual state regulations, forbidding interest rates above a certain amount in order to prevent economic exploitation.

Despite these anxieties about lending and borrowing, as Baker and Sheerin note in their chapters, credit networks were an essential aspect of European economies because the countries experienced frequent coin shortages, especially for lower-denomination coins, primarily because of the global flows of specie. As economies rapidly expanded, the demand for money often outpaced its supply, requiring an alternative system for many transactions. For this reason, systems of credit were employed in the period, the extent of which has been thoroughly documented for England by Craig Muldrew in *The Economy of Obligation* (1998). As I mentioned above, some transactions were carried out by the use of locally produced tokens made of base metal and good only for specific neighborhoods, but the period also witnessed the development of a system of trust, in which people wrote down amounts owed in a ledger and only occasionally settled accounts. For example, as Herman Van der Wee describes, a "shopkeeper would have a current account with the brewer-innkeeper and the latter would keep a reciprocal account with the shopkeeper; periodically the accounts were closed and only the balance was paid in hard cash" (1977: 301–2). One's reputation for paying one's debts was, of course, critical for this system, and, like the tokens, they tended to function only in local settings, towns, or neighborhoods, where everyone knew the trustworthiness of others. If particular people were known not to pay their debts, it would be difficult for them to engage in transactions without ready intrinsically valuable coins. As Baker writes:

> Because most of the participants in a deal would have owed money to some, and be owed money by others, reputation—the communal verdict on a person's trustworthiness, neighborliness, and even godliness—was crucial. It

was this social index that allowed the early modern English to calculate one another's probable economic behavior, and it was this calculation that came first, before the more abstract estimation of profit and loss that we think of as accounting.

Baker finds in this "social index" the main "interpretive" problem for English transactors, who did not have the advantage of modern institutions like global banks and credit-rating agencies to gauge the trustworthiness of people. As Muldrew notes: "Many bargains ... were remembered differently by the parties involved and payments to third parties could also be communicated badly ... Notes were also lost and payments were forgotten. Arguments over the nature of contracts took place, as did disputes over poor or damaged goods" (1998: 199). There was sometimes legal recourse if a party did not pay a debt, as indicated by the prodigious expansion in debt litigation in late sixteenth-century England. But such legal actions were less than desirable and so people needed not only to make sense of a complex system but also to negotiate the complexities of social bonds under conditions of uncertainty.[13]

THE EMERGENCE OF RESERVE-BASED BANKING AND PAPER MONEY

Informal systems of credit relying upon the local reputations of community members would eventually be replaced by formal institutions of credit in extensive banking networks that would employ collateral and measures of credit risk for individual borrowers when lending money. Such large systems did not yet exist in the early modern period, but components of the modern banking structure emerged at various times and places in the period.[14] Most historians believe that European banking originated not with moneylenders or even pawnbrokers, but with money changers, most of whom were merchants as well; they changed money as one component of their overall business (Hunt and Murray 1999: 64). According to Raymond De Roover, the first references to modern banking practices in Europe are found in notarial records from the twelfth and thirteenth centuries in Genoa around the time of the Crusades. These records demonstrate that the *bancherii* were forming partnerships, accepting both time deposits (in which money is deposited for a minimum amount of time and sometimes earned interest or a share of profits, the latter a result of prohibitions against usury) and demand deposits (in which money would be reclaimable upon demand, usually not earning interest), extending credit to some customers, usually by allowing them to overdraw their accounts, and even participating directly in overseas ventures (1974: 200–1).[15]

The main function of banks in the Middle Ages, however, was to maintain deposits of clients for safe-keeping and just to transfer balances between clients in order to settle accounts, the so-called "giro system." In some instances, credit was issued in the case of overdrafts, but these tended only to be granted to select clients, and banking based on fractional reserves (when the actual money in the bank remains lower than the total outstanding credit or obligations) remained illegal in most towns. This system of credit, therefore, remained relatively small (Hunt and Murray 1999: 64). The general emphasis during the period is on banking not as credit but as *exchange*, especially involving exchange of assets between countries. Merchant bankers of the period were typically those, according to De Roover, "who dealt extensively in foreign exchange by means of correspondents abroad" (1974: 206). The rise of modern banking would be defined primarily by a bank's capacity actually to produce circulating currency, in the form of checks or banknotes, backed up only by a fraction of its outstanding obligations in reserves. That is, modern banking went hand in hand with various currencies in paper form.

This shift to paper money as the primary form of currency would not be complete until the beginning of the eighteenth century, when paper forms of money exceeded metallic forms in England, Wales, and Scotland (Davies 2002: 279). But the development of paper forms of currency occurred much earlier. The earliest banknotes are attributed to China under the reign of Hien Tseng (806–21), who felt the need to adopt this form of currency due to a dearth of copper. Other Chinese states followed suit, and paper money continued to be used in various kingdoms of the region—including within Kublai Khan's Mongolian empire, as famously described in Marco Polo's *Travels*—until about 1455, at which point there is no mention of paper money, after several years when the money appears to have been substantially devalued. Persistent issue of these notes would lead to periods of severe inflation, and rigid state control would be required for the people to be willing to use the money—other forms of currency, especially the use of precious metals, had to be strictly forbidden. Such a system was attempted in the Kingdom of Persia in 1294, following a depletion of the king's treasury. A proclamation declared the death penalty for all who refused to accept the paper money, but the experiment only lasted about two months, after which trade and commerce seem to have collapsed within the kingdom (Davies 2002: 181, 184, 183).

In Europe, paper money would emerge not from strict state control, but from the rise of private goldsmith bankers in England during the 1630s. Initially, scriveners—legal experts who would draw up contracts, bonds, mortgages, etc. and often be entrusted with large quantities of money—learned the craft of small-scale deposit banking, accepting money deposits for the purpose of lending it to others. But it was the goldsmiths—who first became involved in currency exchange and served as safe storehouses for the valuables of private individuals—who were in the right place at the right time: England on the verge of civil war around 1640. Insecurities surrounding the war and the lack of need for traditional goldsmith crafts encouraged the goldsmiths to focus more on the banking side of their business. They would not only accept deposits but loan some deposits out, and the demand for more deposits to lend would induce them to begin offering interest on deposits. Meanwhile, the paper used to acknowledge receipt of deposits and loans would lead to the issuing of checks, "inland bills" (a domestic version of bills of exchange),[16] and banknotes (which evolved from the receipt of deposits issued by the goldsmiths). Goldsmiths would also come to engage in the bills of exchange business, diversifying their investments in paper by employing their knowledge of credit risks of various London merchants involved in overseas trade. The first English banknote (or goldsmith's receipt) is dated 1633, and the first still extant English check, which was modeled on bills of exchange, is dated 1659. Eventually, these paper documents would begin to circulate as currency, supplementing the circulating coinage. By the 1660s, bankers had begun issuing the paper as negotiable instruments when making loans, not just as receipts for currency deposits, a move that would introduce fractional reserve banking, a key component for the modern banking practice of money creation through demand deposits (Davies 2002: 250–2). As I mentioned above, by the eighteenth century, paper currency would supplant metallic currency as the primary form of circulating money.

The rise of paper money would be accompanied by the shift from silver as the dominant material for metallic currency circulation to the "gold standard"[17]—the eventual internationally recognized measure of value that would not be supplanted until the twentieth century, when all currencies became, in essence, free-floating, linked in some cases only to the value of another free-floating instrument, especially the US dollar. At that point, the extrinsic value theory of money would come to dominate, since fiat money systems rely on the belief that the printing on this piece of paper is enough to guarantee the stated value: the value of a given unit of currency would always exceed the intrinsic value embodied in the material. And with the emergence of electronic money, even the paper and stamp themselves could be eliminated—only a series of numbers for distinguishing accounts, and amounts within a given account, would be necessary. Such systems would typically continue to rely on the stability of an issuing state, but with the development of technologies like bitcoin, even the state apparatus behind currencies could be eliminated. All that is needed for such currency to continue circulating is the belief that others would be willing to accept it at a stated value.

The shift to electronic money would eliminate from currency the circulation of visual elements: generally, states could not promote certain political and religious values through number alone. Paper currency did, of course, maintain the important iconographic element of money, and paper and credit card (and even electronic) forms of money would continue to be employed for purposes other than exchange, such as in art. The shift to paper and electronic money would eliminate the problems associated with needing ready access to bullion; however, enhancements or devaluations of the currency based on the supply of money released into the economy would continue to affect the reputation of national governments represented by the printing on the paper and the "real" quantities of resources contained within each account. Meanwhile, the ethical and moral concerns about money, such as those related to the problem of usury, would be restricted only to egregious forms of economic exploitation, like excessively high interest rates and forms of bankruptcy protection for consumers who default on debts. Systems of credit and the persistent creation of new financial instruments would greatly expand economic activity, though at times putting the economy in a precarious position due to reliance on faith that loan defaults and runs on banks would not become the norm. The Great Depression and the Great Recession of the twentieth and twenty-first centuries are clear indications that such faith is not always rewarded. By contrast, the Price Revolution in the early modern period and the series of bank failures seem quaint by comparison because the effects tended to be localized—not the potential global catastrophes made possible by large interlinked systems of credit in the contemporary world. Nevertheless, even the comparatively smaller currency systems of the early modern world could produce hopes and anxieties, and the variety of issues surrounding money, as the following chapter shows, suggests that early modern peoples understood the importance of money to their everyday lives.

CHAPTER ONE

Money and its Technologies

Mining, Metallurgy, Minting, and Non-Metallic Monetary Forms

ARTURO GIRÁLDEZ

A GLOBAL MARKET FOR COINS

With the founding of Manila in 1571, a global market was established linking all of the earth's large land masses. The Iberian powers' discovery of oceanic routes and the acquisition of precious metals in Africa and the Americas, in addition to the Columbian ecological exchanges, were the conditions that made such a worldwide economy possible. As Fernand Braudel has remarked, this global economy depended on monetary exchanges: "Over the whole world, the great monetary circuits organized transfer routes, and centres where profitable rendezvous could be arranged between money and the rich trades in 'royal commodities.'" Long-distance trade was the foundation of accumulation: "It controlled the world of the *ancien régime* and money was at its command, following or preceding it as necessary. Trade steered the economies" (1981: 439).

The output of European and East Asian mines and the "flood tide of American silver" contributed to a high rate of inflation from the first half of the fifteenth century to the first half of the seventeenth century—Earl J. Hamilton's "Price Revolution." Long-term movements of population, trade, and finance were also pushing the inflationary trend, but obviously the products of Mexican and Peruvian mines "did quicken and steepen the price rise" (Wernham 1968: 3).

About this crucial period, John Maynard Keynes asserts: "Never in the annals of the modern world has there existed so prolonged and so rich an opportunity for the business man, the speculator and the profiteer. In these golden years modern capitalism was born" (1950: 159).[1]

This early capitalism and its concurrent trade was instrumental to the emergence of empires such as the "Powder Empires"—Safavid Iran, Ottoman Turkey, and Mughal India—or a unified Japan, whose shoguns defeated the feudal lords, *daimios*, with the products of their mines. New European powers like the Iberian and later the Dutch, British, and Russian empires depended upon trade and the silver that came from the Americas and Japan. Likewise, in the sixteenth century, the Habsburg monarchy financed its wars by means of Central European silver and copper, and Gustavus Adolphus of Sweden supported his military forces in the Thirty Years' War with profits from the copper from Swedish mines. Precious metals were behind the Atlantic economy and the European expansion in Asian waters. State apparatuses, large armies, and growing trade required the development of financial institutions and the wide use of fiduciary instruments to facilitate the energized commercial exchanges of "these golden years" (Keynes 1950: 159).

HAMMERED COINAGE

The monetary substances of the fifteenth, sixteenth, and seventeenth centuries were copper, gold, and silver. In the global markets, silver was the most important. These metals were processed in one of the first mass industries in history dedicated to producing uniform coins of approximately similar shape and weight. The lack of standardization was the result of a rudimentary procedure known as *hammered coinage*, used by mints all over the world.

To manufacture coins, metals were refined to the prescribed degree of purity and alloyed with other metals to strengthen them. Copper was added to silver, and copper and silver were mixed with gold in the Spanish Empire. It was common for only copper to be used, such as in the French gold *ecu* of Francis I, which was minted in 1519 and had twenty-three karats, that is, twenty-three parts gold to one part copper (Burzio 1945: 44; Cipolla 1993: 165; see Figure 1.1). Once the metal had the required degree of fineness, the first step was to produce disks called "blanks." Each blank was placed on a die, which functioned as an anvil, and was struck with the other die, which was used as a hammer to engrave in the obverse (top) and reverse (bottom) the figures and legends legally prescribed. Once struck, the coin had to be trimmed with cutting instruments to turn out coins of an approximately circular shape (Munro 2012: 23).

Such basic technology explains why mint regulations did not specify the weight of each coin but rather indicated the number of coins to be struck from a unit of metal, the "marc." Regulations also specified the bullion purity

FIGURE 1.1: Gold French ecu of François I. © cgb.fr, 2012, via Wikimedia Commons.

(fineness). In the case of gold, fineness was measured in karats: twenty-four-karat gold was 100 percent pure. Silver fineness was defined in Europe in terms of weight. For instance, the Castilian marc (230.046 grams) of silver was struck into 67 reals of 930.551 thousandths of silver content. The famous *real de ocho*, the piece of eight reals, was equivalent to 25.5 grams of silver (Burzio 1945: 42).

The nominal value of a coin was determined by the price of its metal, its intrinsic value, plus brassage and seigniorage. Brassage were the fees paid to the mint master for all the expenditures on manufacturing coins—tools, alloys, labor costs, and so on—and seigniorage were levies collected by the sovereign.

Despite state laws and interdictions, copper, silver, and gold coins were commodities searching for markets in which they could fetch the highest value. If the intrinsic value of a coin was higher than the nominal value granted by law, the coin left the realm or was melted down, and taxes and other legal transactions were paid for with cheaper coins. A case in point was changes in the gold currency issued by Charles I of Spain in 1535. Given the flow of Castilian gold coins to France, he decided to pay the troops going to North Africa with new pieces (*escudo*) containing only 91.67 percent gold, a fineness similar to the French and Italian coins. The double escudo was called the *pistole*, a coin of international importance (Carande 1990: 228).

BEFORE AMERICAN SILVER: A CYCLE OF GOLD, 1443–1560

There was a cycle of gold, a predominance of this metal, in global trade from 1443 until 1560. It began when Portugal occupied the island of Arguin on the west coast of Africa and gained access to the gold of Timbuktu. Soon, the Lisbon mint issued the *cruzado* (1457) of 3.54 grams of fine gold, "the first important trading currency of modern Europe" (Porteous 1969: 140; see Figure 1.2). In addition to Arguin, in around 1456, Diego Gomes reached Mali in Central Africa. Soon, gold from America reached Seville, the fleets' terminus point from Spanish America. Until 1560, American gold represented more than half the value of the imported precious metals, but after that year it oscillated by about 8 percent (Vilar 1974: 142). This influx of African and American gold reduced the comparative price of gold to silver (what is called the "bimetallic ratio"), making highly profitable the exploitation of silver mines in Central Europe and Japan. Incidentally, discoveries of gold in the Brazilian interior in around 1693, also stimulated production in the American silver mines (Braudel 1981: 460).

Gold coinage in Europe followed the fineness and weight of Venice's 3.54 grams ducat. In 1497, the Catholic Monarchs—*Pragmática de Medina del Campo*—decreed that the monetary standard was the *marco* or half-pound of Castile (230.046 grams). The half-pound was divided into 65.3 gold pieces of 23.75 karats each (3.5 grams of pure metal); the coin was called the *excelente de la granada* and was equivalent to the Venetian ducat. In 1510, Maximilian I, the Habsburg emperor (1493–1516), modeled the gold coinage of the Holy Roman Empire on the Venetian ducat. Alan Stahl writes that the diverse Europeans coins called "ducats," "represented the closest thing the Western world has had to a unified coinage standard since the age of Charlemagne, and indeed provided Europe with a gold standard that long predated the now more famous gold standard (from the 1720s)" (2012: 49; see Figure 1.3). Economic areas trading with the Mediterranean also joined the area of the ducat. When Muhammad the Conqueror, after the capture of Constantinople, struck the *altun* (1477) and the Safavid kings of Persia minted the *ashrafi*, both adopted the ducat as a model of weight and fineness. Mints from Egypt and Yemen followed the same standard. During the first half of the sixteenth century, these currencies and large quantities of Venetian ducats flowed from the Red Sea in a "river of gold" that dominated the Indian Ocean trade. Such coinage circulated "with great freedom" on the coasts of Western India (Haider 1996: 323).

FIGURE 1.2: 500 reais gold coin ("cruzado"), King Sebastian of Portugal (1557–78). © JFVP, 2008, via Wikimedia Commons.

MONEY AND ITS TECHNOLOGIES

FIGURE 1.3: Transylvania 1681 25 ducat. Courtesy of National Numismatic Collection, National Museum of American History, out of copyright, 2010, via Wikimedia Commons.

Mines in Central Europe became extremely profitable after the Duke of Saxony in 1451 authorized the process of mixing ores with lead to separate silver from copper, while new mining technology was also developed. The plates in Georgius Agricola's *De Re Metallica* beautifully depict these new machines (1950 [1556]; see Figure 1.4). Mining districts were located in Bohemia, Saxony (Luther's father was a miner in Mansfeld), Tyrol, Hungary, Alsace, and Silesia. It was the silver and copper of Tyrol that induced South German merchant houses to go into mining and finance. The most representative of these houses was that of the Fuggers, bankers of the Habsburgs—their loans made Charles V emperor of the Holy Roman Empire—and collectors of the papal indulgences that precipitated the Reformation.

The abundance of silver was at the origin of a new European coinage. The first of these novel coins were inspired by Pisanello's (1395–1455) medals, modeled on classic numismatic portraits and with Roman instead of gothic lettering. The reform began in Venice with the minting of the lira Tron (6.16 grams of silver) in 1472. It showed the semblance of the doge Nicoló Tron in Renaissance style. It was a single exception, the Swiss and the republics of Venice and Florence did not issue coins with portraits. Milan in 1474 minted a heavy coin (9.44 grams of silver), with the face of the duke, Galeazzo Maria Sforza. They were called *testoni* because they carried a half-bust representation of basically the head (*testa* in Italian; (Cipolla 1996: 40). The style spread rapidly in Italy (Torino, Genoa, Firenze, and the Papacy), the Low Countries, France, and England. In 1503–4, the latter inaugurated its modern coinage with Henry VII's *shilling* of 8.63 grams of silver, which carried a likeness of the king by Alexander of Brugsaal from Germany—"the father of the English coin portraiture" (Craig 1953: 98).

FIGURE 1.4: Engraving from *De re metallica* di Georg Agricola, Basilea, 1556. Out of copyright, 2013, via Wikimedia Commons.

Edward Besley remarks that in Germany, instead of portraits in the Italian style, "there was more emphasis on the rank and authority of the issuer, who was frequently depicted on horseback, or half-length in armor, in association with symbols of his power such as a sword" (1980: 189). Until the eighteenth century, Spain and Portugal were exceptions with respect to this fashion. In the case of Spain, the busts of kings and queens were stamped onto the *excelente*; Charles V is represented on some coins of Milan, and Philip II appeared on coins of the Netherlands, but virtually all coinage carried only religious symbols, legends, coats of arms, dates, and the mint's origin without the royal head.

In 1477, Archduke Sigismund of Tyrol ordered the issue of large silver coins, the *Guldiner*, with 29.92 grams of silver, and the *Halbguldiner* with a fineness of 14.96 grams of silver. In Bohemia, in the year 1519, the Count of Schlick, owner of the Sankt Joachimsthal mine, began the minting of a large coin with 27 grams of pure silver. When the mint passed into the hands of Ferdinand of Austria, it was reduced to 26.39 grams of metal. The coin was called *Joachimsthaler*, abbreviated to *Thaler* (see Figure 1.5). Philip Grierson observes that the new pieces "provided the models for new issues which in the sixteenth century spread throughout Europe and transformed the whole appearance of the currency" (1975: 97). It was the case if we add the *pieces of eight* minted for the first time in Mexico in about 1537. The *thaler* met with such "incredible success" that the Dutch *rijksdaaler* and the American *dollar* adapted its name (Cipolla 1993: 41–2). There was an economic basis for minting large coins because they were much cheaper to manufacture: "12 times as much labor was involved in making 12 pennies as in making 1 shilling" (Grierson 1975: 97).

Silver production increased in Central Europe from about 1460 to the 1530s, reached a plateau, and then in the 1560s began a pronounced decline, unable to compete with American production (Nef 1997: 16). Nevertheless, German miners and engineers were at the time the "undisputed masters" of mining and refining technologies (Spooner 1972: 17). Their most important contributions were in assaying and in separating precious metals from other substances. Publications like the *Probierbüchlein* explained how to recuperate silver and gold from coins, clothing and paintings (*Bergwerk und Probierbüchlein* 1949; Bargalló 1955: 108). A crucial development for the future was the application of amalgamation with mercury to refine silver. Vanoccio Biringuccio

FIGURE 1.5: Joachimsthaler, 1525. © Berlin-George, 2015, via Wikimedia Commons.

FIGURE 1.6: Drawing from *De la Pirotechnia*, 1558. © Sailko, 2017, via Wikimedia Commons.

wrote about the procedure in his *De la Pirotechnia* (1540) (see Figure 1.6). He was probably informed of the method by a German expert during one of his visits to the country.

Soon, German metallurgists arrived in the New World after the conquest of Mexico in 1521; and "Between 1527 and 1530 some eighty or ninety miners crossed the Atlantic at the instigation of the Welsers" (Spooner 1972: 25). The Welsers were German bankers to the Spanish Emperor. Bartholomeus V. Welser's loan to Charles V in 1528 was secured, with Venezuela as collateral. The Fuggers also participated in this technological diffusion. It seems that Cristobal Raizer, the Fuggers' agent in Seville, sent German metallurgists to Mexico in 1563 (Bargalló 1955: 94–5). At the time, in exchange for the credit they extended to Charles V, the Fuggers were given control and received the profits of the Almaden mercury mine and the Guadalcanal silver mine, both nearby in southern Spain.

In the viceroyalties of New Spain and Peru, the amalgamation method passed through numerous tests and improvements that culminated in 1555 in a procedure named the *beneficio de patio* of Bartolomé de Medina. In his *Medina Codex*, he acknowledged, "I learned in Spain through discussion with a German, that silver can be extracted from ore without the necessity for smelting it, or refining it" (quoted in Probert 1969: 96). By 1562, there were already 35 such *patios* in Zacatecas. Around 1571, Pedro Fernández de Velasco introduced Medina's process to Peru, adapting it to the conditions of Potosí with the name of *beneficio de cajones* (Bargalló 1955: 112). Peter Bakewell comments, "This slow but sure process sustained the great edifice of silver production, because it allowed cheap refining of the great masses of low-yielding ore available in Spanish America" (1984: 115). A faster way to extract silver was by the *pan amalgamation* method (*cazo* or *fondo* in Spanish), which involved heating the ore in copper vessels with a mixture of salt and mercury. It was Alvaro Alonso Barba, a priest and metallurgist, who invented it. He published his findings in *Arte de los Metales* (1640), the earliest work of mining and metallurgy in America (1817).

The use of mercury was a fabulous stroke of fortune to the Spanish kings because they owned the Almaden mine in Spain and, in Peru, Huancavelica—discovered by the Spaniards around 1563. If necessary, they had access to the mercury of Idrija (today in Slovenia). In a few cases, small amounts of quicksilver arrived from China via the Manila galleons.

CHINESE DEMAND AND AMERICAN AND JAPANESE SILVER SUPPLY

Antonio-Miguel Bernal, a Spanish historian, writes, "The Spanish Empire is considered the most relevant example of mining colonialism, not of industrial nature but just for monetary reasons" (1999: 354). From this perspective, it was a great success. Grierson states: "It was largely through the output of the mints of America, where those of Mexico City and Potosi were opened up in 1535 and 1574 respectively, that coinage in the European tradition came to dominate the world" (1975: 32). Spanish America produced at least 150,000 tons of silver between 1500 and 1800, perhaps exceeding 80 percent of the entire world output over that time span (Cross 1983: 397; Barret 1990: 237), but there was another large producer of precious metals. During the sixteenth and until the first half of the seventeenth century, Japan had the second largest mines in the world. Ward Barret calculates that Japan may have mined about 30 percent of the world's silver in the sixteenth century and about 16 percent in the seventeenth century (1990: 225).

Just as the American miners received German know-how, the Japanese benefited from a new refining technology, the *haifuki*—a cupellation process that had arrived via Korea from China around 1540. The process consisted of placing in a furnace silver ore with a quantity of lead, which resulted in a mass of alloyed lead and silver. The alloy was placed on a cupel or hash-filled hearth. Then it was melted over a fire and, as a result, the lead sank to the bottom and the silver remained in the ashes (Innes 1980: 24).

But the middle of the seventeenth century signaled a sharp decline of output from Japanese mines (Innes 1980: 24–5). Despite their success, the Japanese were well aware of superior American refining techniques. The shogun, Tokugawa Ieyasu (1543–1616), in a conversation with visitors from the Philippines, requested American metallurgists. Rodrigo de Vivero y Velasco, a nephew of Mexico's viceroy, wrote in 1610 that the shogun "begged him to request King Philip to send to Japan fifty miners, men he understood were very skillful in extracting silver in New Spain, because, those in Japan did not procure half the silver the mines were capable of yielding" (quoted in Innes 1980: 91).

In Japan, the Tokugawa Shogunate (1603–1868) introduced a monetary system that improved on developments during the Azuchi-Momoyama period of national unification (1568–1600). At first, they copied Chinese models, but by the end of the seventeenth century, rectangular and oval gold coins took over. The gold ones were the *oban* (large plate), with a weight of 160 grams and were equivalent to ten *kobans* (small plate; see Figure 1.7). Each koban contained 15.64 grams of pure gold; they were large oval plates of cast metal, stamped near the edges with the crest of the *kiri* flower and an inscription in Indian ink, indicating its denomination and bearing the Gold Mint Superintendent's signature. Silver pieces took the shape of "crude bars and lumps." The piece of higher value, *cho-gin*, circulated from 1601 into the nineteenth century. Private paper notes based on silver were widely used in Osaka by 1630, and in 1661 the Shogun authorized the issue of similar notes in other places (Grierson 1975: 67, 69; Cribb 1980: 306–7).

China was an important customer, willing to buy large quantities of the white metal from America and Japan, which made possible the immense profits of the enduring mining enterprise. Vitorino Magalhães Godinho describes China as a

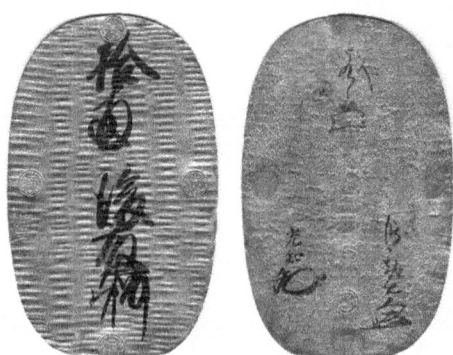

FIGURE 1.7: Tokugawa coin—Tensho oban. Divetobluemarine, courtesy of GFDL, 2007, via Wikimedia Commons.

"suction pump" (*bomba aspirante*) that attracted silver globally for centuries. This demand was apparent in the relative prices of silver and gold in different markets (1984: 1: 432–65). In the early sixteenth century, for example, the gold:silver ratio in China stood at 1:6, while in "contrast the gold/silver ratio hovered around 1:12 in Europe, 1:10 in Persia and 1:8 in India" (von Glahn 1996: 127). In the 1590s, the proportion was 1:5.5 or 1:7 in Canton, while in Spain at that time the exchange ratio was 1:12.5 or 1:14, "thus indicating that the value of silver was twice as high in China as in Spain." Bimetallic ratios were about 1:10 in Japan and 1:9 in Mogul India at the time (Chuan 1969: 2; Boxer 1970: 461). Given the price differential between Japan and China, Innes observes that "the export of gold from China to Japan could have yielded a gross profit of 40 percent or higher on the return trip" (1980: 27).

Chinese authorities had over-issued paper money, and, by 1450, notes had depreciated to a thousandth of their nominal value (Cribb 1980: 300). Everyday commerce required a medium of exchange, and silver became the metal of choice. J.P. Geiss explained why silver was chosen: gold was impractical for most transactions, and with respect to copper, "the value of the coin lay in the metal, not in the mint. . . . While silver could, if necessary, be assayed for purity, copper coins could not. To assay a copper coin entailed its destruction. . . . Silver came to be the preferred medium of valuation and exchange" (1979: 155). Lien-sheng Yang observes that since 1400, silver ingots were employed in large transactions, and, in 1436, a portion of the land tax (*chin-hua yin*) was paid in silver (1952: 2, 46). Taxation on this metal was expanded around 1570, when the emperor decreed the Single Whip tax system. The new law specified the consolidation of a number of levies into a single payment to be made in silver. Merchants, landowners, and poor peasants participated in the empire-wide commercial network, partly due to the payments in silver required by the tax system. The price of silver in the Ming Empire with respect to the rest of the world rose steeply.

In the words of F.W. Mote, China "has always been the largest bloc of the human race, its population larger than that of any other ethnically, culturally, or politically defined unit in world history." There were 155 million Chinese in 1500, 231 million in 1600, and 268 million in 1650 (1999: 473, 475). During the late Ming dynasty, cities like Nanjing had over 1 million inhabitants, while Beijing followed closely with 660,000. When such a large percentage of the world's economy is committed to purchasing a particular commodity, especially one that is highly valued and relatively easy to transport between continents, the impact of that industry is certain to be global.

Because of China's extensive tributary system—countries associated with the empire through diplomatic and commercial relations—domestic use of silver reverberated powerfully outside its borders. In the words of Takeshi Hamashita, "The entire tribute and interregional trade zone had its own structural rules which exercised a systematic control through silver circulation and with the Chinese tribute trade at the center. This network of trade encompassing East Asia was articulated with neighboring trade zones such as India, the Islamic region and Europe" (1994: 97). The forceful combination of the supply side and the demand side implied enormous profits for all involved.

Without the unprecedented supplies of Japanese and American silver, Europeans could not have bought such vast quantities of Asian products like spices, porcelains, silks, and so on. Spanish historian, Antonio Domínguez Ortíz, observes how American silver "streamed into Turkey, Persia and Sumatra—'the Spanish dollars are everywhere current' remarked a traveler there—and finished its long odyssey in China" (1971: 303). The coinage of New Spain and Peru, in addition to that of the Seville mint, virtually made the Spanish Empire "the world's monetary factory" (Bernal 1999: 379).

Surprisingly, the Chinese emperors did not mint coins. Instead, silver ingots stamped by merchants circulated. The ingots, called *tael*, were "small, thick, slightly oval oblongs resembling a Chinese shoe with both ends raised." The empire's weight units were based on the *liang*, known to Europeans as the tael of 37.5 grams—"the common monetary standard of East Asia"—employed as the equivalent of the European units of account, the cruzado and the ducat. Ingots of one tael circulated widely, but there were taels in multiples of up to fifty (Grierson 1975: 61; von Glahn 1977: 133). The Chinese carried with them scissors to cut small pieces of precious metals and a scale to weigh them when it was necessary to employ silver for payments smaller than the tael. In 1626, Father de las Cortes described with admiration the ability of the empire's inhabitants to estimate the fineness of silver. He described also how they collected the smallest fragment of the metal in a bell filled with wax attached to their belts; when enough scraps were collected they melted the wax to recuperate it (Braudel 1981: 454).

PIECES OF EIGHT

Large silver coins like the *rijksdaalder*, first coined in 1575 by the Republic of the Seven United Netherlands, the *leeuwendaalder*, named after the rampant lion on its face, and the *ducatoons* (1659), had an important position in international trade but were not comparable to the peso: "Who owned reals of eight had an acquisition power to spend everywhere in the world," writes Carlo Cipolla (1996: 58; see Figure 1.8). Cipolla's opinion supports Bernal's assertion that "Spain was, for almost three uninterrupted centuries, the minting house of the world," if we understand Spain to refer to the whole of the Spanish Empire (1999: 380).

In accordance with the requirements of merchants in Mexico, a royal ordinance of 1537 set stipulations on pieces of eight in all American mints. This coin's

FIGURE 1.8: Piece of Eight—Potosí 1770. © José Fuertes, 2015, via Wikimedia Commons.

diameter was 40 millimeters and its thickness 3 millimeters; it weighed 27.5 grams and had a fineness of 930.555 thousandths, resulting in 25.5 grams of pure silver. Soon, Spanish mints like Seville also produced such pieces. In 1599, a German traveler, Diego Cuelbis, estimated that "the Seville house was the best of the world and where more money is coined" (2002: 37). When the fleets arrived, merchants preferred to take their bullion there to save time and to avoid the transportation costs and risks implied in sending it to other mints despite the incentives offered by them, particularly in Segovia (Pérez Sindreu 1991: 269).

But the quality of hammered coins was defective in terms of purity, weight, and size, which made them easy to counterfeit. By 1537, native Mexicans had already been falsifying pieces of four reals, and native Peruvians, as well, were using lead and copper mixed with silver to make coins.

When the fleets arrived in Seville, the silver and gold property of the Crown and of private persons were sold to bullion merchants (*Compradores de Oro y Plata*) to expedite the business of coining money. For reasons of expediency, the authorities of the House of Trade (*Casa de Contratación*)—the organization in charge of trade with America—preferred to put private businessmen in charge of refining the precious metals to the legally required level before selling them to the mint. It was a very speculative undertaking because profits came from the differential between the pretended fineness and the real precious metal content of ingots and bars. Clarence H. Haring estimates that "earnings, apparently, were rarely more than four maravedis on a marc of silver, or one maravedi on a peso of gold" (1964: 175). It was already common in the time of Philip II to encounter gold ingots and silver bars with fineness markedly superior or inferior to the legal figure. An occasional source of substantial profits was the silver bars called *guacas*, which contained some gold but were sold to the bullion merchants at the silver price. "In 1561, the silver bars of Peru, property of the Crown, produced half a million maravedis of fine gold" (Sanz 1979: 2: 83, 84), which corresponded to 1,300 excelentes belonging to the Catholic Monarchs—a coin containing 3.52 grams of gold that was equivalent to 375 maravedis. But sometimes bars had only a veneer of silver over a cheaper metal. After 1603, given the high value of gold, merchants bought it only after its fineness had been inspected in Seville (Haring 1964: 176; Pérez Sindreu 1991: 267).

The reason for such a state of affairs was the low technical level of American refiners, particularly in Peru. Silver badly assayed caused grievous losses to the bullion merchants. When the fleets of Pedro Menéndez de Aviles arrived in 1563, the bullion merchants refused to buy silver until it was officially reassayed. Such deficiencies were known in international markets: in 1574, in Florence, there were complaints about the quality of coins from Seville and Toledo; consequently, the mint rejected quantities of reals brought to be reminted in local coinage.

If assaying was faulty, weight was not exact. Coins circulated until they disappeared or were exchanged with new ones. Historians concur regarding the famous pieces of eight, noting that they were poorly manufactured and in massive amounts. Cipolla wondered how such rough and badly minted coin—"*così brutta, così mal coniata*"—was accepted everywhere, and his hypothesis was that "the power of the reals of eight relied primarily on their enormous quantities" (Cipolla 1996: 73; Céspedes del Castillo 1972: 464).[2]

THE OTTOMAN EMPIRE, SAFAVID PERSIA, MUGHAL INDIA

Kirti Chaudhuri clearly describes the power of American pesos in the global trade: "From the Isthmus of Panama to the straits of Bab al-Mandeb and Hormuz, no government was able to declare monetary independence from the piece of eight" (1986: 73).

The Ottomans, after the empire's territorial expansion, including the occupation of Syria and Egypt, found themselves controlling intercontinental trade routes, whose taxes became crucial for their economy. To facilitate traffic, all customs duties on silver were removed, and from the 1580s the white metal "flooded the Levantine market" to continue its march to be exchanged for other commodities (Inalcik 1995: 139). The "Price Revolution" linked to this river of silver generated price inflation and contributed to the deterioration of the Ottomans' monetary system. In the time of Suleyman the Magnificent (1494–1566), the small silver *aqches* were unpopular in Syria and Iraq; consequently, by 1592, the mints were striking large silver *dirhams* with regional designs. By the end of the seventeenth century, the silver coinage was suffering continuous devaluations, and only a small number of mints remained open (Broome 1980: 271).

The growth of the Safavid Empire's economy was linked to Iran's position between Europe, India, and Central Asia. The Silk Road, which passed through northern Iran, was revitalized in the sixteenth century, and there was direct trade with England and the Netherlands. The main currency was in silver, the Persian rulers charged high seigniorage, and coins circulated at values above the price of their precious metal content. The main silver coins were the *abassis*, which were of high quality and weight. The *two-shabi* provided small change for everyday transactions, and the bent silver bars were called *larins*. In 1587, one ducat was equivalent to 6 larin, and at the end of the seventeenth century, 5 larin could be exchanged for one piece of eight. Conducted down the "river of gold" in the second half of the sixteenth century, the larin "expanded enormously" in the Indian Ocean trade (Broome 1980: 273; Haider 1996: 304).

In India, the final era of hammer-struck coinage was inaugurated after the rule of Sher Shah (1540–5) and Akbar (1556–1606). Babur introduced in 1542 the silver *rupee*, a coin originally of 11.5 grams, and the copper *dam* of 21.4 grams, which became the standard coins of the realm, and he increased the number of mints to over twenty (Grierson 1975: 50). Bullion and foreign specie acquired through trade were brought to the mints to be struck into rupees and gold coins, *muhrs*. The variety of coinage with different degrees of precious-metal content and fineness required the expertise of moneychangers, *sarrafs*, who, as buyers of imported metal (like the merchants in Seville), assayed bullion and coins and determined their value on the market (Haider 1996: 327).

The Portuguese trade with the Monomotapa Kingdom (today, in Zimbabwe and Mozambique) resulted in a flow of gold to Indian markets. In Goa, an enclave belonging to Portugal, the authorities minted the gold *saotomés* (its name taken from the stamp of an image of Saint Thomas), similar in weight and fineness to the Indian *pagoda* of about 3.5 grams (Vilar 1974: 127; Grierson 1975: 51). The gold half-pagoda was called *kashu*, but this name "was applied to a copper coin of the same weight which became in Portuguese caixa, in English cash, and was subsequently applied to the copper coinage of all South-East Asia and eventually to that of China" (Grierson 1975: 52). Colonial powers in India tended to copy local coinage. The East India Company minted coins of Mogul type for trade in northern India, while at Madras it struck gold *pagodas* and silver *fanams* for trade along the Coromandel Coast. The French at Pondicherry followed Indian models, yet their fanams were stamped with a crown and fleurs de lys (Porteous 1969: 209).

India, like the Ottoman Empire and the Persian Safavids, participated in a global economic network with China as the low-pressure region in terms of silver. The bimetallic ratio of coins from this period proves that silver was re-exported from India to China and Southeast Asia to pay for these regions' imports (Chaudhuri 1978: 180).

TECHNOLOGY FOR A UNIFORM COINAGE

Johannes Gutenberg's printing press of around 1540 inspired the idea of using machines to manufacture better coins. The lack of uniformity in coinage preoccupied well-known artists of the Renaissance. Leonardo da Vinci (1452–1519) wrote, "All the coins should be a perfect circle, and to do this a coin must before all be made perfect in weight, size and thickness" (quoted in Usher 1959: 234). Grierson specifies the requirements for fulfilling da Vinci's request: (1) obtaining a circular blank of uniform weight, (2) making the edges clear to prevent fraud, and (3) producing a clear stamp. "These problems were not new, but they had all become more serious as a result of the introduction in the late fifteenth century of much heavier silver coins" (1975: 112).

Donato Bramante (1444–1514) had adopted a screw-press to enhance the stamping of the papal crest upon the lead seals to be attached to official documents. Da Vinci left mechanical drawings showing that he had conceived a rolling mill and a press for shaping blanks. In his designs, water moved a mill consisting of seven hammers attached to a single shaft. Ideally, this machinery would have been able to mint better coins in large numbers. The resulting coinage was called "milled money" (Davies 2002: 180). Da Vinci was occupied at the papal mint during his stay in Rome, "though there is no record of any coins struck under his supervision" (Usher 1959: 235). Abbot Usher summarizes his contribution to minting: "His work thus consisted in defining the problem and elaborating the various mechanical alternatives opened up by such a new conception of the process" (1959: 236).

It is accepted that Benvenuto Cellini (1500–71) was aware of previous mechanical developments and used them first for making medals and later for producing coins in several Italian mints. In 1529, he was appointed *Maestro delle stampe* (Master of the Stamp) at the papal mint. Later, in 1533, he engraved the dies for the silver *testoni* of the Duke Alessandro de Medici. Charles V at Milan employed the sculptor, Leone Leoni, to engrave his *testoni* of 1551. John Porteous observes, "Never before, except perhaps in fifth century Syracuse, had such eminent artists been content to work in this field.... The resulting coinage was somewhat mannered, suitable only as long as it was not wanted in great quantity." But large numbers of silver coins were required by trade and finances, which made such artistic endeavors unfeasible (1969: 174).

Cellini communicated his expertise on how to improve coinage to Francis I of France (1494–1547), but the new technology was only adopted by his son, Henry II (1519–59), via Germany (Craig 1953: 118; Usher 1959: 235). In 1550, his ambassador reported from Augsburg the existence of machinery to mint coins (Grierson 1975: 118). A skilled engineer, Aubin Olivier, was sent to look into it, and he bought the devices that came to Paris accompanied by a German technician. The new equipment "comprised rolling mills, draw-benches, cutting and striking presses; a very few Paris coins of 1555 and later years even have raised letters on the brim, which shows that some kind of segmented collar had been contrived" (Craig 1953: 118). The mills were moved by the water of the Seine.

In England, Elizabeth I (1533–1603) decided to exchange all coinage in circulation for currency of good silver in a time span of about ten months—December 1560 to October 1561. It was a propitious moment because the price of silver had been falling since 1551. Sir Thomas Gresham in Antwerp negotiated a loan to secure bullion to supplement the silver collected from the debased coinage; in the same year, 1560, he signed a contract with a German company to separate copper from the precious metal of old coins. That was not all; the following year, Eloi Mestrel, an employee of the Paris mint, offered to install machinery at the Tower of London to help with the recoinage. The quality of the newly milled coinage was exceptional, and the coins of Elizabeth I, in the words of Grierson, "stand out from the rest by the reason of the circularity of their flans and the high quality of their striking" (1975: 118; see also Porteous 1969: 181; Davies 2002: 206). Notwithstanding the excellence of their output, the milling machinery was discontinued in 1572.

German mints used a rolling press instead of the French screw press. The energy to move these machines came from horses or water. In the Habsburg Empire, the important mint of Hall in Tyrol employed such machines. Impressed by its reputation, Philip II, a cousin of the Habsburg emperor, imported the milling devices that arrived from Genoa in the company of German technicians. In Segovia, a city near Madrid, the king opened up the new establishment, which would become known as the *Ingenio de la Moneda* (Engine of Coinage) and which was moved by the river Eresma. The *Ingenio* was highly superior to all the mints in the Spanish Empire, producing the magnificent silver fifty reals of Philip III (1578–1621) and Philip IV (1605–65) for use as presentation pieces, while technical improvements were appearing not only in Germany but in Spain as well. The Spanish numismatist Tomás Dasí quotes a royal document of 1598 contracting Baltasar Vellerino de Villalobos to install in the mints of Santo Domingo, México, Lima, Potosí, and Bogotá an "*Ingenio de tijera*" (Engine of Scissors) that had been invented by one Miguel de la Cerda. Such an *Ingenio* was already in use at the Madrid mint (Dasí 1950: 2: LIX, LXX.).

The increase in the production of precious metals was accompanied by a deterioration of coinage. Mints in America—the worst was Potosí—produced extremely poor coins, but those from Antwerp, Genoa, and London were not much better. The best coins of the late sixteenth century were Italian or were struck at remote mints such as Edinburgh and Danzig (Porteous 1969: 177).

The new milling technology had its disadvantages. It was very expensive to install and operate because it broke down easily, caused more accidents to the workmen than the previous method, and was extremely unpopular among the moneymakers from fear of unemployment. In addition to its greater costs, milled coins could only be issued as part of a national recoinage such as those that took place in France in 1643 or in England in 1696–7 (the latter paid for with a tax on windows), to avoid the disappearance of high-quality coins. The problem of marking the edge to avoid clipping was finally solved by France in 1645, where the fully mechanized coin appeared with its milled edge (Craig 1953: 242). Years later, in London, the Roelters mill and screw press issued coins whose edges, in the case of larger coins, bore the legend "*decus et tutamen*"—"an ornament and a safeguard" (Chown 1994: 61). It is relevant to mention that the Dutch, whose economic practices in the seventeenth century were the most sophisticated in Europe, did not adopt the new machines until 1670 (Porteous 1969: 181; Grierson 1975: 117). Coins were merchandise, whose value was basically its precious metal content, and what was of consequence on the global market were their quantity, not their perfection, which partially explains the delay in implementing new minting technologies.

Hammered silver and gold coinage remained prevalent in Europe, with the exception of Germany, up to the last decades of the seventeenth century. Still, in 1686, the merchants of Seville complained to the king about the inconvenience of the new milling machines. In America, hammered coinage continued until the first half of the eighteenth century (Burzio 1945: 48; Pérez Sindreu 1991: 214).

COPPER COINAGE

Braudel classifies the three monetary metals in Europe according to their functions: "In fact every metal played its part: gold, reserved for princes, large merchants (even the Church); silver for ordinary transactions; copper naturally for the smallest. Copper was the 'black' money of people of small means and the poor. Mixed with a little silver it blackened quickly and deserved its name" (1981: 458).

The adoption of copper coinage during the modern period followed the minting pattern of Greece and Rome. Renate Pieper indicates that, in 1415, Portugal was already issuing pure copper moneys (1999: 435). Numismatists commonly mention the Naples copper *cavallo* of Ferdinand I (1458–94), "the first successful modern copper coinage of Europe" (Besley 1980: 182), soon to be imitated in the rest of Italy. The Low Countries introduced this coinage into their system in 1543 and France in 1572. In England, the manufacture of copper farthings was a private business and was officially licensed in 1613; finally, in 1672, the mint began issuing copper halfpennies (Grierson 1975: 33).

Pure copper coinage appeared in German regions around the Kipper and Wipper period (1619–22) during the Thirty Years' War, but soon after that, small change began to be made with a mixture of copper and silver. In Spain, copper was initially alloyed with a small amount of silver (billon); billon coins (*vellón*) remained until 1598, when pure copper ones took their place. Pieper observes that the regions closely integrated in the silver circuits of the Atlantic economy were the first to issue copper coins. Central Europe's regions, like Austria, adopted copper coinage only in the mid-eighteenth century (1999: 436).

Copper arrived in Spain from Tyrol and Hungary and later from Sweden. In early modern Europe, warfare provided the essential cause for monetary alterations. In Spain's case, the piece of eight was a global commodity based on its content of pure silver, and the monarchs' seigniorage and other taxes depended on its acceptance by merchants, so its depreciation was uneconomical. Only copper currency was to be manipulated. The Crown collected copper coins and reissued them at a higher nominal value, generating devastating periods of inflation. Surprisingly, with the exception of the island of Hispaniola during the second half of the sixteenth century, American merchants rejected the minting of copper rather than risk monetary devaluations. In fact, Charles II's monetary reform in 1687 kept the colonial piece of eight at its long-existing value while devaluing silver coinage in Spain: "From now on, the colonial money was completely separated from the Spanish one" (Gil Farrés 1959: 259).

European copper had a new competitor in 1629, when significant quantities of Japanese red metal brought by the Dutch East India Company arrived in Amsterdam, causing the prices to fall (Glamann 1977: 498). This circumstance explains Sweden's strange copper coins. In 1644, during the reign of Christina (1632–54), the mints, suffering from a glut of copper, issued copperplate money, *plåtmynt*, which contained its full metal market value. The largest, the ten-thaler piece, had a weight of 19.7 kilograms. This was a scheme to market the abundant copper, and issues of plate money continued until the middle of the eighteenth century (Besley 1980: 205).

The quality of Chinese copper coinage varied, depending on the purity of their metal, because sometimes they were heavily alloyed with lead. The coin was cast to have a small projecting wedge at its rim, where the molten metal had entered the mold; coins with a four-sided center hole were fit onto a square piece of bar and the resulting cylinder of metal filed to remove irregularities and render the coins circular. This coin commonly circulated on strings, with a deduction of three to five coins to pay for the threads (Grierson 1975: 59, 60).

East Asian countries, including Japan, the Ryukyus, and Vietnam, used Chinese currency. In the second half of the fifteenth century, there was a proliferation of private coinage, and authorities in China and Japan allowed the use of these coins. According to Richard von Glahn, "Beginning in the 1520s, the silver boom in Japan transformed the monetary regimes of both Japan and China. Yet the infusions of bullion did not obviate the need for fractional currencies" (1996: 97). Starting in 1524, for three years, Ming authorities made private coinage legal, acknowledging that it was unable to control the coins in circulation. After 1541, the state closed the mints for over a decade because the costs of minting had overtaken the value of the coin; the Court in 1564 discontinued coinage once more. "The Ministry of Revenue, while deploring the market's usurpation of the power to determine the value of coin, conceded its own impotence and recommended that currency rates be allowed to float." Due to rising copper prices and corruption in the management of the mints, seigniorage never generated the expected profits (von Glahn 1996: 104, 110, 187). Counterfeiting led to a severe decline from the standard of 1,000 copper coins per 1 tael of silver to 6,000 coins (Fairbank and Goldman 1998: 134).

Japan at the end of the sixteenth century "was probably the world's leading producer and exporter of the red metal" (Innes 1980: 10). Japanese copper, known as *yang-t'ung*, "foreign copper," was an essential import for the duration of the Ming Empire (Yang 1952: 38). German copper-refining technology played a role as well. The *nanban-buki* method (liquation or the Seiger process) was invented in the early fifteenth century in Nuremberg. The Portuguese-taught Soga Riemon Jusai (1572–1636), the founder of the Sumitomo family, further developed the lead-intensive *nanban-buki* for refining copper and extracting silver as a by-product, which created a large demand for lead from Europe and Siam (Eiji 2013: 19).

In Japan, copper coins had been imported from China since the Tang period (618–907 CE), but the increase in copper production made large-scale minting of the *Kan'ei tsūhō* possible. Bearing similar features to Chinese coins, it was a cast circular coin with a square hole in the center and a high rim; it contained between 2.0 and 3.7 grams of copper (about 80 percent) mixed with lead and tin. It remained legal currency until 1953. After 1670, the circulation of Chinese coins was prohibited (Eiji 2013: 14–15).

OTHER SMALL CHANGE AND MONEYS OF ACCOUNT

In this period, copper was not the only material used for small change; other items included, for instance, bitter almonds (*badam*), which were used in Gujarat and imported from Iran, or the coins or moneys of the land (*monedas de la tierra*) in America. But most important was the cowrie shell collected in the Maldives Islands (*Cypraea moneta*) and from East Africa (*Cypraea annulus*) (Johnson 1997: 193; see Figure 1.9). Filipino islanders harvested cowries and sold them to Siam, Cambodia, Malaysia, and Bengal, "where they are used as money and a means of trading, as happens in New Spain with the cocoa-bean," wrote Antonio de Morga (1559–1636), a Spanish bureaucrat with experience in the Philippines (1971: 171). Cowries were also in use in Yunnan—a territory in southern China—up until the second half of the seventeenth century, when Han Chinese settled the region and copper and silver became widely used. Bing Yang speculates that the high price fetched by cowries from the Indian Ocean "may have resulted in the outflow of cowries from Yunnan" (Yang 2004: 311). In the same years, cowries were in great demand for buying textiles and rice in Bengal and slaves in Africa (Boomgaard 2008: 21).

FIGURE 1.9: Cowrie shells. © Bin im Garten, 2011, via Wikimedia Commons.

Chronicler João de Barros estimated that since 1515, Portuguese carracks brought 2,000 to 3,000 quintals' worth of cowries to Africa as ballast for trade; 2,000 quintals of shells amounted to over 1,000 million cowries. Once the Dutch took over Ceylon, cowries entered Dutch ledgers, and large quantities appeared after the middle of the seventeenth century. At the end of that century, one African slave was purchased with about 100 pounds of cowries (Johnson 1997: 195–6, 243).

In Mesoamerica (México, Guatemala, Nicaragua, El Salvador, and parts of Honduras), cacao beans were used as coins. Gonzalo Fernández de Oviedo, a sixteenth-century historian, explained that "even with those almonds there exist fraudulent practices such as including a portion of hollow almond shells which have been filled with dirt or some other substance and cleverly sealed so as to appear whole" (1944: 247). The Spanish colonial monetary system integrated Aztec currencies because the tribute imposed on native populations required it. Outside the central area of New Spain, cacao beans were paid as such a tax in places of cacao production. Similarly, with the exception of important trade routes and large cities in which the use of bullion coins was prevalent, local products, the coin of the land, such as mate tea (*hierba mate*) and bundles of tobacco leaves, became the effective means of paying tribute and other levies. This practice was prevalent in the provinces of Buenos Aires, Paraguay, and Tucumán. In 1574, at Tucumán in Argentina, the City Council (*Cabildo*) decided that goats (equivalent to one peso) and horseshoes (one and a half pesos) served as moneys. As late as 1618, Phillip III acknowledged the situation and allowed the payment of taxes in such currencies (Burzio 1945: 37).

The diversity of currencies required a standard of value—money of account— to make equivalences among different coins for accounting purposes and to make payments. For instance, in the Spanish Empire, it was the maravedi. The Low Countries adopted the guilder or florin by a decree of Charles V, and after Amsterdam became a predominant business center, the coin given the name of "Dutch guilder" remained in use in the northern and southern Low Countries. During the fifteenth and sixteenth centuries, at the end of the fairs of Geneva, Lyons, Besançon, and Piacenza, final payments had to be made in a money of account representing a fixed weight of precious metal (Van der Wee 2012: 88).

Units of account were related to the coinage used widely by society. When economic conditions required extraordinary expenses, Herman Van der Wee explained, "the authorities could expand the volume of the current money of account in a fairly simple fashion by successive debasements of the basic coinage, without impairing the stability of high finance and of the international economy" (1977: 298). Rulers followed such policies consistently. Between 1440 and 1760, there was a devaluation of the main European moneys of account in terms of precious metals (García Guerra 1999: 576).

CREDIT AND BANKING

Braudel's observation is fundamental: "A clear frontier separates money (in all its forms) from credit (taking into consideration all instruments of credit). Credit is the exchange of two promises separated in time: I will do something for you, you will pay me later" (1981: 478). Credit entered all levels of society and all kinds of economic transactions during this period. In all of Europe, there were many parishes with a "common stock" of cattle, wool, and tools that could be loaned to people in need. In England, "improvement funds" existed to provide loans at low interest to young apprentices so that they could set up for themselves (Cipolla 1993: 305; Parker 1997: 536). The *monti di pietá* appeared in Europe with the purpose of protecting poor people from usury. The first of such institutions opened in Perugia in 1462. From the end of the fifteenth century, the *arcas de misericordia* in Navarre and the *monte frumentarii* in Italy were already in existence. These were corn banks that lent seed or provided other aid to farmers on favorable terms. The Italian *montepios*, the Spanish *positos*, and other municipal pawnbroking establishments often also performed the function of land banks.

Consumer credit expanded during this period. Peasants and workers received credit against harvests or future labor. Another form of credit was the extension of payments: "The shopkeeper would have a current account with the brewer-innkeeper and the latter would keep a reciprocal account with the shopkeeper;

periodically the accounts were closed and only the balance was paid in hard cash" (Van der Wee 1977: 301). It was also common for businessmen to settle their transactions by transferring moneys from one account to another in a local bank. In America, in spite of the abundance of silver and gold, business was done on credit, and when metals were refined, merchants compensated for the difference in silver or gold (Céspedes del Castillo 1972: 350).

All kinds of instruments of credit that had already been developed in antiquity were employed everywhere in the modern era: bills of exchange, promissory notes, letters of credit, banknotes, check, and so on. On the routes from the Mediterranean to the Indian Ocean, deposit banking, moneylending, and financing commodity trade were common. In India, the sarrafs advanced moneys (*dadani*) to primary producers and negotiated bills of exchange (*hundi*) and respondentia (risk-sharing loans) (Haider 1996: 299).

On all continents, there were a large number of professional pawnbrokers and moneylenders willing to advance sums of money. Goldsmiths, silversmiths, jewelers, and moneychangers acted as bankers. In Ming and Ch'ing times, pawnshops provided credit closely regulated by the government on their rate of interest and the period allowed for redemption. Another credit institution was the cooperative loan society, a temporary organization of friends or relatives to finance its members with rates of interest lower than those offered by moneylenders or pawnbrokers. Banking functions were performed largely by the gold- and silversmiths and money shops. Ordinary shopkeepers would also receive deposits from customers, and capital was given to wealthy businessmen like salt merchants or pawnbrokers, who could expect an equitable interest rate (Yang 1952: 6–7).

In Europe, the system of payments centered on fairs that were held periodically in a number of countries during the sixteenth and seventeenth centuries but that developed into permanent establishments in the most important commercial cities (Antwerp 1531, London 1571, Seville 1583, Amsterdam 1611). In 1542, as a portent of things to come, a commercial tract complained about merchants in Flanders hedging exchange rates: "They wager among themselves on the rate of exchange in the Spanish fairs at Antwerp. They call these wagers parturas according to the former manner of winning money at a birth (parto) when a man wagers whether the child shall be a boy or a girl." Bills of exchange for amounts of 200,000 or 300,000 ducats were invested in such operations (Ehrenberg 1963: 244).

The increase in mercantile activity required the institutionalization of business practices that took place in the Netherlands. The Dutch East India Company established a stock market in Amsterdam in 1602. Braudel maintained that the Mediterranean (and its futures market, bonds, annuities, stocks, etc.) was "the cradle of the stock market. But what was new in Amsterdam was the volume, the fluidity of the market and publicity it received, and the speculative freedom of transactions" (1982: 101). Soon, in 1609, the Wisselbank, whose precedent was the Venetian Banco della Piazza di Rialto (1587), opened for business.

THE END OF THE GOLDEN YEARS

The global economy originated with the enormous profits of the silver trade. Price differentials among economic regions drove economic exchanges for a century. Because of the accumulation of tens of thousands of tons of silver production worldwide, silver's price on global markets declined up to about 1640. Adam Smith writes, "Between 1630 and 1640, or about 1636, the effect of the discovery of the mines of America in reducing the value of silver appears to have been completed" (1937: 192). As a result, the Price Revolution ended, merchants' extraordinary profits disappeared, taxes collected in silver lost their value, and empires all over the world suffered devastating losses. To the disasters resulting from the Little Ice Age and its concurrent famine, epidemics, and wars, the fall of silver profits added another cause to the miseries of the global crisis of the seventeenth century.

During the 1690s, gold was discovered in Minas Gerais (Brazil) and, by 1711, the annual amount of gold legally shipped to Portugal was about 15,000 kilograms; as a result, Portuguese external trade boomed, and the main beneficiary was Britain. In the words of A.R. Disney, "In the eighteenth century the tendency for gold to flow from Portugal into British hands was seemingly irresistible" (2009: 253). The first decades of this Brazilian gold bonanza coincided with Isaac Newton's tenure as Master of the Mint (1696–1727). Under his mastership, mint operations switched to manufacturing gold coins and neglecting silver coinage—during the whole of the eighteenth century only £1,254,000 of silver was minted, whereas from 1695 to 1640 some £17,000,000 of gold was coined. A new monetary era had been born. In the words of Glyn Davies, "When the principle so firmly established by the great reform, namely that the pound sterling was a given a weight of metal, became linked with the revealed coinage preferences of the public, ... then the gold standard had practically arrived, silently a century or more before its legal enactment" (2002: 248). The City of London became the center of a new political economy regulated by the legal possibility of converting the pound to gold.

CHAPTER TWO

Money and its Ideas

Justice, Sovereignty, and the Idea of Money as Commodity

BRADLEY D. RYNER

During the period of the time covered by this volume, thinking about money fundamentally changed. It is not just that people's ideas about money changed; rather, the intellectual, institutional, and stylistic frameworks for thinking about money changed. Gradually, writing about money became less concerned with money's relationship to moral theories of justice and more concerned with empirical questions of the causes and effects of changes in monetary value. Mercantile writers, active participants in commerce, began to take up debates about value that had originated with scholastic writers, trained in philosophy, theology, and canon law. The rise of mercantile writing laid the foundations for what would later become the field of "political economy," a term used for the first time in 1615 by the French mercantile writer, Antoine de Montchrétien, in his *Traicté de l'œconomie politique*. Rather than devoting their efforts to explicating a concept of the just value of money, which a monarch was morally obligated to enforce, mercantile thinkers began to conceptualize monetary value as the result of complex international relationships, subject to political decisions made within the bounds of global economic forces. This chapter sketches the shift from scholastic to mercantile modes of writing and thinking. It begins by examining the uneven emergence of money as a practical problem for late scholastic writers, such as Martín de Azpilcueta, and early humanist writers, such as Jean Bodin. It then looks in detail at how this shift inflected the debates between so-called "bullionists" (Thomas Milles and Gerard de Malynes) and free-trade advocates (Edward Misselden and Thomas Mun) in England.

MONEY AS MEASURE, MONEY AS COMMODITY: MARTÍN DE AZPILCUETA AND THE SCHOLASTIC LEGACY

In the medieval scholastic tradition, writing about money had primarily concerned itself with moral questions. By the sixteenth century, scholastic writers had begun to struggle in more systematic ways with empirical questions about money, such as how the influx of gold and silver from colonization of the Americas affected prices globally. In such writing, the idea began to take root that money is not just a measure of other commodities, as the prevailing Aristotelian tradition maintained, but a commodity itself.

The dominant concept of money as a measure derived primarily from Aristotle's *The Nicomachean Ethics*, where it was deeply bound up with his concepts of justice. Aristotle had delineated two types of justice: distributive justice (*dianemetikon dikaion*) and commutative justice (*diorthotikon dikaion*).[1] Distributive justice applied in cases when things were to be divided "in accordance with geometrical proportion," so that the more deserving would get the greater share, whereas commutative justice applied in cases when things were to be divided "in accordance with a mathematical proportion," so that all parties would get an equal share (Aristotle 2009: 1131a10, 1131a25). But determining whether things are distributed equally or unequally first requires a way of equating unlike things, making all goods measurable in a common unit. Aristotle took this common unit to be "need" and understood money as a conventional "representation of need" (2009: 1133a25–30). He reasoned that "if men did not need one another's goods at all, or did not need them equally, there would be either no exchange or not the same exchange," but when exchange took place, it attested to an equal valuation in so far as the buyer's need for a good was equal to the seller's need for whatever other good could be purchased with the money: "Money, then acting as a measure, makes goods commensurate and equates them; for neither would there have been association if there were not exchange, nor exchange if there were not equality, nor equality if there were not commensurability" (2009: 1133a25–30, 1133b15–20). Aristotle offered simple examples of money making unlike goods commensurate: "Let A be a house, B ten minae, C a bed. A is half of B, if the house is worth five minae or equal to them; the bed, C, is a tenth of B; it is plain, then, how many beds are equal to a house, namely, five" (2009: 1133b20–30). However, he did not devote space in *The Nicomachean Ethics* to more complex types of economic transactions, in which the value of goods and money or the probity of the exchange might be legitimate subjects of dispute.

Building on Aristotle, medieval schoolmen began to address more contentious questions about money as they debated what determined the "just price" of a good. Most influential were those associated with the University of Paris, especially Thomas Aquinas (see Wood 2002; Langholm 1992). Aquinas began the section of *Summa Theologica* titled, "Of Cheating, Which is Committed in Buying and Selling," with the question: "Whether it is lawful to sell a thing for more than its worth?" Among the putative support for the lawfulness of selling a good above its worth, he included an argument based explicitly on Aristotle's account of utility in friendship in *The Nicomachean Ethics* and implicitly on his argument that the value of money correlates to need:

> according to the Philosopher (*Ethic*. viii. 13), in the friendship which is based on utility, the amount of the recompense for a favor received should depend on the utility accruing to the receiver: and this utility sometimes is worth more than the thing given, for instance if the receiver be in great need of that thing, whether for the purpose of avoiding a danger, or of deriving some particular benefit.

Rejecting this argument, Aquinas contended that, although one should rightly recompense friends based on the "the usefulness accruing" from their favors, buying and selling must be governed by commutative justice, which works to make the price "equal to the thing bought." Aquinas took as axiomatic the Aristotelian definition of money as a common measure:

> the quality of a thing that comes into human use is measured by the price given for it, for which purpose money was invented, as stated in *Ethic*. v. 5. Therefore if either the price exceed the quantity of the thing's worth, or conversely, the thing exceed the price, there is no longer the equality of justice: and consequently, to sell a thing for more than its worth, or to buy it for less than its worth, is in itself unjust and unlawful.

This does not mean, however, that Aquinas conceptualized just price as an immutable property of a good. Although a seller should not take advantage of a buyer who has greater need of a good than other buyers, Aquinas maintained that if the seller "has great need of a certain thing," then that seller might justly charge "more than [the good] is worth in itself, though the price paid be not more than it is worth to the owner" (1947: II–II, Q.77 A.). The just price, then, was assessed with primary consideration of the thing itself, but with the understanding that the same good might justly be valued differently in different circumstances.

The notion that the just price of a good can vary was crucial to Aquinas' understanding of why profits from trade were lawful. Answering the question,

"Whether, in trading, it is lawful to sell a thing at a higher price than what was paid for it," he duly followed Aristotle's *Politics* (1.3) in condemning profit-seeking as an end in itself. He concluded, however, that "nothing prevents gain from being directed to some necessary or even virtuous end, and thus trading becomes lawful." A merchant can rightfully "seek gain, not as an end, but as payment for his labor," which also benefits his country. The price of a good may lawfully rise between its purchase and resale, "either because [the buyer] has bettered the thing, or because the value of the thing has changed with the change of place or time, or on account of the danger he incurs in transferring the thing from one place to another, or again in having it carried by another" (Aquinas 1947: II–II, Q. 77, A. 4). In contrast to usury, which Aquinas condemned for immorally realizing profits by unnaturally distorting the value of money, he presented the profits from trade as the result of a natural alteration of value.

Later scholastic writers became increasingly concerned with the practical details of how the value of goods and money changed in the course of trade, although their overarching concern was still the moral implications of trade. Martín de Azpilcueta's *Commentary on the Resolution of Money* (2007 [1556]) is especially illustrative of the emergence of more sophisticated descriptive analysis within the framework of prescriptive moral literature. Azpilcueta (regularly referred to by his contemporaries as Navarro) was a doctor of theology and canon law at the University of Salamanca. In the sixteenth century, Salamanca became a hub for innovative economic thought in response to the dramatic inflation that Spain experienced with the influx of gold and silver from the colonization of the Americas (see Grice-Hutchinson 1952, 1978; Alves and Moreira 2010; Vilches 2010). Azpilcueta's *Commentary* has a strong claim to being the first work to coherently articulate a quantity theory of money—the concept that an increase in the supply of money will result in a rise in prices, or, as Azpilcueta phrased it, "the rest being the same, in those countries where there is a great lack of money, less money is given for marketable goods, and even for the hands and work of men than where there is an abundance of it" (2007 [1556]: 70). However, the *Commentary* was not originally published as a stand-alone economic treatise, but as an appendix to a confessional handbook, the *Manual de confesores y penitents*. The overt aim of Azpilcueta's appendix was to delineate licit economic exchanges from illicit ones that would require penance. Thus, insights about how economic transactions functioned were subordinated to arguments for the probity of such exchanges based on their correspondence to established notions of justice.

Throughout the treatise, traditional modes of exegesis and disputation mix with an emergent emphasis on analyzing the observable operations of commerce. The opening chapter of the *Commentary* consists of a thorough explication of one sentence from Pope Gregory IX's 1236 decretal condemning usury,

Naviganti de usuris, used to foreground the ambiguity of what specific types of exchange are usurious. Each subsequent chapter then addresses a specific facet of exchange ("Concepts and Types of Exchanges," "The Origins and Functions of Money," "Exchanging as a Profession," "Exchanging by Buying, Bartering, or Innominate Contract," etc.), identifying key classical or patristic authorities on each topic, summarizing points of dispute among subsequent scholastic writers, and justifying Azpilcueta's own conclusions as to what is licit and illicit. Amid this seemingly timeless debate over principles of justice, however, the focus shifts at key moments to practical questions about the workings of commerce, at which points Azpilcueta grounds his assertions firmly in what can be inferred from observing the operations of commercial transactions, past and present. Early in the text, he supports the conventional idea that currency exchange naturally developed "because the currency of a land was worth less there than somewhere else" with the topical instance: "today almost all the gold and silver currency from Spain is worth less there than in Flanders and France" (2007 [1556]: 34). Likewise, he supports his assertion that prices increase with increased supply of money by appealing to what "we can see from experience in France where there is less money than in Spain" as well as with a historical comparison of prices in Spain before and after "the discoveries of the Indies covered it in silver and gold" (2007 [1556]: 70). The *Commentary* foregrounds information on the variability of currency value and exchange rates, and in one striking instance, Azpilcueta prefaces an explanation of how international credit transactions work with the assurance that "I have learned [how they work] at my expense" (2007 [1556]: 82). The assumption that firsthand participation in commercial transactions could yield important insights about their workings succinctly distinguishes the intellectual milieu in which Azpilcueta was writing from that of the previous generation of scholastic writing.

Established modes of scholastic disputation and emergent modes of economic analysis come together in the *Commentary*. In framing this argument, Azpilcueta had to contend with the fact that the two predominant touchstones of scholastic thought, Aristotle and Aquinas, plainly considered money to be a measure of commodities, not a commodity itself. As Azpilcueta put it, Aristotle "thought it was wrong to exchange and trade with money because he did not think [trafficking in money] was natural nor brought any benefit to the republic but that of profit, which is an end without an end"—that is, a vain end not serving a greater good (2007 [1556]: 34). Azpilcueta flatly contradicted Aristotle's argument but did so by using one of Aristotle's own examples against him:

> It is not true that using money to obtain a profit by exchanging it goes against its very nature because, even if it is a different use than the first and main one for which is was created, it is still apt for a less principal and secondary use.

> This happens, for example, when shoes are used to make a profit, which, although is a different use than the primary one for which they were created (which was to wear on feet), does not go against their very nature.
> —Azpilcueta 2007 [1556]: 34

Aristotle had used the example of the distinction between the primary use of shoes (wearing) and its secondary use (selling for profit) to mark the second as less ethical than the first because it made profit an end in itself. Patently ignoring the ethical valence of the example, Azpilcueta presents what it is possible to do with an object as what is natural and, therefore, licit. This naturalization of profit was part of a larger trend in scholastic thought to accept the status quo of commercial exchange as de facto moral. This trend was already visible in Aquinas, whose writings required little nuancing to be brought in as support for Azpilcueta's position. Azpilcueta noted that even though "Saint Thomas said that any art of exchange whose main purpose was only to obtain profit was illicit," he also held that "the art of exchange is licit if its purpose is a moderate profit to support oneself and one's home and if the art of exchange brings about some benefit to the republic." Therefore, Azpilcueta concluded, profiting from buying and selling money was both natural and licit, so long as it was undertaken "honestly and modestly" to "support oneself and one's home" (2007 [1556]: 34).

Azpilcueta clarified that he held it licit to buy and sell money not only "as a piece of metal, and as gold, silver, or broken copper" but also "as money" (2007 [1556]: 56). In an age when money existed primarily in the form of coined precious metal that had significant market value independent of a coin's face value, thinkers tended to conflate the material and nominal values of money. It had long been understood that the commodity prices of gold and silver fluctuated, giving a coin a value independent of its face value. Azpilcueta, though, understood that money as a purely nominal marker of value within a country, irrespective of its metal content, "can be worth more of less than the price that the law establishes" (2007 [1556]: 56). The care with which Azpilcueta makes this distinction makes it clear that he attributed inflation not merely to an influx of bullion but to an increase in the amount of money available as a medium of exchange. Moreover, anticipating a purchasing-power parity theory of international exchange rates, Azpilcueta recognized that the price of currency on an international market depends not on its material composition nor on its face value but on the value of goods and services that money buys in different places (2007 [1556]: 71–6).

If the market value of a unit of currency in a given place is taken as its "just value," then profit may be made licitly from trafficking in money "as with other merchandise, collecting it through exchange of its just value where or when it is worth less to exchange it where and when it is worth more" (Azpilcueta 2007

[1556]: 65). In traditional moralistic language, Azpilcueata counseled confessors to warn those who profit by exchanging money that they "walk toward Paradise through high and rocky grades from where the tumbles [that come] from the great love and attraction of great profits may easily hurl them down deep ravines of sins and such thick bramble patches of restitutions that late or never will they pick themselves up and get rid of them" (2007 [1556]: 89). But, for Azpilcueta, the moral "tumbles" resulted from selling money above its fair market price, not merely from trafficking in it for profit. Like other thinkers of his time, he had ceased to conceptualize money in Aristotelian terms, as a way of measuring the value of all other objects so as to ensure their equitable exchange. Rather, the abstraction of money itself was starting to be understood as commodity in its own right, from which profit could justly be made.

MONEY AND SOVEREIGNTY: JEAN BODIN'S HARMONIC JUSTICE

A shift to conceptualizing money as a commodity outside of the framework of Aristotelian notions of justice was troubled in part by the political implications of doing so. The monarch traditionally had been understood as the ultimate authority guaranteeing the just valuation of money. Investigating the forces that caused the commodity value of money to fluctuate not only necessitated losing recourse to a simple rhetoric of a stable just value, but also meant confronting the possibility that even an absolutist monarch is powerless to alter market forces. These tensions are especially evident in the writing of the French humanist Jean Bodin, who demonstrated exceptional skill at investigating the empirical causes of price fluctuations but who, nonetheless, argued for policies aimed at maintaining money as a consistent measure of value and who argued simultaneously for the absolute authority of the monarch and for the monarch's direction by "harmonic justice," a concept that is ultimately hard to differentiate from unconstrained market forces.

Bodin shares with Martín de Azpilcueata the distinction of being generally recognized by modern scholarship as having a strong claim to being the first writer to offer a recognizably modern articulation of the quantity theory of money. In *Response to the Paradoxes of Malestroit* (1997 [1568]), Bodin set out the idea more clearly than Azpilcueata, although also more than a decade later than Azpilcueata had. The concern of both men with the systemic effects of an influx of money speaks to the larger global economic context shared by the two. Bodin also shared with Azpilcueata a scholastic heritage. After abandoning a career in the Church (having been released from vows he had taken as a Carmelite), Bodin studied at the Collège de France and at the University of Toulouse (where Azpilcueata himself had taught some twenty-five years earlier) before entering political life in Paris (Bodin 1997 [1566]:

11–14). Bodin's education would have involved reading many late-scholastic writers within an emergent Renaissance humanist framework, and he came to emblematize Renaissance humanism's imperatives of systematizing information and analyzing it with an eye to its historical situation (see Franklin 1963; Blair 1997).

Bodin's most sustained work on economic questions began with his attempt to disprove the claims that Jean Cherruies, Lord Malestroit, had made in a 1566 treatise titled *Paradoxes*. Malestroit's first claim, which he deemed "paradoxical" because it was "very remote from the opinion of the vulgar," was that despite the perception that "the price of everything in France has increased," in fact, "no prices have increased during the past 300 years." Malestroit held that gold and silver were "the true and fair measure of the cheapness or dearness of all things," and that goods had consistently sold for the same amount of gold and silver (Bodin 1997 [1566]: 39, 41). The difference, he maintained, was that the metal content of coins had been reduced so that it now took more coins to deliver the same amount of precious metal. His second paradox was that "much can be lost on an *écu* or other gold and silver money, even though it is paid out at the same rate as that at which it was received." Malestroit's concern was that landowners who collected rents specified in silver coinage, for example, fifty *sols*, were receiving less value now that fifty *sols* exchanged for one golden *écu* than they had when an *écu* exchanged for only twenty *sols* (Bodin 1997 [1566]: 44). Thus, Malestroit concluded, although "the price of everything, for the king and his subjects, is the same as it was in the past," in terms of what quantity of goods gold and silver will fetch, the king, like other landowners, "does not receive as great a quantity of gold and fine silver now as his predecessors did in payment of his domanial and other rights" (Bodin 1997 [1566]: 47). Malestroit's treatise proffered a fantasy of stability based on two central tenets. First, gold and silver were the essence of money as a measure of value. Second, the values they measured would always be constant as long as the exchange rate between silver and gold was constant.

Bodin skillfully refuted Malestroit in ways modern economists can still appreciate: by showing his data to be incorrect or incomplete and his methodology to be insufficient. Malestroit had used velvet as his chief example of a commodity whose nominal price had risen but was still exchanged for the same amount of precious metals. Bodin countered that Malestroit lacked evidence about the historical prices of velvets and was fundamentally mistaken to think that velvet was available for purchase at all in France any earlier than a century prior. Moreover, Bodin argued that "velvet must not be taken as an example of other Latin merchandise, and still less of goods in general" (1997 [1566]: 55). He then called on the evidence of a range of historical documents, such as the property register of Toulouse and records of the *Chambre des comptes*, to show that the rise in prices of various commodities and land did not correspond proportionally to reductions in the precious metal content of coins. Additionally, he showed Malestroit to have been "mistaken as to the standard of money minted in this kingdom during the last 300 years," invoking more complete records and faulting Malestroit for basing his calculations on "a year when money was strongest and [setting aside] the years when money was weakest" (Bodin 1997 [1566]: 77, 79). While Bodin attributed inflation in part to currency debasement, he argued that its primary causes were the greater abundance of gold and silver, the growth of monopolies, and the greater scarcity of certain commodities (1997 [1566]: 59).

Bodin had a clearer understanding of the multiple forces affecting the value of money than Malestroit did, but he shared with Malestroit the sense that attending to the nominal value and exchange rates between silver and gold currency was an essential duty of a king. Although Bodin did not believe that reductions in the precious metal content of coins had significantly contributed to inflation, he, nonetheless, opposed such debasements and championed "the stability of money" (1997 [1566]: 93). The second edition of the *Response* asserted that:

> if money, which ought to govern the price of everything, is changeable and uncertain no one can truly know what he has: contracts will be uncertain, charges, taxes, wages, pensions and fees will be uncertain, fines and penalties fixed by laws and customs will also be changeable and uncertain; in short, the whole state of finances and of many public and private matters will be in suspense.
>
> —Bodin 1997 [1566]: 102

Bodin claimed that because monarchs "are the custodians of justice and owe justice to their subjects" and are "subject to the law of nations," they cannot "without incurring the infamy of counterfeiter, alter the weight of his coin to the prejudice of his subjects, and much less to the prejudice of foreigners who treat with him and trade with his people" (1997 [1566]: 102). In this way, Bodin continued the Aristotelian line of thought that conceived of money as a measuring tool necessary for ensuring of justice. To this end, he recommended minting three different types of coins (gold, silver, and copper), with exacting purity standards and consistent exchange rates.

Bodin incorporated the bulk of his *Response to Malestroit* into book six of his *Six Books of the Republic* (1962 [1576]), where his ideas about money took up an uneasy relationship with his absolutist theory of sovereign authority. Bodin held that sovereign power, categorically, must be absolute and unqualified and, therefore, must be held by a single group or individual. He argued this it was ultimately most beneficial to a commonwealth when sovereign power belonged not to all people (democracy) or to a subset of them (aristocracy) but to one supreme individual (monarchy). Unanswerable to any earthly authority, the sovereign monarch for Bodin was constrained only by limits intrinsic to the maintenance of sovereignty itself (*leges imperii*) and, more broadly, by natural laws derived from God. The monarch could not, for example, constrain his successor directly, although fiat or by exclusion from succession, or indirectly, through the alienation of royal domain. The natural laws that Bodin understood as limiting the monarch's authority included respect for the freedom of his subjects and their rights to own property. Although for Bodin the monarch was only accountable to his own conscience for violations of natural law, he was at pains to stress that the sovereign should feel bound to ensure just economic transactions, going so far as to argue that raising taxes without public consent violated a natural right to property (see Franklin 1973: esp. 86–9; Bodin 1992: esp. xxv–xxvi). Ultimately, despite the unchecked power that Bodin attributed to the sovereign monarch, he still assumed that natural laws would direct the use of this power toward greater justice. He reasoned that: "if justice be the end of law, and the law is the work of the prince, and the prince is the lively image of almighty God, it must needs follow that the law of the prince should be framed unto the model of the law of God" (Bodin 1962 [1576]: 113).[2] Bodin's recommendation to mint gold, silver, and copper coins of precisely regulated purity was aimed at ensuring that money remained the reliable measure that the Aristotelian tradition identified as necessary for evaluating the justness of transactions. The *Six Books of the Republic* culminates in a consideration of how an absolute monarch should most justly govern a commonwealth: "whether by justice distributive, commutative, or harmonical" (Bodin 1962 [1576]: 754). Thus, Bodin situated traditional paradigms of justice in new relationship to sovereign authority, but still maintained their primacy in evaluating transactions within a commonwealth.

Bodin rejected Aristotle's assertion that some exchanges should be judged in accordance with commutative (arithmetic) justice while others should be judged in accordance with distributive (geometrical) justice. The Aristotelian tradition that predominated scholastic thought held that the arithmetic equality of commutative justice was appropriate "when question was of the goods of any one in particular, or for the recompensing of offences and forfeitures" but distributive justice's proportional differentiation based on "the good or evil deserts and the quality or calling of every man" was appropriate "if question were of common rewards to be bestowed out of the common treasure, or for the division of countries conquered, or for the inflicting of common punishments" (Bodin 1962 [1576]: 756). Bodin argued that a strict application of either form of calculation in any case posed problems of fairness and that, instead, each case should be judged by a "harmonic justice" that simultaneously incorporated aspects of commutative and distributive justice. Bodin reasoned, for example, that attempts to establish a fine properly equal to an offence or penalty would necessarily prove unfair because the rich would be less severely affected than the poor—a point that he illustrated with the fable of Naratius, a wealthy ancient Roman who, realizing that he could easily afford the established fine for battery, strolled through the streets, giving "a good and sound buffet or box on the ear" to whomever he pleased, followed by his slave carrying his purse to pay the fine immediately (1962 [1576]: 775).

At the same time, Bodin contended, strictly proportional justice was also inadequate because even the smallest fine levied against a very poor person would amount to an excessively punitive amount if scaled up proportionally to a wealthy person's estate. By contrast, Bodin's harmonic justice promised to alleviate the unjustness of each by combining the two, just as the progression of numbers in a sequence such as 3, 4, 6, 12 "harmonizes" an arithmetic sequence (3, 9, 15, 21, 27) with a geometric one (3, 9, 27, 81). His model here is musical harmony, which allows for tremendous variability of specific elements in a sequence so long as each element holds a certain concordant relationship to the other elements. Just as countless different arrangements of musical notes satisfy the conditions of being harmonically pleasing, so to a just society, for Bodin, accommodates a great variety of value distinctions between individuals and within transactions.

Despite presenting harmonic justice as "the model of the law of God" enacted on earth through the monarch as "the lively image of almighty God," the driving force for creating the multitudinous gradations of value distinctions Bodin describes is, by and large, not the monarch but the market (1962 [1576]: 113). It was, for example, market forces that caused a long-established fee to fail as a deterrent to battery in the case of the rich Naratius. Bodin tells us that at the time the pertinent law was crafted, "the poverty of men was so great" that "a fine of twenty-five asses, or small pieces of brass ... by arithmetical proportion indifferently exacted of all men" was a sufficient punishment for battery. However, as "men's wealth increased," this relatively small sum no longer fairly measured the pain inflicted by "a blow upon the face" (1962 [1576]: 775). Bodin shows how one must respond to these changing market conditions by revaluing things with multiple examples of people taking more or less in exchange in one circumstance than they would in another, such as creditors who settle for less money from a bankrupt debtor or laborers who charge more to the wealthy. He asserts that this flexibility in valuation accords with "a certain natural reason" (1962 [1576]: 781, 783).

As Bodin explains, a surgeon, led by this natural reason, might take five crowns from a poor man for removing a gall stone but five-hundred from a rich man for doing the same. This fee scheme not only violates commutative justice by charging unequal amounts for the same service, but also violates distributive justice by charging the poorer, but no less deserving, man a greater proportion of his estate:

[the surgeon] in effect takes ten times more of the poor man than of the rich, for the rich man being worth fifty-thousand crowns, so pays but the hundredth part of his goods, whereas the poor man, being but worth fifty crowns pays five, the tenth part of his substance.

Bodin concludes that: "if we should exactly keep the geometric or arithmetic proportion alone, the patient should die of the stone, and the surgeon for lack of work starve; whereas now, by keeping the harmonic mediocrity, it goes well with them both, the poor man cured with the rich, and the surgeon so gaining wealth" (1962 [1576]: 783). As the surgeon's profit attests, the "natural reason" at work here might equally be called the logic of the market. As with the scholastic notion of "just price," the category of harmonic justice is ostensibly moral, but its criteria for evaluation quickly collapse into the mercantile.

MERCHANDIZING EXCHANGE AND THE BALANCE OF TRADE: ECONOMIC JUSTICE FOR ENGLISH MERCANTILE WRITERS

The first half of the seventeenth century in England, as the English were struggling to bolster their presence in global commerce, saw a flurry of treatises written by firsthand participants in commerce: Thomas Milles was a customs officer; Gerard de Malynes was an employee of the Royal Mint and a minor merchant; Thomas Mun was a merchant in the English East India Company; while Edward Misselden worked both for the Merchants Adventurers and later for the English East India Company. English mercantile treatises drew conceptually and stylistically on both scholastic and humanist modes of writing about the economy while pioneering their own modes of analysis and representation (see Magnusson 1994; Finkelstein 2000; Ryner 2014). They still invoked Aristotelian concepts of justice, but these concepts had ceased to provide a coherent analytical framework for key questions of debate, such as what factors contributed to profit and loss in international commerce and, most importantly, what the role of the state and the sovereign should be in promoting profitable trade. Scholars disagree about whether or not these mercantile treatises constituted a coherent "mercantilist" ideology that understood economic policy as an instrument of state power (see Amussen 2012; Matson 2012; Newell 2012; Pincus 2012; Stern and Wennerlind 2013; Magnusson 2015; Barth 2016). They were certainly part of a larger cultural discourse that linked questions of economic value to questions of national identity and royal sovereignty (see Harris 2003; Kitch 2009; Deng 2011; Landreth 2012).

Competing notions of sovereignty manifest as arguments over whether money should be conceptualized as a measure of value or as a commodity.

Milles and Malynes, frequently termed bullionists because of their position that the monarch should prevent precious metals from being exported in greater quantities than they were being imported, held to the traditional Aristotelean idea that money must remain a stable public measure of commodities, not a commodity itself. The "balance or traders," Misselden and Mun, took the opposite position, arguing that nothing especially distinguished money from any other commodity in the course of trade and that by exporting bullion, England did not deplete English wealth so long as the English could gain more in value for their exports (or re-exports) than they spent on imports that did not generate additional profit.

English mercantile writers unevenly integrated new modes of economic analysis into the established frameworks for conceptualizing justice. Whereas Bodin had seen distributive and commutative justice as harmonized by market transactions, Malynes and Milles attempted futilely to differentiate the two as they became intertwined in their accounts of economic activity. Malynes's claim at the start of *Lex Mercatoria* that "every man of judgment knows that [traffic] is comprehended under justice commutative" (1622: sig. F6v) would have been thoroughly uncontroversial: for English mercantile writers, the notion that well-ordered commerce is properly a subset of commutative justice was a truism. However, their analyses helped to undermine this habit of mind. For Milles and Malynes, following the truism, distributive justice did not bear directly on proper commercial transactions, but was, nonetheless, essential in providing the context of social harmony in which equitable commercial transactions could take place. Distributive justice ensured that the monarch occupied a privileged place from which to regulate commercial activity. In other words, they saw the *inequality* between monarch and subject as necessary to maintaining the *equality* of measurements in commercial transactions. However, Milles and Malynes also gave voice to fears that the reverse might be true, that rather than exchange being dependent on the monarch, the monarch was in fact beholden to larger commercial forces. Their opponents, Misselden and Mun, largely embraced the latter idea, positing the true value of money as outside the strictures both of royal authority and justice.

Despite Milles's and Malynes's efforts to present social stratification and commerce as two distinct domains governed by different models of justice, these two domains regularly collapsed into one another in their writings. In *The Custumers Alphabet and Primer* (1608), for example, Milles asserted that he will leave "the duties of all our distributive justice to those most worthy and most honorable persons that . . . discern and decide the cases and questions of special right and of general reason, as well between subject and subject as [between] the Sovereign and his vassals" (1608: sig. C1v). Nonetheless, he then went on to argue that ensuring that commerce is governed by commutative justice is necessary in order for the king to receive the honors he is due by distributive justice. By virtue of distributive justice, he argued, the king is due revenue from customs and subsidies, just as God is due adoration and tithes; however, if commerce is diminished by a failure of commutative justice, Milles maintained, these dues would dwindle (1608: sig. C2v). Although there is no need to doubt Milles's ardent belief in the divinely sanctioned authority of the protestant monarch (Kimbro 2015), here the conflation of king and God that James I's absolutism shared with Bodin was disconcertingly undercut by the king's dependence on commerce.

Malynes, in more intricate ways, also tried to separate commutative from distributive justice but ultimately presented the actualization of the latter as dependent on commercial activity ordered by the former. Malynes helped to inaugurate England's seventeenth-century print debate about economics in 1601 with the publication of two treatises, *Treatise of the Canker of Englands Common Wealth* and *Saint George for England, Allegorically Described*. His third published treatise, *England's View in the Unmasking of Two Paradoxes* (1603), offered loose translations of Malestroit's *Paradoxes* and Bodin's response to it as well as Malynes's own critiques of both Malestroit and Bodin, and an elaboration of his own theory of the value of money. Malynes began *England's View* by looking back at his two 1601 treatises and retrospectively associating each with a different theory of justice: distributive justice in *Saint George for England* and commutative justice in *Treatise of the Canker of Englands Common Wealth*.

His alignment of the argument of *Treatise of the Canker of Englands Common Wealth* with commutative justice is straightforward. Starting with the precept that "by justice properly called commutative is the commerce and traffic with other nations maintained," Malynes contended that "this kind of equity is interrupted and overthrown by merchandizing exchange, as in the treatise of *Treatise of the Canker of England's Common Wealth* is declared" (1603: sig. A6r–v). Like the scholastic writers who deeply influenced Malynes (see De Roover 1974: 346–66), he used the term "merchandizing exchange" to mean buying and selling of money as a commodity. In marked contrast to Azpilcueata, who had deemed merchandizing exchange licit, owing in no small part to its just profitability, Malynes condemned merchandizing exchange on the grounds that it was necessarily unjust and unprofitable to one party in an exchange. Moreover, he argued, treating money as a commodity with a fluctuating market value impedes the ability of the monarch to regulate how much precious metal is flowing out of the country in exchange for the coins and goods that flow in. His proposed solution, set out in *Treatise of the Canker of Englands Common Wealth* and emphatically repeated in each subsequent treatise, was to apply commutative justice to currency exchange in the form of a par of exchange that would require coins to be exchanged only for other coins containing the same amount of precious metals. The par of exchange was grounded in the notion that:

money must always remain to be the rule and square to set a price unto everything, and is therefore called *publica mensura*, the public measure whereby the price of all things is set to maintain a certain equality in buying and selling to the end that all things may equally pass by trade from one man to another.

—Malynes 1603: sig. A7v

The proposed par would ensure the measuring power of money that made assessing commutative justice possible.

Malynes' claim that *Saint George for England* treats distributive justice is more vexed. He asserted, "By justice properly called distributive is the harmony of the members of a commonwealth maintained in good concord," but argued that when "usury is tolerated," this harmony is "much hindered" with "some few waxing thereby too rich, and many extreme poor, the operations of effects whereof are declared by me under certain similes or metaphors in the *Treatise of Saint George for England*" (1603: sig. A5v–A6r). As this summary suggests, *Saint George for England* is concerned with an apparent violation of distributive justice: a meritless few have grown "too rich" while many have undeservedly suffered "extreme" poverty. However, in Malynes's account, this violation of distributive justice was ultimately an effect of a violation of commutative justice: usury. Moreover, "usury" for Malynes encompassed much more than the charging of excessive interest on loans roundly condemned by scholastic writers. By the term, he instead designated any transaction the end result of which was the exchange of one amount of money for a greater amount of money, as routinely happened in international currency exchanges of the sort that Aquinas would have tolerated and Azpilcueata positively endorsed. For Malynes, the maintenance of distributive justice depended on the maintenance of commutative justice, and the manifest threat to commutative justice was the animating notion of the international money market: that money is itself a commodity.

The international dimension of the money market was salient for Malynes. He contended that, although Bodin understood the workings of money better than Malestroit, Bodin nonetheless failed to fully understand money's fluctuations in value because he had not given sufficient attention to its function in a global context. One might have expected Malynes to largely agree with Malestroit's treatise. Both men thought that money was properly a measure of commodities and that this function depended ultimately on the precious metal content of coins. Malynes, however, argued that Malestroit was only correct in one fundamental proposition ("when moneys do alter in weight or in fineness or in valuation or in all three, the price of things does alter only by denomination if the valuation be made accordingly") and wrong in essentially everything else (1603: sig. D7r). He noted that Malestroit's claims that France had experienced no real price rises but that the king and aristocracy were receiving less value were self-contradictory because "the course of money is all alike between the king and the subject" (1603: sig. D5v). Malynes had evidently missed Malestroit's point that the king and aristocracy were constrained by the terms of their landownership to receive rents figured in silver rather than gold currency. Even had Malynes caught this part of Malestroit's argument, though, he would still have fundamentally disagreed with Malestroit's claim that the real price of goods had been stable for 300 years. To be sure, Malynes desired such stability but saw in the historical record radical fluctuations in the value of money. Malynes approvingly rehearsed all of Bodin's arguments for real inflation, but claimed that his multifaceted explanation "is of small moment" because Bodin had failed to make:

> a comparison of the enhancing of the price of the commodities of one country with the price of the commodities of other countries, and thereby to find out whether things are grown dear with us in effect and whether we pay more proportionally for the foreign commodities within the aforesaid time of three hundred years than we do receive for the price of our home commodities.
> —1603: sig. E3v

Malynes's notion that there is no real price increase as long as the price of exports rises in step with the price of imports is clearly wrongheaded as the purchasing power of individuals does not necessarily increase as the price of exports increases.

Malynes presented a xenophobic conspiracy narrative based on an observable phenomenon that he found fundamentally disconcerting: in the course of international exchange, money was not simply an independent measure of commodities but a commodity itself with a market value. Malynes imagined the prices of imports and exports being rigged against the English by foreign rulers, bankers, and merchants partly by manipulating currency exchange rates. In his account, sinister individuals recognized money "to be the measure and mean to command and obtain all other things" and "practice[d] to be master of that measure, so that no man can come by it but with their consent and paying well for it." Buying and selling money, they "[made] the money to become a merchandise ... whereby the measure between [countries] is become falsified" (Malynes 1603: sig. K8r–v). Malynes imagined foreign bankers and merchants acting with the blessing of foreign sovereigns, but argued that such practices undermined royal sovereignty itself. He wrote that: "money ... being the public measure to maintain a certain equality in buying and selling, must therefore have [its] standing valuation only by public authority of princes, as a matter annexed to their crowns and dignities" (1603: sig. L3v–L4r). For "private men" to "give or receive any money *in specie* above the price of their valuation imposed by the authority of the prince" undermined both the measuring function of money and elevated the authority of the subject above that of the prince, thus violating both commutative and distributive justice.

In an artful turning of Malynes's own moral-philosophical framework against him, Edward Misselden argued, in *The Circle of Commerce* (1623), that a royally mandated par of exchange designed to give English coins the same purchasing power as a like amount of precious metal stamped as foreign coins actually violates the principles of commutative justice. Endorsing the received notion that commerce was properly governed by commutative justice, Misselden noted that commutative justice's allocation of things "with respect to the quality of the thing, not the person," put "the buyer and the seller ... upon equal terms" (1623: sig. Ce3v). "Therefore," he coyly pointed out, "you break this law, Malynes, when you will have the taker of money ruled by the deliverer" (1623: sig. Ce4r). There is nothing conceptually novel about Misselden's argument here. Reasoning about the value of money from Aristotle through the scholastics to the humanists had held that just value in an exchange depends on both parties freely agreeing to the transaction. However, deploying this logic in the context of a debate on how English monarchs can intervene in international commerce had the effect of pointedly subordinating royal authority to the operations of a market that equates all men with one another, kings and subjects alike. Misselden's use of the logic of commutative justice, though, was patently opportunistic. Although he was very familiar with the scholastic tradition and still considered its invocation in economic writing appropriate and effective, it was insufficient to ground his arguments about the actual operations of commerce. The "balance of trade" that concerned Misselden operated independently of the applications of ethical theories of justice.

For Misselden and Mun, the balance of trade was "a pair of scales" that weighed money and commodities interchangeably (Misselden 1623: sig. Dd1v). In response to arguments that England should aim to limit the exportation and increase the importation of coined money, Misselden argued that what was important was the *value* of exports and imports, not their substance as money or goods. If English merchants sold merchandise worth "one thousand pounds of our money in value," they could receive this value indifferently in "money or merchandise; if not in money, then in merchandise, if not in merchandise, then in money, and consequently, the more comes in in money, the less in merchandise, and the less in merchandise, the more in money" (Misselden 1623: sig. Dd2r). He warned that if this value circled back in the form of non-durable commodities, England would lose the value once these commodities had been consumed. He therefore advocated, in line with English East India Company practice, purchasing foreign commodities that could be "exported again into foreign trade" for a net profit. In *A Discourse of Trade*, Thomas Mun contended that for

"£100,000 in money exported," the English East India Company could purchase "about the value of £500,000 in wares from the East Indies" (1621: sig. E1v). In *England's Treasure by Forraign Trade*, he clarified that he promoted exporting money because "money begets trade and trade increases money." The profit of exported money was realized only after the purchase and reselling of wares that "in the end become an exportation unto us of a far greater value than our said moneys were" (Mun 1664: sig. D3r). For Mun and Misselden, the profit that could be made by buying and selling goods in different locations did not need to be validated by a theory of justice: it existed as an observable fact.

They stressed the importance to the state of carefully monitoring the balance of trade. Misselden wrote, "if a king would desire to behold from his throne the various revolutions of commerce within and without his kingdom, he may behold them all at once in the globe of glass, the balance of trade" (1623: sig. Gg2v). Mun advised that "this balance of the kingdom's account ought to be drawn up yearly, or so often as it shall please the state to discover how much we gain or lose by trade with foreign nations" (1664: sig. B7r). Monarchs should undertake this monitoring, they held, in order to promote the conditions that allowed merchants to generate more in value than is destroyed in domestic consumption. Most forms of royal interventions in the market, however, they held to be ineffective. Mun devoted successive chapters of *England's Treasure by Forraign Trade* to demonstrating that the value accrued to or lost by a kingdom was not ultimately affected by altering the metal content or denomination of coins, enforcing different currency values for foreign coins, forcing foreign merchants to take return on transactions in wares rather than money, forcing English merchants to take return on transactions in money rather than wares, or under- or overvaluing currency in bills of exchange. The market would adaptively respond to each of these policies. Mun did argue that the kings should not attempt to profit from currency manipulations because "money is not only the true measure of all our other means in the kingdom but also of our foreign commerce with strangers, which therefore ought to be kept just and constant to avoid those confusions which ever accompany such alterations" (1664: sig. F4r–v). But, unlike Malynes, Mun argued for maintaining money as a "just," "constant," and "true measure" not because doing so was necessary to ensuring fair valuation in economic transactions, but because failure to do so would cause temporary "confusion" as the valuation of currency in the market adapted to the change.

Likewise, Mun gave attention to "how the revenues and incomes of princes may justly be raised" as a legal and ethical question but with a prevailing sense that the monarch, like his subjects, was always constrained by larger economic forces. He concluded that "the great revenue of the king" ultimately depended on "foreign trade" but little could be done to enforce the profitability of trade (1664: sig. P6r–v). The monarch is not ever granted prominence of place in the litany of economic practices not effecting national prosperity that Mun uses to build to his conclusion:

> let the merchants' exchange be at a high or at a low rate or at the *par pro pari*, or put down altogether; let foreign princes enhance their coins, or debase their standards, and let His Majesty do the like, or keep them constant as they now stand; let foreign coins pass current here in all payments at higher rates than they are worth at the mint; let the statue for employments by strangers stand in force or be repealed; let the mere exchanger do his worst; let princes oppress, lawyers extort, usurers bite, prodigals waste, and lastly let merchants carry out what money they shall have occasion to use in traffic. Yet all these actions can work no other effects in the course of trade than is declared in this discourse.
>
> —1664: sig. P5v–P6r

The actions of "His Majesty" here are undistinguished from those of "foreign princes," "merchants," and "exchangers," all of whom are powerless to overcome the market forces that determine value and direct the movement of goods and money "by a necessity beyond all resistance" (Mun 1664: sig. P6r).

This subordination of the monarch to the market greatly accounts for the decreased emphasis on received theories of justice. Such theories are of central importance to economic thought if one believes oneself to be living in a world in which the monarch's maintenance of just economic exchange through the mechanism of money ensures prosperity. If one conceives of the value of money as established not by royal authority but by its nature as a commodity responding to national and international market forces, theories of justice can be relegated to a domain of ethics distinct from economic analysis. Economic writing from this period demonstrates an uneven shift from one worldview to the other. In tracing the genealogy that stretches from late scholastic writers like Azpilcueta, through humanistic writers like Bodin to the English mercantile writers, we see how reframing of the question of money as an empirical rather than a moral one allowed for the emergence of a concept of money as commodity that, in turn, helped to subordinate royal sovereignty to the forces of international economics.

CHAPTER THREE

Money, Ritual, and Religion

God's Stamp and the Problem of Usury

STEPHEN DENG

In Matthew 22:15–21, the Pharisees and Herodians attempt to trick Christ into an act of treason by asking whether it is right for Jews to pay their taxes to Caesar:

> Then went the Pharisees, and took counsel how they might ensnare him in [his] talk. And they send to him their disciples, with the Herodians, saying, Master (or Teacher), we know that thou art true, and teachest the way of God in truth, and carest not for any one: for thou regardest not the person of men. Tell us therefore, What thinkest thou? Is it lawful to give tribute unto Caesar, or not?
> But Jesus perceived their wickedness, and said, Why tempt ye me, ye hypocrites? Shew me the tribute money. And they brought unto him a penny. And he saith unto them, Whose is this image and superscription? They say unto him, Caesar's. Then saith he unto them, Render therefore unto Caesar the things that are Caesar's; and unto God the things that are God's.
> —Abbott 2014: 255

The Flemish painter Maerten de Vos's 1602 painting depicts the biblical passage (see Figure 3.1). As with all scripture, the passage has been interpreted in

FIGURE 3.1: Maerten de Vos, Render unto Caesar, 1602. Out of copyright, 2016, via Wikimedia Commons.

disparate ways, but one key line of interpretation is that it indicates a clear separation between Church and State, between spiritual and secular matters. For example, James Barr notes that Jesus' answer "makes one striking point, which differs in essence from the theocratic image: there is at least something, somewhere, that is Caesar's, not everything is God's . . . There is thus a certain dualism in society: not everything can be derived from one sole principle" (2013: 203). If the coin itself is Caesar's then this would suggest that money is one such category that is not the concern of God. According to this interpretation, the material object issued by Caesar is irrelevant to the world of the spirit. Christ craftily eludes the trap by implicitly permitting the Pharisees and Herodians to continue paying their tribute as usual, as long as they leave all spiritual matters to God.

However, as I argue in this chapter, this division between spiritual and secular matters was not so clear-cut in early modern Christian thought, at least in relation to the category of money. Indeed, some early commentators see in the passage a metaphor for the relation between God and humans—God stamps his image in humans just as Caesar stamps his image on his coins. The coin, therefore, becomes a model for the conferral of spiritual value in God's favored creatures. And, yet, such an image enables conceptions of potential problems associated with coinage and money, such as debasement, counterfeiting, and hoarding. For example, the conflation of a similar metaphor, deriving from Aristotle, of humans as coins receiving the father's stamp in the mother's material introduced the potential for *illicit* coinage, akin to the production of counterfeit coins. In such versions of the metaphor, how might people conceive of a counterfeit or even debased coin stamped by God Himself? While the image might evoke the ideal of what coins *could* be, the actual experience of coinage saw an array of problems primarily connected to the greed associated with the love of money being the root of all evil.

Moreover, the image of God stamping his image in humans provokes the question of a coin's use and its etymological connection to usury, especially when considering another passage in Matthew: the Parable of the Talents. The parable suggests a potential justification for and even valorization of usury as interest-bearing in the story becomes a metaphor for using one's "talents" for the glory of God. However, other allusions to usury in the Bible emphasize its sinfulness, primarily because of its suggestion of greed and lack of brotherly compassion. And, yet, attitudes toward usury were changing in the early modern period, as the needs of business culture started to influence theological discourse, especially within Reformation theology. A key figure for this transformation was Jean Calvin, who reinterpreted scripture in order to differentiate between *types* of usury, those destructive versions indicated by the Hebraic term "*neschech*," and the more productive version called "*tarbit*," which merely connotes increase. The eventual establishment of a legal rate of interest differentiating "usury" from the more neutral "interest" would correspond to Calvin's emphasis on destructive vs. productive versions of moneylending with interest. Overall, intersections between theological and monetary concerns would persist in the early modern period despite attempts to differentiate between the spiritual terms of religion and the worldly terms of economy.

GOD'S STAMP

The passage from Matthew in which Christ responds to the question of whether or not taxes should continue to be paid to Caesar has been a key point of debate about the extent of separation between Church and State or spiritual and secular realms. Some commentators use the passage to differentiate jurisdiction over the two realms. For example, John Foxe, in his influential *Acts and Monuments* (first published 1583), describes a conversation in Paris in 1329 between prelates, clergy, and members of the king's council. One participant, Lord Peter de Cugner, speaking on behalf of the king, took up the passage from Matthew as his theme, interpreting two points in the passage: first, "the reuerence and subiection of the Prelates, that they ought to haue to the king their soueraigne," and, second, "the deuision of the temporall iurisdictio[n] from the spirituall." In support of the second point, he invokes Luke 22, which refers to two swords signifying two different jurisdictions, as well as

> mans law, where it is sayd, 2. great gifts are bestowed, Priesthood and Empire: The priesthood to rule ouer matters diuine: the Empire to beare domination ouer humaine matters. wherby he co[n]cluded, that when these iurisdictions are distincted of God: The one being geuen and limited to the church, and the other to the temporalty.
>
> —1583: sig. HH4r

Cugner cites scripture to establish the power of the state as separate and distinct from that of the Church. But the State's power was often thought to derive *from* God, complicating the distinction between "temporall" and "spirituall" jurisdictions. Richard Ward interprets the passage as an indication that God and Caesar are both magistrates, but that Caesar's magistracy is *subordinate* to that of God: "God and *Caesar* are not contrary, but subordinate Magistrates; GOD is the chiefe, and *Caesar* subordinate. And therefore render to both of them what is theirs" (1640: sig. Eeee3r). Other commentators invoked the passage to establish the idea that Caesar's (or a king's) power is granted directly by God and therefore has divine sanction. For example, Philipp Melanchthon reads the passage as a sign of Christ "comfyrmyng the auctoritie of princes, commaunding also to gyue, pay, and rendre vnto Cesar all that doth belonge to the emperyall crowne and dignitie of the Emperoure," adding also a reference to Paul who commands "vs to be obediente to kinges and magystrates, addinge thereto a cause of oure necessary obedience, declaringe that he is nat ordeyned of man but of God, as the hygh minister and officer of god, and that he beareth nat the swerd in vayne" (1548: sig. M5r). Both "temporall" and "spirituall" jurisdictions derived their authorities from God, and each would therefore need to establish the will of this authority in various matters to define clear boundaries between their respective realms, a division of authority that was not always so clear-cut.

Rather than a separation of jurisdictions, David Landreth interprets the passage as an instance of separating the substantial or "real" things that are God's from the insubstantial or mere "images" that are Caesar's, a play on the nature of the coin which is real material that becomes usable as currency only when it receives the surface stamp. Landreth finds in this "riddle of the penny" an "accommodation" between "revolutionary church" and "indifferent empire," which elevates the penny "into the discourse of ontology" that "bifurcates the penny into two aspects, material and formal, of which only the former is real" (2012: 11). Ultimately, it is the gold or silver that is the real substance merely carrying the insubstantial signifier that constitutes Caesar's claim despite that it is a coin only by virtue of the stamping process:

> The riddle of the penny articulates the tension between divine and human authorities as a feature of the coin's makeup. It is a penny by virtue of the image impressed upon it to give it form, which is that of human authority, Caesar. But "the things which be God's," read ironically, relegates the imprint of Caesar to the status of epiphenomenon, or surface effect. Given that everything is God's, "the things which be Caesar's" becomes a merely notional category, an empty set, constituted by insubstantial images. Substance, then, is God's claim on the coin. Insofar as the penny bears Caesar's "image and superscription," it is Caesar's. Insofar as it exists in the universe, it is God's.
>
> —2012: 10–11

In this instance, Jesus is able to negotiate the trap by verbally identifying a "realm" that belongs to Caesar, but this identification ultimately constitutes a verbal trick to maintain God's claim on the coin in its substantial components. Caesar's claim remains merely on the insubstantial realm of images.

Jesus' response to the question of Caesar's coinage in these examples serves to examine whether the emperor maintains certain jurisdictional rights over real substance (or merely insubstantial imagery), in general. However, Nicholas Oresme uses the passage to limit the king's rights in producing coinage, *in particular*. In his treatise from the 1350s called *De moneta* ("On Money"), the nominalist scholar states that the passage is usually interpreted as meaning, "'The coin is Caesar's because Caesar's image is stamped upon it,'" and therefore Christ is instructing those raising the question to return to Caesar what is properly his. But because Oresme wrote his tract in response to debasement of the coinage by French kings, he questions the nature of ownership of the coin. Oresme reinterprets the passage to suggest the coin is Caesar's only because he was the "person who fought the battles of the state" not as an indication that he can do whatever he likes to coinage, including reducing its precious metal content (1956: 11). Caesar in this reading should receive coins as tribute for the services he has rendered, not because the coin bears his image; the stamp merely indicates authenticity and not ownership. Oresme uses what is typically understood as a distinction between spiritual and worldly realms to establish universal laws preventing abuse of the money supply.

The questions of ownership and potential abuses of coinage complicate a common metaphor of humans as coins produced by God's stamp. G.W.H. Lampe suggests that in the passage from Matthew about the tribute money, "a reference to the divine image in man may have been originally intended by Jesus" (1951: 254). The passage enables such a metaphor by seeing humans as bearing God's image, as coins stamped by God. In one sermon, Augustine implores Christians:

> Regain, therefore, the likeness to God which you lost through your sins. For as the image of the emperor on the coin is one thing and his image in his son another: for there are different kinds of images; but the image of the emperor is engraved in the coin in one way, in the son in another, and in solid gold even in a different way: so you too are a coin of God; and even better since you are God's coin with reason and life, so that you know whose image you bear and according to whose image you are made: For the coin is not aware of bearing the emperor's image.
>
> —Quoted in Schleiner 1970: 113

In his sermon, Augustine alludes to three kinds of stamps: the emperor's stamp on his coins; the emperor as father's stamp on his son; and God's original stamp on the sinner. He suggests that sin alters the coin granted by God, and only by recalling the value of one's stamp can one follow the path of redemption and restore the coin to full weight. The second stamp, that of the father, alludes to Aristotle's metaphor in *De Generatione Animalium* that in procreation, "the female always provides the material," while "the male always provides that which fashions the material into shape," that is, the stamp of the soul (1953: 185). Aristotle's metaphor is that of a wax seal, but the image was often extended to coinage as well.[1] For example, in Shakespeare's *Cymbeline*, Posthumus describes acts of adultery in terms of illicit coinage production:

> We are all bastards,
> And that most venerable man which I
> Did call my father, was I know not where
> When I was stamp'd. Some coiner with his tools
> Made me a counterfeit . . .
>
> —2.5.2–6[2]

Believing his love, Imogen, unfaithful to him, Posthumus assumes that all women are false and involved in producing illegitimate children from the material of their bodies and the stamp of someone other than their husbands'. Posthumus' particular employment of the metaphor calls attention to the potential for "immoral" versions of producing both coins and children.

This potential for illegitimate production unsettles the metaphor of humans bearing the stamp of God. Later in *Cymbeline*, Posthumus uses another coining metaphor that suggests he is a previously legitimate coin with a divine stamp that has been altered, rather than being born a counterfeit coin. Regretting having accused Imogen of being unfaithful, after he believes she is dead, he pleads to the gods to accept his own life in exchange for restoring hers:

> For Imogen's dear life take mine, and though
> 'Tis not so dear, yet 'tis a life; you coin'd it.
> 'Tween man and man they weigh not every stamp;
> Though light, take pieces for the figure's sake;
> You, rather, mine being yours; and so, great pow'rs,
> If you will take this audit, take this life,
> And cancel these cold bonds.
> —5.4.22–8

In Posthumus' first speech, he has received an illicit stamp from a man other than his mother's husband. In the second, he has been granted the stamp of the gods, but his life's metal has become "light" because of what he has done. Posthumus in this second instance sees himself as akin to a clipper, one who has clipped metal from the edges of coins, which was a common practice in the early modern period. And, yet, he hopes that the original stamp would allow him to maintain his life's value despite his actions. Whereas he at first believed his mother had offered her metal to another man's stamp in producing his counterfeit life, the guilt he feels about Imogen's putative death transforms his thinking, now believing he was born a legitimate, full-bodied coin but that he had altered his divine gift through immoral acts.

In a sermon given on Christmas of 1622, John Donne crafts a similar conflation between God's and the father's stamp in his application of the metaphor. Donne employs the image of a son receiving the father's stamp in order to compare Christ to a newly minted coin receiving the Holy Ghost's stamp within the mint of the Virgin. He expands upon this idea by conceiving of the coin being used to redeem the debts of humans—a common conflation between financial and spiritual "debt"—who have altered and abused the coins they were lent originally:

> First, he must pay it in such money as was lent; in the nature and flesh of man; for man had sinned, and man must pay. And then it was lent in such money as was coined even with the Image of God; man was made according to his Image: That Image being defaced, in a new Mint, in the wombe of the Blessed Virgin, there was new money coined; The Image of the invisible God, the second person in the Trinity, was imprinted into the humane nature.
> —1953–62: 4:288

In Donne's metaphor, Christ's birth restores the standards of the current coinage: his life is a gift that offers the wealth needed for redeeming the original loan. However, his allusion to a new stamp provided by the Holy Ghost intimates that this coinage is even dearer than the original coins granted to humans. The store of human wealth has therefore increased as a result of Christ's redemption, a financial version of the Fortunate Fall.

Again, the metaphor of God's stamp was likely informed by the passage from Matthew in which Christ is asked whether tribute should be paid to Caesar. Lampe finds the metaphor in early sources such as Gregory of Nyssa and Macarius and suggests that Early Church Fathers found in the passage Jesus' intention to compare the image of Caesar on the coin to the divine image and inscription of God's name engraved in the believer, who "becomes the Lord's coin and receives the royal χάραγμα [charisma]." For Lampe, the illegitimate coin represents the soul of the unbeliever, who "does not bear the image of the Spirit" and thus "cannot be put into the royal treasuries of the Kingdom of Heaven" (1951: 254). Such a reading is supported by a passage in one of Macarius's homilies:

> As the golden coin, if it does not receive the imprint of the king's image, does not come upon the market, and is not stored in the king's treasuries, but is discarded, so the soul, if it has not the image of the heavenly Spirit in light unspeakable, even Christ imprinted on it, is not fit for the treasuries above, and is discarded by the good merchants of the kingdom, the apostles.... This is the mark and sign of the Lord imprinted upon souls, being the Spirit of light unspeakable.
>
> —1921: 225

While Posthumus had described himself as a counterfeit coin produced by his mother having received the stamp of one who was not her husband, Macarius uses the concept of the counterfeit coin to describe the non-Christian who has not received the true stamp of Christ's grace but the false stamp of some other religion. Such deployment of coinage imagery establishes a representational connection between morality and legitimate production of coinage, which partly authorizes the monarch and state as the rightful producer of money employed by subjects, but also partly limits the power of the state in coinage production, especially by curbing the temptation to extract value from the people by debasing the coinage. The divine gift of the monetary stamp is not something that should be exploited and abused.

The idea of God's stamp and grace as a monetary gift from Christ recalls another passage in Matthew, the Parable of the Talents, which adds yet another monetary practice to the already complicated mix: usury. An etching by Lucas van Doetechum from the mid-sixteenth century depicts the story (see Figure 3.2). In this parable, a master gives to three of his slaves a certain number of "talents," extremely valuable coins, each was worth about 6,000 *denarii*

FIGURE 3.2: Lucas van Doetechum (1530–84), Parable of the Talents etching. © Fine Art Images/Alamy.com, 2017.

(1 denarius was about a day's wages for a common laborer) (Hultgren 2000: 274–5). The first slave received five talents, the second slave two talents, and the third slave one talent. The first two slaves took the talents and "traded with them" (Matthew 25:16), thereby doubling the money.³ But the third slave who received one talent "went and dug in the ground and hid his master's money" (Matthew 25:18). After some time, the master returned and "settled accounts with them" (Matthew 25:19); each slave, in turn, presents the talents they now have to him. The master responds to the first two: "'Well done, good and faithful slave; you have been faithful over a little; I will set you over much; enter into the joy of your master'" (Matthew 25:21). But the third attempts to rationalize his decision to bury his talent: "'Master, I knew you to be a hard man, reaping where you did not sow, and gathering where you did not scatter [seed]; I was afraid, and I went and hid your talent in the ground'" (Matthew 25:24–5). He presents the master with only the one talent he had been given, and the master subsequently rebukes him for his decision: "'You wicked and lazy slave! You knew that I reap where I have not sowed, and gather where I have not scattered? Then you ought to have invested my money with the bankers, and at my coming I should have received what was my own with interest'" (Matthew 25:26–7). He has the lone talent taken from the slave and

gives it to the one who had originally received five talents (Matthew 25:28). The master then summarizes the lesson that should have been learned in the decisions of the three slaves: "'For to every one who has will more be given, and he will have abundance; but from the one who has not, even what he has will be taken away. And cast the worthless slave into the outer darkness; there people will weep and gnash their teeth'" (Matthew 25:29–30).

The general sense of the parable, that one must employ the gifts or "talents" that God has granted, especially in support of God's will, is pretty clear. In his commentary on the parable, Arland Hultgren states that it "reminds the Christian community that God has bestowed various gifts, and gifts in various measure, to all," though he qualifies that rather than pure gift, the talents might be understood as "money entrusted to them" because "all the gifts of God are temporary; they are like funds entrusted to people but for a while" (2000: 279). The problem with the slave who had one talent is that his burying of it "signifies lack of use, acting in such a way that nothing has been entrusted at all" (2000: 280). The image meshes with general warnings about the dangers of monetary hoarding, which removes from circulation money needed for economies to run smoothly. Money, in this conception, was meant to be used in exchange and not hoarded for the purpose of wealth accumulation.

However, the imagery in the parable also suggests that the "use" of money, or taking of interest with it, may be permitted, going against other biblical prohibitions of usury. There is some ambiguity in the source of monetary return for the slaves who received five and two talents, respectively. The parable mentions that the slaves "traded with" their talents. There are no biblical prohibitions of trade or merchants, generally; the idea of making money through the exchange of goods was permissible and sometimes lauded as a willingness to trust in God's providence in the face of financial risk. But, unlike the risk-bearing merchant, the usurer is promised riskless return on money, a return that does not rely on faith in providence. Generally, such acts were deemed contrary to Christian principles, especially when greed seemed to be the primary motive for charging interest. And, yet, in this one parable, the master rebukes the third slave that he "ought to have invested my money with the bankers, and at my coming I should have received what was my own with interest." The parable clearly works as a lesson about using one's talents for the glory of God, but the particular admonition in support of interest seeking seems counter to Christian ideals.

Nevertheless, during the early modern period, Christian countries were beginning to reconcile biblical attitudes toward usury with the growing needs of business and commerce for gaining access to interest-bearing money markets. Some Reformation figures—Jean Calvin, in particular—were critical for establishing a distinction between forms of usury that were beneficial to Christian society ("*tarbit*") and forms of usury that were destructive ("*neschech*," which has various other spellings, including *"neshech," "neshekh,"* and *"neshek"*). The command to seek interest in the Parable of the Talents might be interpreted as an example of the former, more productive form of usury.

USURY

Usury had been prohibited in most Christian countries because of biblical injunctions against it, as in Exodus 22:25: "If thou shalt geve monie to lone unto my poore people which dwelleth with thee, thou shalt not be instant upon him as an importunate wringer, neither shalt thou oppresse him with usurie," or as in Deuteronomy 23:20–1: "Thou shalt not increase monie upon thy brother by usurie, nor corne, nor any other thing: but do that to thine enemy" (quoted in Jones 1989: 7). The latter suggested the possibility of lending at interest to those *not* considered your brothers, or "others." Nevertheless, the practice was typically condemned in general as a form of avarice that could be detrimental to the soul, as depicted in allegorical *memento mori* such as Jan Provoost's *Death and the Miser* (see Figure 3.3). In addition to biblical prohibitions, anti-usury discourse cited classical sources, especially Aristotle. For Aristotle, the Greek term for usury, *tokos* or "offspring," connoted a kind

FIGURE 3.3: Jan Provoost, *Death and the Miser*, early 1500s. Web Gallery of Art, out of copyright, 2013, via Wikimedia Commons.

of unnatural breeding that perverted the notion of naturally produced offspring. Usurers in the early modern period were often represented as being more interested in producing money than progeny, or caring more about their wealth than their children, as in the case of Shylock, who conflates his stolen "ducats" and his lost "daughter," according to an account in one scene of *Merchant of Venice*.

Before the sixteenth century, the scholastic debate about usury hinged primarily on the difference between usury (*usura*), which was sinful in all cases, and interest (*interesse*), the latter of which was often categorized as either *damnum emergens*, the loss from failure to repay a loan, or *lucrum cessans*, the loss of potential profit on the money loaned by the lending party. The latter, which modern economists describe as the "opportunity cost" of money, would gradually become the justification—from an economic perspective if not from a moral perspective—for why interest should be charged on money loans. The interest rate is, in effect, the price of money in terms of a possible return foregone. In the Middle Ages, the two terms remained points of contention, with Aquinas permitting the first (*damnum emergens*) but refusing to legitimize the latter (*lucrum cessans*). Nevertheless, by the mid-fifteenth century, the idea of risk involved in making a loan provided a rationale for the charging of interest even while usury in principle remained a sin (Jones 1989: 11).

Controversy arose especially around the "triple contract"—which permitted one party to pay another party to assume the risk of a loan. By the 1480s, such contracts in effect became partnerships between only two parties (despite the term "triple-contract"), the lender and borrower, so that, as Norman Jones writes, "the borrower was insuring the lender against loss in return for a lower, but guaranteed, rate of return on the loan" (1989: 11). The concept somewhat resembles our contemporary "credit default swaps," which allow financial institutions, especially insurance companies, to buy the risk on mortgage-backed securities—or technically, to sell instruments alongside mortgage-backed securities, according to which they contractually assumed the risk on these securities. Some maintained that triple contracts constituted usury because the hedging (in modern parlance) made it such that there ended up being no risk on the loan.[4]

Controversy over the triple contract arose once again in the late-fifteenth and early-sixteenth centuries, when the issue of *intention* complicated the debate. In response to claims that triple contracts constituted usury because of the guaranteed return, the "Tübingen school" of Gabriel Biel, Conrad Summenhart, and Johann Eck—who had been influenced by Jean Gerson's emphasis on intention in gauging whether acts should be construed as evil—argued that intention should also determine whether loan contracts are classified as usurious. They insisted that there is no usurious intention in the triple contract, either because it merely produces a partnership entailing the co-ownership of money, and thus there is no true loaning of money (Summenhart), or because the partner solicited the loan from the lender for legitimate business purposes and was able to make a profit from it (Eck). Eck, in particular—whose patron was Jacob Fugger, of the great mining and banking family—created significant controversy by claiming in his *Tractatus contractu quinque de centum* (1515) that *any* contract, in Jones' description, "was completely legal, so long as the interest was modest and it occurred in a *bona fide* business situation" (1989: 12). Eck even suggested that a reasonable rate of 5 percent interest (apparently a common going rate for such contracts in Augsburg) should be authorized for legitimate business purposes, as long as there is no intention of oppressing the poor.[5]

The position of those defending certain forms of lending with interest gained strength during the mid-sixteenth century with the work of Charles du Moulin and especially with the authority of Jean Calvin, whose response to Deuteronomy, Benjamin Nelson claims, "spelled the dislodgement of the millennial theory of usury" (1949: 69; see Figure 3.4). In his *Tractatus contractuum et usurarum, reditumque pecunia constitutorum et monetarum*, written in 1542 and published in Paris in 1547, du Moulin argued that loan contracts should be (according to Jones' description):

> judged by the circumstances of the borrower. If the request came from a poor person one must lend freely expecting nothing in return. If it came from those who, though not indigent, were temporarily in need, one must lend freely, expecting only the principal to be returned. If it came from a rich person one might charge interest because the money will be used to make more money, and one has a right to a share in the profits. As long as the interest charged is reasonable, says du Moulin, there is nothing wrong with lending at interest to people who will use the money productively. These distinctions became the stock-in-trade of those English who supported lending at interest.
> —Jones 1989: 16

Du Moulin was clearly following the line of the Tübingen school in emphasizing intention within the loan contract. As long as any person entering a loan contract followed the golden rule, the contract would not be sinful and, in fact, could be virtuous if the loan is made out of charity. And, like Eck, he argued for the authorization of a "reasonable" rate of interest, which he also set at 5 percent. Moreover, he adds to these concerns the important element of the borrowers' specific financial circumstances in deciding whether loan contracts should be permitted. While lending to those in need should be done with no expectation of obtaining interest or even the principal, money and interest should flow freely among the rich because they can employ the money for creative and productive purposes.

FIGURE 3.4: Anonymous (Hans Holbein?), Jean Calvin, 1550s. Public domain, 2017, via Wikimedia Commons.

In a 1545 epistle, Jean Calvin similarly argued for the need to consider the circumstances of those borrowing in a loan contract, and more importantly he reinterpreted scripture to support this position. Jones points out that Calvin's letter of advice was not intended for the public, but as an expression of his own opinions to a friend. It was not published for some years after its composition. In fact, in the letter, he admonishes the friend not to publicize these opinions because he was concerned it would be used as a promotion of all usury. Nevertheless, as Jones writes, "Calvin's stature among reformed theologians made his opinions on usury well known in Elizabethan England" (1989: 19). In his epistle, Calvin proclaimed that: "if wee condemne Vsurie altogether, then doe wee laye a heauier burthen vpon mens consciences, than GOD himselfe doeth in his worde" (1616: sig. F3r). He set out to demonstrate that careful interpretation of scripture disproves the claims that the bible prohibits all lending; no testimony of scripture, he argued, ever condemned usury completely. For example, he reads verse 35 of Luke, "*Lende one to another, looking for nothing againe*," as a commandment "to lende to the poore, rather than to the rich. And so for all this, wee see not Usurie altogether forbidden" (1616: sig. F3v, F4r). Again, from scriptural example, Calvin finds that usurers are forbidden "onelie so farre as they are repugnant to equitie and charitie" (1616: sig. F4v–G1r). At the end of his epistle, he lists seven caveats that loan contracts should follow. The third caveat is that "there bee no condition insert, or put in the couenant of lending, but that which agreeth with naturall equitie, and is agreeable with CHRISTS commandement, to wit, *Whatsoeuer ye would haue men doe to you, doe yee likewise the same to them*" (sig. G2v). Like du Moulin, Calvin saw no problem with a loan contract as long as the lender followed the golden rule and intended no harm to the person of the borrower.

However, Calvin's most significant contribution was his observation that Hebraic scripture, especially in a verse from Ezekiel, used the two different terms for usury with which we are already familiar: *neschech* and *tarbit*:[6]

> But the Prophet EZECHIEL goeth yet farther: for whilest hee reckoneth out the abhominations for which the wrath of GOD was kindled among the IEWES, hee useth two sundrie wordes, of which the one [*neschech*] signifieth Vsurie, and is deryued from a certaine Verbe, which doeth also signifie gnawing or byting, and the other [*tarbit*] signifieth encrease or augmentation.
> —1616: sig. F4v

Calvin was especially concerned that usury should not bite the poor, and in fact he makes the "biting" connotation of *neschech* synonymous with damage specifically *to* the poor. In his sermon on Deuteronomy, he writes that the term *neschech* was employed in scripture, "Bicause it byteth and wasteth a poore man which is charged with it" (1583: sig. Zzz3v). And in his 1545 epistle he makes as his first caveat "That Vse bee neuer required of needie and poore men, nor that anie that are in necessitie and miserie bee compelled to pay Vse" (1616: sig. G2r). Similarly, the second caveat expresses concern about a lender's addiction to interest profit, while disregarding the effect on the poor, such that "in taking securitie for his money, he haue no regarde of his poore brethren euen in lending to them" (1616: sig. G2r). The suggestion from Calvin's comments is that scripture intended *neschech* to refer specifically to those usurious loans that oppressed the poor, not to all loans in general.

Moreover, the second term *tarbit* might indicate a positive side to loan contracts. Calvin's interpretation of scripture argues against those like the later commentator, Henry Smith, who claimed there was only one word for usury in the Bible: "If there were one byting vsurie, and another healing vsurie, then vsurie should have two names; one of byting, & another of healing: but all vsurie signifieth byting, to shewe that all vsurie is vnlawfull" (1591: sig. A6v). Calvin shows that, in fact, there *were* two words for usury, although whether *tarbit* should be interpreted with positive valence remained a point of controversy. While the implication of the first term, *neschech*, is clearly destructive, the meaning of the latter term, *tarbit*, is not as clear. For example,

Philipp Caesar reads *tarbit* as akin to *tokos*, an unnatural increase: "By Tarbis is ment an ill encrease, because Vsurers make that to fructisie whiche is fruitles, whiche by the witnes of Ethnikes is contrarie to nature" (1578: sig. C1v). In his commentary on Calvin, Jones believes Calvin interprets *tarbit* to mean "to take legitimate increase" (1989: 18), but from the context of the epistle alone its valence remains unclear despite the fact that he generally argues that not all usury is forbidden. However, Calvin's sermon on Deuteronomy provides further information about his view:

> Nowe for all this God forbiddeth not all manner of gaine, so as a man may not make any profite at al. For were it so, we must lay aside all Marchandise, and wee might not lawfully buy and sell one with another. But hee forbiddeth the profite or encrease which a man getteth by deliuering out his owne goods without his owne losse, and yet notwithstanding will sucke another mans substance: and careth not whether he harme his neighbour or no, so that he may enriche himselfe.
>
> —1583: sig. Zzz3v

From the sermon we find Calvin arguing that increase in itself is not bad as long as it does not come at the expense of the borrower. Commerce and exchange benefit both parties, so why should the lending of money not be allowed if it also can benefit both? If the borrower can use the money loaned productively and reap a return at least as high as the interest charged, the increase going to the lender should be considered legitimate.[7]

Calvin's position on usury was developed independently by Martin Bucer, who around 1550 famously debated the Master of Pembroke Hall, Cambridge, John Young, on the question. Although the exact date and location of the debates are unclear, Bucer published his arguments on usury in his 1550 *Tractatus de usuris*. The controversy emerged primarily because, in 1545, Parliament began its own debate over whether a 10 percent rate of interest should be permitted in England. Young assumed the conservative position that all usury was sinful. On the other hand, Bucer, like Calvin, argued that the Bible does not prohibit all usury. Like Calvin and the line of apologists for usury before him, Bucer argued that in loan contracts the lender should follow the golden rule in considering the particular circumstances of the borrower: the poor should not be exploited and therefore nothing should be expected in return. However, if you are lending to a merchant, you could still follow the golden rule in expecting a return since the merchant would presumably profit from the use of the money (Jones 1989: 19–22).

Again, as Calvin argued, it is only *neschech*, the type of loan contracts that "bite" borrowers, which should be classified as a kind of theft and therefore prohibited by scripture. Indeed, following Justinian's code, England may lawfully permit a ten percent rate of interest. Whereas Roman law permitted a 12 percent rate of interest, Germans permitted 5 percent, and Zurichers allowed 3 percent, England permitted 10: "In every case, however, the community has licensed and moderated what is recognized to be a necessity" (Jones 1989: 21).[8] It was therefore Bucer who first made the explicit connection between a legitimate 10 percent rate of interest and the prohibition only of "biting" usury. *Implicit* in his response is that any rate higher than this might be considered biting whereas 10 percent or below could be construed as non-biting, as long as the circumstances of the borrower are taken into account. Calvin had included as his seventh caveat, "That we exceede not the measure or extent of the vse agreede vpon in anie Countrey or Commonwealth," as well as the point that not all loans should be made at the legal level "for that is often suffered, which by no Ciuill Ordinance can bee amended, or restrained: The rule of righteousnesse is therefore first of all, and chiefelie to bee regarded" (1616: sig. G2v–G3r). But, for Calvin, *neschech* was primarily the exploitation of the poor, while for Bucer, *neschech* meant not only the exploitation of the poor and needy by charging any interest, but also the exploitation of merchants and other businesspeople by charging too *high* a rate of interest. Summarizing the perspective of apologists for usury, Jones writes that while "[c]ondemning 'biting' loans, they were willing to tolerate loans at interest for legitimate business purposes" (1989: 19).

The result of the debates in Parliament was a statute in 1545 repealing an earlier ban on usury and permitting interest on lending of up to 10 percent. The debate did not end there, however. A 1552 statute repealed the 1545 one permitting certain loans, and once again banned all lending with interest. Then, in the 1570s, the debate heated up once again, and the metaphors that had previously been used to justify certain forms of usury were once again deployed. According to the Parliamentary debate that led up to the usury statute of 1571, the Queen's Latin Secretary, Sir John Wolley, defended the practice of charging interest on loan contracts by invoking the same scriptural passages as Calvin and Bucer (though using the Latin term "morsus" rather than the Hebraic), and mentioning supporting interpretations by early biblical scholars:

> As for the words of the Scripture, he [Wolley] saith, the Hebrew soundeth thus in Answer of this Question; *Qui non dat pecuniam suam ad morsum*: so it is the biting and over-sharp dealing which is disliked and nothing else. And this, he said, was the opinion and interpretation of the most Famous Learned Man *Beza*, and in these days, of *Bellarmine* and divers others; who say, that the true interpretation of the Hebrew word is not *Usura*, but *Morsus*.
> —D'Ewes 1682: sig. Z2v

Thomas Wilson, who later wrote the famous *Discourse Upon Usury* (1572), then cited Augustine's saying, "that to take but a Cup of Wine, is Usury" in order to argue that all usury is in fact "*Morsus*," and another, Mr. Norton, argued in the final speech:

> all Usury is biting; as in the word *Steal* is contained all kind of injurious taking away of a mans goods: and as slanderizing is said to be murthering or homicide; so is Usury justly ever to be said biting, they being both so correlated or knit together, that the one may not be without the other.
> —D'Ewes 1682: sig. Z2v, Z3v

Yet, again, the debate concerned the question of whether there are two types of usury with different valences, or whether any usury proves destructive to a commonwealth. Those unwilling to compromise by permitting *any* form of interest taking wanted to establish a unitary principle of usury, which is always in itself a violation of Christian morality.

Despite the arguments against usury, the 1552 statute banning usury was repealed, primarily because the ban created more problems, and in fact produced more cases of exploitative usury, than would otherwise have been the case. The compromise of permitting once again a maximum 10 percent rate of interest was justified on the grounds that it was in the interest of the commonwealth as a whole. In his sixth caveat in the epistle, Calvin had mentioned the importance of taking into account the overall welfare of the commonwealth. He argued that in considering usury laws, we should "regarde also what may bee expedient for the Commonwealth: for the Vsurie which Marchandes paye, it is a publicke tribute. There must a care, therefore, bee had, that the couenantes bee drawne as maye stand rather with the good, than hurt of the Commonwealth" (1616: sig. G2v). Francis Bacon later picked up on this perspective of the Commonwealth's interest, while also employing the language of *neschech*, in his proposal that there be two rates of interest, "the one free, and general for all," which Bacon suggests at 8 percent and "the other under licence only, to certain persons and in certain places of merchandizing," which should be set by the market (2002: 423). In fact, Bacon uses the implications of the metaphor in order to defend legalized usury, contrasting the mere "gnawing" that usury would create with the lack of commerce from banning usury, which would eventually devour people:

> were it not for this easy borrowing upon interest, men's necessities would draw upon them a most sudden undoing; in that they would be forced to sell their means (be it lands or goods) far under foot; and so, whereas usury doth but gnaw upon them, bad markets would swallow them quite up.
> —2002: 422

The ability to borrow actually prevents people from being consumed. However, the rate should be chosen so that such gnawing should be moderate. In specifying a reasonable rate of interest common to all, therefore, Bacon suggests "that the tooth of usury be grinded, that it bite not too much" (2002: 423).

Also writing in the 1600s, Andrew Willet employed the metaphor but suggested that a moderate rate of interest would not bite at all: rather than grinding the teeth, it would remove them all together.[9] Moreover, a moderate rate would not even be considered usury, which, like the earlier opponents of legalized usury, he makes synonymous with *neschech*:

> interest which is received must be moderate, not excessive: *Yee shall not oppresse him with usury*: the word is *neschech*, biting: it must not bee a biting, nipping, or devouring usury . . . So the lawes of this land doe moderate excessive usury: to take above two shillings in the pound, and ten in the hundreth, is a forfeiture both of the principall and interest.
> —1633: sig. Oo4v

Like the earlier scholastic commentators on usury, Willet distinguishes between "interest" and "usury," but he does so in an entirely new manner. Whereas interest had previously been determined qualitatively—by designating the losses from a loan either in non repayment or forgone profits—Willet now makes the distinction quantitatively. Any rate under ten percent would be considered "interest" and perfectly legal, while a rate above that would be considered "usurious." This resembles our contemporary differentiation between "interest" and "usury." We find in Willet a clear articulation of the link between the moral position that usury should not be biting and the economic perspective that a ten percent rate of interest may be deemed "reasonable."

The establishment of a differentiation between "usury" and "interest," with the former indicating only *excessive* interest-taking, relies upon this distinction between productive and destructive versions of usury embodied in the terms *tarbit*, which suggests "increase," and *neschech*, which connotes "biting" usury. The latter term featured prominently especially in attempts to legitimate certain types of lending with interest. Whereas *any* breeding of money according to the notion of *tokos*, no matter how small the interest rate, would be considered "unnatural," supporters of loan contracts with interest would refer to *neschech* in order to differentiate between destructive forms of usury, those that "bite," and non-destructive or even beneficial forms. For example, Jean Calvin, whose epistle on usury—which had not been intended for public consumption but nonetheless proved an important influence in the later debate—differentiated between the two biblical Hebraic terms used for usury: *neschech* and *tarbit*, the latter of which has a sense of "increase" akin to Aristotle's *tokos*, but without the necessary "unnatural" connotation: it has often been interpreted as "legitimate increase." Whereas *neschech* represented the deleterious form which should be banned, *tarbit* encompassed beneficial forms of lending that had been recognized throughout much scholastic discourse. The compromise within England in 1571 (which upheld an earlier statute under Henry VIII) of a lawful 10 percent rate of interest constituted, in effect, a designation of the boundary point between *neschech* and *tarbit*. A common argument for setting a maximum rate of interest was that loans should not bite the borrower, especially if the borrower is poor, but that lending at reasonable rates of interest could benefit commerce throughout the commonwealth.

The famous passage from Matthew in which Jesus declares, "Render therefore unto Caesar the things which are Caesar's; and unto God the things that are God's," provoked various considerations about the boundaries between those things in the world that are of immediate concern to God and those that are not. Money and coinage would seem to be one such category of concern only to the state and secular authorities, but as I have demonstrated in this chapter, the metaphors of coinage and the morality of monetary increase would become key sites where divine and worldly interests converged and often produced tensions concerning the realities of monetary use. In its ideal forms and practices, money could offer a productive conceptualization of God's relation to humans as well as communal relations that could benefit all members. In its realistic abuses, however, such as the practices of counterfeiting, clipping, debasement, hoarding, and "biting" interest-taking, the conceptualization reveals the moral problems of money for which "rendering unto Caesar" alone would seem insufficient for upholding Christian ideals. This tension provoked by monetary abuses would persist as long as Christian values continued to have bearing on economic practices. It would only be when economy finally divorced itself from its moral and ethical underpinnings (to the extent that it ever has remains a question of debate, however) that Jesus' pronouncement could be interpreted as clearly designating two distinct non-conflicting realms of jurisdiction.

CHAPTER FOUR

Money and the Everyday

Reputation, History, and Symbolism on the Eastern African Coast

STEPHANIE WYNNE-JONES

This chapter asks the question, "What is money for?"[1] The occasion for this question is a study of the coins of the precolonial Eastern African coast. During the period covered by this volume, this coast was a fully integrated part of the Islamic world, with connections to and knowledge of a network that extended from China in the east to the Mediterranean in the west. Yet, the study of Eastern African coinage is interesting because the people of this coast—known collectively as the "Swahili"—remained on the margins of the Islamic world. Although fully cognizant of people and practices in the heartlands of Islam, the Swahili were independent of direct control, and maintained their own unique practices. Coins were minted in only a few places on this coast, but in those places they were energetically adopted. The coins minted in centers like Kilwa Kisiwani and Mogadishu were also widely distributed along the coast and between residents of the towns. Coins are associated with all centuries of coastal occupation, linked to the trading society that developed here from the eighth century onwards.

In this chapter, the focus is on the fourteenth to sixteenth centuries, coinciding with the era known elsewhere as the Renaissance. On the eastern coast of Africa, this was the peak of commercial prosperity in a precolonial trade network around the Indian Ocean world, in which the Swahili were active participants. This was a time on the Eastern African coast associated with the construction of grand townscapes at some of the trading towns, apparently dominated by a wealthy merchant elite. Those groups were Islamic, highly cosmopolitan, and very aware of material and symbolic practices elsewhere in the Islamic world. This is a fascinating period to explore material objects in this region, linked to the golden age of precolonial Swahili prosperity. This is also a period from which we have particularly high-resolution data, from recent excavations at the site of Songo Mnara on the southern Tanzanian coast (Wynne-Jones and Fleisher 2010, 2011). Contextual information for the coins found in the archaeological record has given a new insight into the ways that coins were valued and used, as part of the everyday life of the site rather than as part of the town's trade in bulk commodities such as gold, ivory, and cloth (Fleisher and Wynne-Jones 2010; Wynne-Jones and Fleisher 2012).

Here, the focus of attention is not on the monetary uses of coins. Instead, this chapter will explore other ways that coins were used. These were as stores or markers of value; as structured deposits in the foundations of houses; as offerings on tombs; as decorative objects for adornment and display; and as mnemonics for the creation and maintenance of history. By looking at the full range of what people did with coins, we can begin to think about the question posed at the start—what is money for? On the precolonial Swahili Coast, money was not the only possible option for any of these uses. Why then was it adopted, and why did people find coinage useful?

This is, of course, a set of discussions and data that relate to a very specific time and place. At the end of the chapter, the issues raised for the Swahili Coast are positioned within the world of Islamic coinage more generally. Eastern Africa emerges as a place with some particular characteristics, but with some insights that might shed light on the uses of coins elsewhere in the world. In particular, it extends some of the insights about the relationship between coinage and authority; expands on the ways that different parts of the Islamic world developed their own esoteric bronze coinages; and forces us to explore the reasons and mechanisms for the adoption of money in many parts of the world that had previously had no tradition of coinage. Islam brought coins and systems of value to many of those places.

COINAGE AND VALUE ON THE COAST OF EASTERN AFRICA

Swahili coins were minted at a number of locations along the eastern coast of Africa. This littoral is and was home to a series of urban centers, often known as "stonetowns" due to the vernacular tradition of coral-built architecture that they contain (see Figure 4.1; Kusimba 1999; Horton and Middleton 2000; Wright 1993). Towns on the Swahili Coast have a long history of development, from initial settlement around the seventh century AD. The earliest sites were built entirely of mud and thatch architecture, yet were from the start extremely complex and sophisticated settlements. They were home to a multi-ethnic

FIGURE 4.1: Map of Eastern Africa showing major sites mentioned in the text. Drawing by Stephanie Wynne-Jones.

population supported by a diverse set of economic practices: agriculture, pastoralism, and a range of crafts. They were also connected from the start to trade networks with partners in the deep hinterland of Africa and across the Indian Ocean. These trade relationships came to define the Swahili in some important ways; as the towns developed from these early roots they continued to look outwards and the inhabitants positioned themselves as middlemen between Islamic merchant networks and webs of connection with African neighbors.

There is evidence that Muslims were present in coastal sites from as early as the eighth century (Horton 1991, 1996; Fitton and Wynne-Jones 2017), the ancestors of a long tradition of Islamic scholarship and practice on the coast that continues to this day. From the eleventh century, the start of building using coral and lime allowed the shaping of the unique townscapes of this region, with mosques, tombs, and later grand houses, populating the spaces of coastal settlement (Garlake 1966). Throughout, Swahili people engaged in a range of relationships across wide webs of connections, including interactions based on trade, religion, and kinship with others around the Indian Ocean rim. Naturally, these connections were shaped by larger economic trajectories. The eighth-century explosion of trade at the time of the Abbasid caliphate at Baghdad coincides with the first significant upswing in trade for the Swahili, and settlements on the coast can be seen to wax and wane in line with developments around the ocean rim (Horton 1987). By the fourteenth and fifteenth centuries, coastal towns had trading connections with the Persian Gulf, Fatimid Egypt via the Red Sea, ports on the west coast of India (notably in Gujarat), and as far afield as China. Zheng He's early fifteenth-century voyage touched the Swahili Coast at a number of locations, and evidence is starting to emerge for this in the archaeological record (Qin and Yu 2018).

The production and use of coinage in Swahili towns was a part of this engagement with the Islamic world. The initial idea of coinage would have arrived with other knowledge about that world, and some characteristics of Swahili coinage are also linked to the Islamic sphere. Most notably, perhaps, Swahili coins are inscribed in Arabic and they invoke the name of Allah and the virtues of piety and Islamic adherence. Yet, the style of coins is unique to the Swahili world (Brown 1993). They do not bear dates or the details of a mint. Instead, they have a rhyming couplet from obverse to reverse, with the name of a particular sultan or ruler, and a phrase extolling his virtues. The only parallels for this format are found among the seventh- and eighth-century coins of the rulers of Sind (Hawkes and Wynne-Jones 2015: 13ff.) and on some amulets from Egypt (Brown 1993).

Mints and Rulers

The earliest Swahili coins seem to have been minted at Shanga, of silver. They date to the eighth to tenth centuries, and establish some of these standards with inscriptions relating to Muhammad and Abdallah (Brown 1992, 1996). There are no histories of Shanga that can cast light on the status of these persons, or their claims to authority at Shanga. The coins are only 20 in number, and presumably of limited circulation and use. In contrast, the most prolific mint on the coast was at Kilwa Kisiwani, whence many thousands of coins are known from the eleventh century onwards. These are predominantly struck in copper alloys, although precious metals are also known. A hoard of 2,000 silver coins, including 30 of Ali ibn al-Hasan—the earliest known minter of coins at Kilwa—is known from Mtambwe Mkuu on Pemba (see Figure 4.2; Horton Oddy, and Brown 1986), supplementing rare finds from early levels at Kilwa Kisiwani itself (Chittick 1973). Copper coins of Ali ibn al-Hasan are some of the most numerous and dominate coinage throughout the history of the town (see discussion below). In the fourteenth and fifteenth centuries, these early issues continued to circulate, alongside a host of other issues (Fleisher and Wynne-Jones 2010). By then, no silver issues seem to have been circulating, and only copper coins are found in the archaeological strata of Kilwa Kisiwani, and related sites at Songo Mnara, and on Mafia Island. Although other sites of the second millennium AD minted coins, no other town rivalled Kilwa for the quantity or spread of its coins; Kilwa-type coins typify Swahili coinage and are found at sites along the Eastern African coast. One was even found at Great

FIGURE 4.2: Silver coins from the Mtambwe Mkuu hoard, with Ali ibn al-Hasan coin inset. Photograph by Mark Horton, courtesy of Mark Horton.

Zimbabwe, a contemporary trading town in the Zimbabwe plateau far to the interior (Huffman 1972).

Numismatic study of Kilwa-type coins has a long pedigree (Walker 1936, 1939; Walker and Freeman-Grenville 1956; Chittick 1965, 1973; Freeman-Grenville 1957, 1958, 1971). They were initially recognized via a series of hoards and collections, and dated by comparison with the Kilwa Chronicle. The latter is an indigenous history of the town of Kilwa Kisiwani, one of a few that exist for the Swahili Coast and the earliest to have been transcribed (Freeman-Grenville 1962). It existed in oral form and was transcribed by Portuguese chroniclers in the sixteenth century. A later version—similar in most respects—was transcribed in Arabic in the nineteenth century. The Chronicle relates the origin story of Kilwa Kisiwani and a record of the ruling dynasty over several centuries. Debate over how to use such histories is far from resolved, with aspects of the narrative perhaps best regarded as allegorical, some relating to the circumstances in which it was transcribed, and some apparently historically accurate and verified by other sources. The coins provided a sort of check on the veracity of the Chronicle and many—although not all—of the names found on the coins can be located in the story of Kilwa. In the absence of dates on the coins themselves, the histories provided a means of relative dating. This was then compared with the archaeological contexts from which some of the coins were recovered, and a tentative chronology was reached, albeit one that was subject to revision as archaeological data were refined and augmented (see Table 4.1).

By the fourteenth-fifteenth century, a large number of Kilwa-type issues were in circulation. Part of the reason for this diversity was that coin types seem to have continued in use long after they were first struck. This may have been due to continued minting, or immobilization, of popular issues (Fleisher and

TABLE 4.1: Chronology of major Kilwa-type issues

Coin issuing rulers at Kilwa	Dates of minting as currently understood (Perkins 2013: 228)
Ali ibn al-Hasan	c. 1100
Da'ud ibn al-Hasan	End c. 1150
Hiatus	1150–1275
Sulaiman ibn al-Husain	post-1275 due to close stylistic resemblance and die-crossover with Sulaiman ibn al-Hasan
Sulaiman ibn al-Hasan	c. 1300
al-Hasan ibn Sulaiman	c. 1330
Da'ud ibn Sulaiman	c. 1340
al-Hasan ibn Talut	Uncertain positioning
Nasir ad-Dunya	Post-1350, pre-1400

Wynne-Jones 2010); however, recent elemental analysis of the copper alloys suggests instead restricted periods of minting followed by extremely long use-lives for the coins (Perkins 2013). Thus, in these centuries, one of the most numerous types of coin is those of Ali ibn al-Hasan, the eleventh-century sultan/ruler discussed above. Many thousands of coins must have been struck during his lifetime. To these are added an array of other types, most notably those of Hasan ibn Sulaiman, an early-fourteenth-century sultan/ruler, who is famed for his generosity and largesse. This was the sultan encountered by Ibn Battuta when he visited Kilwa in 1331 AD, and yet his coins are still much in evidence throughout the fifteenth century.

Context and Archaeology

The coins are found scattered through the archaeology of the site of Kilwa Kisiwani, in every level and context. Although the excavator of the site used the archaeological and numismatic evidence as a check on each other, there were drawbacks to his methodology that make these excavations less useful for exploring the everyday uses of coins (Chittick 1974). The main problem is that deposits at Kilwa were not excavated with much spatial control—the emphasis was on exploring chronology and development rather than thinking through daily life—thus, it is not possible to position the coins with respect to daily life or practice at the site. Archaeological deposits were excavated wholesale without sieving, meaning that many fewer coins were found than might otherwise have been the case (beads and other small artefacts would have been similarly poorly recovered; Wood 2000, 2011). In addition, the fourteenth and fifteenth centuries, the peak of Kilwa's wealth and prominence, were not really the focus of the massive excavations at the site, which were instead concerned with origins and development. Until recently, the best collections for understanding Kilwa-type coins were those often called hoards, but they were often in fact collections made by colonial officials, which became available for study during the course of the twentieth century (often by circuitous routes; Perkins 2013). These offered a cross-section of Kilwa's coinage, as well as giving a sense of their distribution, with a wide but sparse spread along the littoral and a focus on the sites under Kilwa's dominion: Songo Mnara and Mafia prime among them (Sutton 1993, 1997).

Recent large-scale excavations at Songo Mnara, a town dating exclusively to the fourteenth and fifteenth centuries, on an island adjacent to Kilwa Kisiwani, have provided new insight into this old area of study (Wynne-Jones and Fleisher 2010, 2011, 2016). These excavations have explored the uses of space across the site and have for the first time positioned the coins in their contexts of deposition, making it possible to think through the uses and value of Kilwa-type coins (Wynne-Jones and Fleisher 2012). This would have seemed self-evident to previous scholars, but excavations have shown some patterns that make Kilwa's coinage unusual and privilege the everyday uses of coins, not all of them pecuniary. The types of coins found, and the ratios of different issues known, suggest particular importance for some of the symbolic aspects of coinage and links with rulers or powerful individuals. Find spots, which range from mundane domestic contexts, to ritual locations, to hoards removed entirely from circulation, point to the power of coins to act in multiple different spheres.

INTERNATIONAL STANDARDS AND THE TRI-METALLIC SYSTEM

All of these insights relate to Kilwa's copper coinage, which is the most widely distributed and presumably the most prolific type. These coins did, however, exist within a tri-metallic scheme that also included silver and gold issues. As such, the coins of the Swahili Coast fitted within the broader monetary world of Islam, where gold dinars and silver dirhams, as well as lower denominations of copper, set the standard for international measures of value (Mitchiner 1977; Broome 1985). Gold and silver coins on the Eastern African coast may have been more plentiful than we now recognize; typically these metals would survive less well in the archaeological record. Yet, gold and silver coinage is known from many archaeological contexts across the globe, and it would be strange for no trace to remain if gold and silver had been in common currency in coastal Eastern Africa. Instead, it seems that Swahili minting in precious metals might have been more sporadic and particular. Silver coins of Ali ibn al-Hasan have already been mentioned. The largest number are known from a hoard at Mtambwe Mkuu (Horton et al. 1986), although isolated issues are also found in the Kilwa assemblage from the eleventh century (Chittick 1974). None are known from later centuries. This points to a chronological variation that might be related to the availability of metals (Perkins 2013: 205–18). The silver coins may also have served a different function than the copper, as suggested by their different distribution. The hoard found on Pemba, in the Zanzibar Archipelago, suggests that they travelled further than copper issues, mostly used around Kilwa, and may have been linked to interregional exchange. Gold issues are only known from three isolated examples (Brown 1991), all dating to the fourteenth century, and all attributed to al-Hasan ibn Sulaiman, the wealthy ruler mentioned above. Al-Hasan ibn Sulaiman is known to have made the pilgrimage to Mecca, and Brown (1991) suggests that these unique issues might have been created for distribution along the way. The format is different than the copper issues, using al-Hasan ibn Sulaiman's nickname, "The Father of Gifts," rather than his name.

The tri-metallic system of the Swahili Coast is therefore not the same as the hierarchical system of dinars, dirhams, and bronze coins found elsewhere in the Islamic world. The existence of gold and silver coins is discontinuous and apparently related to particular types of interaction, rather than to the daily life of the coastal people. Silver was probably scarce in this region and at this period (Perkins 2013: 144), but gold was one of the major export goods through Kilwa and is known to have been used in other ways.

Kilwa and the Gold Trade

When the Portuguese arrived at Kilwa in the opening years of the sixteenth century, they recorded a sumptuous town, with richly dressed inhabitants and many outward signs of material wealth. The women of Kilwa were reported to be lavishly decorated with jewelry of gold, as well as beads and fine imported fabrics (Pallaver 2009). One of the Portuguese sailors who plundered Kilwa in 1505 AD stated: "We found therein such great booty of gold, of silver and pearls, of golden pieces, and of sundry precious wares, that it was impossible to reckon their value" (Vespuccius, quoted in Prestholdt 1998: 38). The gold trade funneled through Kilwa from Southeastern Africa was one of the main Portuguese ambitions in the region, and they were ultimately to capture supply directly from the Mozambique Coast and eclipse Kilwa's role as middleman. In the short term, they reported on the value of gold in the region in terms that referenced international standards, especially the *mithqal*, which was approximately 4.2g, the weight of a Cairo dinar (Freeman-Grenville 1962: 108).

This has led some to assume that a true tri-metallic system of coinage must have operated in the region (Horton and Middleton 2000: 92–4). Based on the known weights of Kilwa-type coins, Horton and Middleton calculate a ratio of 1:10:1,000, attempting to position Kilwa's mint within known standards of weight and measure. In fact, this is difficult to sustain as Swahili coins are extremely variable in weight. Brown (1993) suggested that size was probably the more important feature of coins here, constrained by the die that was used, with variable amounts of metal poured in, leading to the lack of standardization on weight or metal content. This has obvious ramifications for standardized systems of specie, and suggests that value was not tied to metal content in any consistent way (Wynne-Jones and Fleisher 2012).

Instead, then, the Swahili Coast seems to have been a region in which an esoteric system of coinage existed. It was tied to the conceptual world of dinars, dirhams, and Islamic systems of commerce, but was not a part of that system. Instead, the idea of coins was used in some varied ways. Differences existed between metals and the ways they were minted and used. Coins struck from copper alloys seem to have been the only ones that might be thought of as a currency, circulating within daily exchange. It is only now, with data from Songo Mnara on the contexts of use and deposition of Kilwa-type coins, that it is possible to begin exploring the ways that those currency objects were used and understood in daily practice.

COINS AND HOW THEY WERE USED

As discussed, copper coins of the Kilwa type have a wide distribution in areas that were part of Kilwa Kisiwani's sphere of influence. In the fourteenth and fifteenth centuries, this extended to Songo Mnara and Sanje ya Majoma, which were both sites in the immediate archipelago of Kilwa, probably parts of the same urban configuration (see Figure 4.3). Kilwa also had a broader sphere of influence, with control claimed over the Mafia archipelago, and the towns of Kua and Kisimani Mafia found there, as well as sites of the Mozambique Coast, whence gold was transhipped for onward commerce out of Kilwa. Thousands

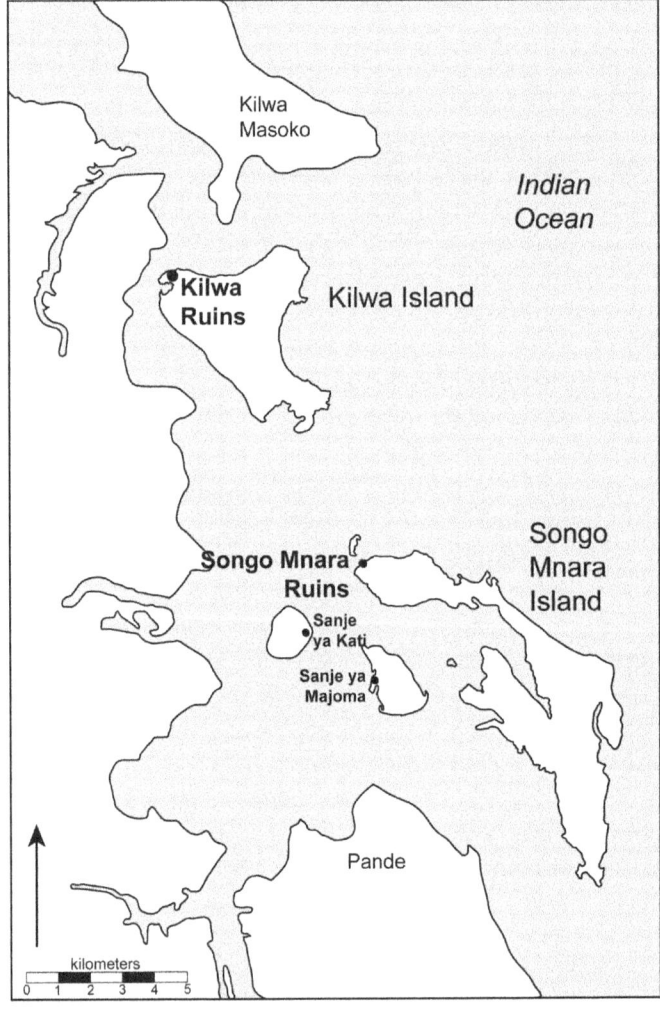

FIGURE 4.3: Map of Kilwa Archipelago, showing sites of Kilwa Kisiwani and Songo Mnara. Drawing by Stephanie Wynne-Jones.

of copper Kilwa-type coins are known from Mafia and from Kilwa Kisiwani (although not from Mozambique, which may simply reflect a lack of research in that region; Album 1999). It is only from Songo Mnara that coins have been recovered in their contexts of use, giving a unique insight into the circulation and use of these coins during the fourteenth and fifteenth centuries (Wynne-Jones and Fleisher 2012).

Excavations at Songo Mnara since 2009 have recovered a corpus of 1,039 copper coins. They come from a wide range of contexts across the site (see Table 4.2). Excavations have been targeted at exploring the uses of space, both inside and outside the built structures of the town, and coins occur across every type of place excavated: houses, mosques, tombs, middens, wells, and open areas. This points clearly to the conclusion that they were in circulation around the site, supported by the specific places where concentrations were found. Large numbers were located in domestic settings, and particularly where there had been sandy or earthen floors. Where structures had plaster floors there were fewer finds in general, and fewer coins in particular; presumably daily objects were more easily lost on earthen floors. In addition, coins were recovered in exterior sites of domestic activity, such as surrounding the well, or in midden deposits outside the walls of houses. Coins were thus apparently part of the world of mundane activity, incorporated into the daily commerce of the town. This might seem obvious, but it is a point that can be made on the Swahili Coast, where towns have been interpreted as having international trade as their primary function (cf. the approach to coins in Horton and Middleton 2000: 93, specifically targeted at locating Swahili coinage in the sphere of international commerce). It is thus necessary to demonstrate that coinage—even though derived from international concepts and standards—was a very domestic phenomenon, used in the daily round of activity, rather than part of the world of international commerce evoked by the discussion of *mithqal* weight standards and caliphal mints. The relationship with petty local exchange is further emphasized by the numbers of coins that were clipped—often halved and quartered—presumably to create smaller denominations. The need for smaller units again suggests that coins were part of a world of small-scale cash transactions, rather than being transferred in large numbers for grand-scale commodity purchase.

In addition to the daily commerce implied by the coins' spread within the site, significant numbers were incorporated into non-monetary activities. Most notably, these include ritual activities: coins were used as offerings on tombs and graves at Songo Mnara, they were also incorporated into a foundation deposit beneath one of Songo Mnara's stone houses. This deposit (Perkins, Fleisher, and Wynne-Jones 2014) included 360 coins, along with a string of imported carnelian beads, interpreted as a household investment in the building of a home. This has especial resonance on the Swahili Coast, where the

TABLE 4.2: Coins at Songo Mnara by context type

		# of coins		
excavation unit	description	2009	2011	2013
SM002	outside stonehouse adjacent to wall	2		
SM004	entrance room of House 44	1		
SM005	Iron working area in centre of site	3		
SM006	well	1		
SM007	wattle and daub house	3		
SM010	back room of House 44	36		
SM011	wattle and daub house	8		
SM012	tomb	7		
SM013	base of stairs of House 23	2		
SM015	Room in House 23	1		
SM016	entrance room of House 31 (stonehouse)		8	
SM017	back room of House 31 (including buried deposit)		378	
SM018	room next to courtyard of House 34 (previously cleared)		0	
SM019	external area between houses		5	
SM020	external courtyard of House xx		10	
SM021	back room of House xx associated with courtyard		6	
SM022	test pit in southern open area		1	
SM023	back room of House 40		50	
SM024	tomb		5	
SM025	tomb		0	
SM026	tomb		0	
SM027	tomb		3	
SM029	test unit in southern open area		5	
SM030	central mosque		5	
	shovel test pits in southern open area		9	
SM031/SM035	wattle and daub house			76
SM032	wattle and daub house			157
SM033	stepped court of House 18			8
SM037	entrance room of House 18			7
SM039	room in House 18			1
SM050	western mosque			2
SM054	gatehouse in western wall			1
SM055	room in House 18			1
	shovel test pits in northern open area			12

ownership of and residence in a stonehouse is one of the key markers of prestige and rank in urban contexts (Allen 1979). The burial of a deposit of coins and beads was thus a powerful statement about investment in place, probably part of what gave the house value (Wynne-Jones 2013; see also Krmnicek 2012).

MULTIPLE ROUTES TO VALUE

The qualities of Kilwa-type coins, along with their contexts of use, suggest that they held value in many different ways (Wynne-Jones and Fleisher 2012). The sultans or rulers represented on the coins are extremely unevenly distributed. Two names are disproportionately represented. Ali ibn al-Hasan, the earliest ruler to strike coins at Kilwa (also linked to the Mtambwe silver coins discussed above), was active in the eleventh century, but his coins still accounted for 18.2 percent of the identifiable assemblage in fifteenth-century Songo Mnara. Al-Hasan ibn Sulaiman, the early-fourteenth-century ruler, whose gold coins were discussed above, accounts for 33.3 percent, with other names much less commonly represented (Table 4.3). These rulers are well remembered in the oral traditions of Kilwa, as founders and key leaders of the Shirazi and Mahdali dynasties respectively. Their prominence may have contributed to both the quantity and the value attributed to their coins. It is also possible that the numbers of coins with these rulers' names on them might have influenced their place in history, as the common circulation of their names would keep them alive in the shared imaginary of the town.

The coins themselves also had qualities that would have led to them being valued by the inhabitants of Kilwa and Songo Mnara. As mentioned, they were linked to the Islamic world, through their very existence and through their use of Arabic script and Islamic formulas in their inscriptions. These links were highly valued in the Swahili world, and connected to the ways that wealth and civility were expressed in a coastal milieu. The metal of their manufacture may also have been part of their appeal, as copper has always been sought after in Eastern Africa, linked to concepts of power and kingly authority (Herbert 1984). Rather than a poor relation of the gold and silver coins, the copper coinage of Kilwa Kisiwani might have been deliberately struck in this metal that evoked local aesthetics and value systems, as well as connections with a lucrative trade with interior regions of Africa.

WHAT WERE SWAHILI COINS FOR?

The function of Swahili coinage is discussed by John Middleton (2003) as part of a more general consideration of how trade and exchange worked on the precolonial coast. His analysis of the uses of coins was informed by the numismatic work of Horton (Horton and Middleton 2000: 93) and Freeman-

TABLE 4.3: Proportions of sultans/rulers on Kilwa coins

	Songo Mnara	Songo Mnara (without unknowns)	Hoard A (Walker 1936)	Hoard C (Walker 1936, 80–81)	Hoard 1 (Walker 1939)	Hoard 2 (Walker 1939)	Hoard 3 (Walker 1939)
ʿAli ibn al-Hasan	9.4%	18.2%	25.7%	20.6%	32.3%	33.3%	
Dāʾūd ibn al-Hasan			2.6%	0.6%	2.4%	1.8%	
Hasan ibn Ṭālūt			0.1%			0.9%	
Sulaimān ibn al-Hasan	3.1%	6.1%	0.2%	9.4%	17.3%	17.5%	17.4%
Dāʾūd ibn Sulaimān	1.6%	3.0%	5.6%	2.8%	6.3%	0.9%	
Sulaimān ibn al-Husain	3.1%	6.1%	14.2%		0.8%		
Muhammad ibn Sulaimān					0.8%	0.9%	
al-Hasan ibn Sulaimān	17.2%	33.3%	49.0%	22.8%	32.3%	43.0%	2.2%
Unknown	48.4%		2.5%	8.3%	7.9%	1.8%	80.4%
Nasir al-Dunya	17.2%	33.3%		35.6%			

Grenville (1971) as well as by anthropological theory on sources of value (particularly, Hart 1986). The specifics of his argument were also provided by a series of contemporary informants. The result is one of the only attempts to understand the rationale for coinage on the Swahili Coast, yet it is difficult to find support for his arguments in the archaeological evidence. Middleton discusses the tri-metallic system, which he takes as having "corresponded to those of gold, silver, and copper used throughout the Indian Ocean and Middle East (and also to the Portuguese gold coins), in that like them they were in the proportions of 1:10:1,000 in value" (Middleton 2003: 515). He moves beyond this in some important ways, as he attempts to account for the different functions of gold and silver coinage vs. the copper coins that were used in petty exchange. He sees the coins in precious metals as having been distributed by the ruler to his merchants, who then kept them in secret vaults inside their houses, to act not as currency in international exchanges, but more as a form of guarantee. They were physical evidence of "comparable oceanwide standards of value of different commodities," displayed in trade negotiations so as to make "direct exchange of commodities possible and easy" (2003: 515).

Elsewhere, I have suggested that the different aspects of value in Swahili society—symbolic value and currency value—were actually more closely bound than Middleton suggests (Wynne-Jones and Fleisher 2012). Ultimately, his argument is let down by inadequate archaeological data. There is no evidence at all for these transactions, or stores of precious metals, in the fourteenth and fifteenth centuries, and the suggestion that ratios of value of 1:10:1,000 existed is not sustainable in light of the coin data themselves (Fleisher and Wynne-Jones 2010), making the links to ocean-wide systems of value difficult to support. Yet, Middleton's analysis was an entirely justified attempt to understand Swahili coinage as part of an international world of coinage and commerce. His work is also good for thinking through the fact that coins were not just coins, and that they were used and valued in ways not connected with commodity exchange.

As described above, the data from Songo Mnara allow us to explore the question of what coins were for on the Swahili Coast on a much more solid foundation. Money was for lots of things, in practical terms. Gold and silver issues clearly performed a function on a broader stage, and seem to have had connections with moveable wealth and with the practice of spreading prestige through redistribution; the gold coins may have been tokens distributed by an especially wealthy ruler on his travels around the Islamic world. Copper coins were for more common and everyday transactions, probably including the purchase of daily commodities. Yet, they were not simply mundane objects, solely for "petty" exchange within the towns. They, like the more precious metals, had symbolic and aesthetic value which would have been bound up with their value in use as well as with their contributions to history.

Coins were also not used in every Swahili town. Kilwa Kisiwani was unique in the quantity and ubiquity of its minting tradition, with more sporadic production at towns elsewhere. Some of the grander Swahili towns of the fourteenth and fifteenth centuries did not mint any coins. Gede, on the coast of Kenya, is a key example of this. The quality and range of imports at the site suggests it has nothing to do with a lack of wealth or of trade. Other currencies may have been in operation; the excavator suggested that cowries may have been a currency at precolonial Gede due to their ubiquity in the deposits (Wynne-Jones and Fleisher 2015).

Thus, rather than coins having a range of uses, we might envisage a range of everyday object roles that were—at Kilwa and its satellites—fulfilled by coins. Why was it coins that were used for those things? Once the connection with international standards of weight and value is broken, what made them suitable as stores of value, symbols of power, and items of daily exchange? This chapter has suggested a series of answers to that question, all of them residing in the realm of daily life and the experience of using and owning the coins.

The copper coins of Kilwa had strong links to Islam, a crucial aspect of Swahili self-identity from earliest times. The first mosque on the Eastern African coast has been identified in levels dating to the eighth century (Horton 1991; see also Fitton and Wynne-Jones 2017). For approximately 1,000 years, Islam remained, in this region, an urban and coastal phenomenon, claimed by the coastal elite as a key marker of their status and their differentiation from the pagans of the hinterland. The material culture of Islamic trade therefore always carried high status in this region and the fact that the *concept* of coinage was here derived from that world would have contributed to the reasons for its adoption (Wynne-Jones 2016: 186). The more specific links to Islam, and the ways that the text of coins simultaneously invoked the name of Allah and of the ruler in question, would have made them valued links between the secular power of Kilwa's rulers and religious power.

In and of themselves, Kilwa's coins had important characteristics as things. The aesthetic properties of copper when shiny, and red, would have made these objects stand out and recommended them as stores of value. They had sonorous properties, too, making them appropriate objects of adornment (see Kus and Raharijaona 2008, for comparable discussion of Marie Therese dollars on Madagascar). Many Kilwa coins are pierced (see Figure 4.4; an average of 4.95 percent in museum collections, up to 15.64 percent for one collection at the Fitzwilliam museum in Cambridge; Perkins 2013: 265), suggesting that they were worn, in which role their aesthetic and sonorous properties would have combined in people's experience of them. Finally, all metals had a high status. Metal objects are rare in the archaeology of Songo Mnara and Kilwa, as they were valued, conserved, and reworked through time, meaning that few objects survive in the archaeological record. The particular enthusiasm of Kilwa for

FIGURE 4.4: Pierced Kilwa-type coin from excavations at Songo Mnara. Photograph by Stephanie Wynne-Jones.

minting coins thus also comes into relief, as there is a continuing association of Kilwa with mineral wealth, with evidence for iron production in its earliest phases, before copper working began in earnest in the eleventh century. Kilwa's role as the largest exporter of gold on the Eastern African coast should not obscure the fact that they were clearly working copper and silver also, necessitating a web of connections with ore-producing areas in the African interior. Kilwa dominated these connections more than any other town, so their use of metal resources for everyday functions (such as might have been fulfilled by cowries, or beads, elsewhere; Pallaver 2009, Wood 2011; Sinclair Ekblom, and Wood 2012) is explicable in these terms. In an African context, the mineral wealth of Kilwa Kisiwani would have been crucial to its status, as both metals and the technical skills required to work them have always been highly valued on the continent (Herbert 1984; Killick 2009).

EAST AFRICA AND THE ISLAMIC WORLD

As described above, connections with the Islamic world were important for Eastern Africa. Yet, the Swahili Coast remained outside the realm of direct control of Islamic caliphates. Unlike most other regions that minted a form of Islamic coinage, the Eastern African coast was converted to Islam by contact and trade rather than by conquest. There was thus no requirement among the autonomous authorities on the coast to conform to Islamic standards of weight or of form. Yet, the relevance of Kilwa's coinage to the broader world of Islam might be greater than is immediately obvious. This is particularly true for the copper coinage.

Islam and Islamic Coinage

Islamic coinage is a huge area, and few reliable overviews exist that can cover all Islamic lands throughout the period under study here (although see Broome

1985). The majority of scholarship on Islamic numismatics is focused on the earliest periods: the Ummayad and Abbasid caliphates of the first centuries of Islam. It is in this period that Islamic coins could be studied as a more unified phenomenon. An initial period of experimentation was based on earlier prototypes in the Islamic lands, establishing a system of gold dinars, silver dirhams, and copper *fulus* (sing. *fals*). Coins of the caliphate were then standardized at the end of the seventh century CE by the Ummayad caliph 'Abd al Malik. He established a format for the style and content of dinars that was to persist for centuries thereafter, invoking the name of Allah as a form of legitimacy for the coins (Maurer 2005). It was the caliph's prerogative to mint gold dinars, and 'Abd al Malik set a standard weight formula of 4.25 g for gold dinars and 2.85 g for silver dirhams. The weight of copper coins was never standardized (Grierson 1960: 246–7), probably because they were normally minted locally, according to local weight standards (Grierson 1960: 254; Lowick 1990). By the tenth century, gold and silver were increasingly also subject to regional weight standards, which would be distinguished by the mint at which they were struck rather than by a centralized authority for the entire Islamic realm. From the twelfth century, one of the key reference points was created by the Cairo mint, whose dinar was commonly used throughout the Indian Ocean world as the *mithqal* standard. The gold coins of Kilwa, from the fourteenth century, are actually quite close to the weight of a Cairo dinar, suggesting again that Swahili rulers and their mints were fully involved in the Islamic world and cognizant of international practice.

Where the Eastern African coast is unusual, then, is in the fully developed system of copper coinage that was in operation at Kilwa Kisiwani. Copper issues, or fulus, were known throughout the Islamic world. As discussed, they could be extremely variable in both weight and style as they tended to be based locally (Perkins 2013: 119). During the Ummayad period, fulus differed stylistically from gold and silver coins, as they did not mention the mint or name a ruler. Later, some elements of the higher denominations were added, but they did not resemble dinars or dirhams (Schindel 2010). Under Abbasid rule, fulus were rarer, and of simple design without the ornamental symbols used during Ummayad rule (Broome 1985: 13–18). In later periods, copper coins seem to have dropped away from the repertoire in the main Islamic mints. The Cairo mint created no known copper coinage, dealing mainly in gold dinars. Copper coins were part of a much more diverse set of coinages created by local authorities for local purposes. They are not often reported in detail, yet the diversity of these might be illustrated by the lead coinage minted at Siraf: a unique local tradition using a base metal. The value of these coins was thus not obviously based upon specie value but instead on the *idea* of coinage, creating systems that worked locally (Lowick 1985). Local systems were also not always about creating smaller denominations; the Ottoman Empire of the fifteenth century actually created a whole series of higher denominations of silver coinage to deal with larger-scale transactions.

Islamic Coins and Everyday Life in the Fourteenth and Fifteenth Centuries

By the fourteenth and fifteenth centuries, the Islamic world was enormous and diverse, encompassing multiple powerful centers from the Mughals in the east to the Ottoman Empire that dominated the Mediterranean world. In all of these regions, though, forms of coinage existed that drew on Islamic standards and prototypes. As discussed, the copper coinages had always been more varied, and thus were even more subject to regional manipulation. By this period, they were not common elsewhere in the Islamic world. At Kilwa Kisiwani, copper was developed into a fully functioning system of currency, which circulated at the site for multiple purposes. It seems that many of the ways these coins were used, and the ways they derived their value, were based in everyday uses. The ongoing circulation of issues relating to powerful rulers would have reconfirmed Kilwa's position in history to the population as they used the coins. As well as being locally powerful, these rulers were also internationally active, embodying links with the Persian Gulf and the Arabian Peninsula through their claimed origins and via pilgrimage and scholarship. The material objects of the coins and their associations would therefore also reaffirm links with the Islamic world. Many of the aesthetic qualities of the coins would have positioned them within prized categories of wealth and display at Kilwa Kisiwani, and the use of coins for adornment and jewelry would again have been part of what gave them value. Finally, the particular qualities of coins as offerings in ritual contexts—in structured deposits beneath house foundations and on the tombs of important ancestors—would have added to the ways that they were valued and understood, not only as tokens of exchange but as potential repositories and symbols of value. Both of these aspects of coinage have parallels in more recent periods in Eastern Africa. On Madagascar, the Portuguese introduction of *thalers* was hampered by the movement of these coins out of the circulation to be used as jewelry (Kus and Raharijaona 2008). Later indigenous coinage of the Merina dynasty was valued as a means of approaching and encountering royalty, and was prized in ritual contexts (Lambek 2001). It is suggested here that these very local, everyday uses at Kilwa might not have been so unusual in a very diverse Islamic world of the fourteenth and fifteenth centuries, where people were brought together by common beliefs, but also by common practices and interactions with the material world (Wynne-Jones 2016). Few have considered coinage in this light, as it is often seen as part of the economic realm, rather than in the world of things. Yet, Flood (2009), for example, has written about how objects acted as mediators across the Islamic world and at its eastern edges, drawing on evidence of art and architecture that created a mutually intelligible world. The coinage of Kilwa is particularly well developed for a local tradition, perhaps because of the status awarded to copper in the African context (Herbert 1984). Yet, it might be indicative of some of the other regional traditions seen across the Islamic world at this time.

Returning to the original question of this chapter then, and asking what coinage is for, the Kilwa coins have raised a series of interesting suggestions that might not be immediately obvious in studies of money. Coins are not simply tokens of exchange, they are also well suited to a variety of different purposes due to their aesthetic and material qualities, but particularly due to their associations. There are few studies that consider the role of coins in non-literate societies, or where literacy was linked fundamentally with religion and religious elites. On the Swahili Coast, links to the Islamic world were always valued, but, in fact, the power of the written word would have been a broader phenomenon. In the world of fourteenth- and fifteenth-century Songo Mnara, coinage held a series of associations that linked inhabitants to their own urban tradition, and to a wider world of scholarship, travel, power, and interaction which was a powerful source of pride and esteem. Coins are therefore well suited as stores and symbols of value due to their multiple resonances in symbolic and material ways. Links to power and authority are well explored, as the "two sides" of the coin (Hart 1986), yet it is in the everyday uses of coinage that inhabitants of the Swahili Coast found value in coinage and all that it could offer.

CHAPTER FIVE

Money, Art, and Representation

Text, Image, and Message

BARRIE COOK

INTRODUCTION

In 1606, in England, an account was published of Sir Henry Middleton's recent expedition to the East Indies, *The last East-Indian voyage*. In it was described an encounter with the captain of a Portuguese fort, who was unaware of the immense changes that had occurred in Europe:

> The 11 day our Generall sent a letter by *Iohn Rogers* to the captaine of the Fort . . . the effect of our Generals letter, was to certifie him of the death of our *Queen,* & peace between *England* and *Spaine,* . . . & for better confirmation of truth, he sent the captain of the fort, our kings Maiesty & the princes pictures, with diuers of his Maiesties new coine, & in conclusion as there was peace with our Princes and their subiects in Christendome he desired that the like might be between vs, for that our comming was to seeke trade with them and the *Amboynians* which he hoped he would not deny him.
>
> —1606: 15–16

This is an exceptional record of the impact of coin designs, here used to defuse tension and advance political and commercial interests. The designs and inscriptions of the coins themselves said nothing explicitly about peace or war: virtually no coinage of the age would have offered such specific information. However, they did present manifest evidence of regime change to support the English claims and reassure the Portuguese (subjects of the king of Spain since 1580).

Such anecdotes are unusual, even for the seventeenth century, in providing evidence for the role of coin design beyond inference from the objects themselves. This instance indicates in the European tradition that what coin designs might do had changed hugely between 1400 and 1600. The location of the encounter is also significant. Coins of James I were accessible on the other side of the world, where European coinage now encountered that of equally old and very different monetary traditions (Figure 5.1).

The design of a coin is the essential thing that makes it money, the stamp of authority that changes a piece of metal from commodity to currency (Cribb 2009: 499–503). The appearance of a coin can reflect the power, the authority, the self-image of the issuing ruler or state, and hence has the potential to respond to current artistic trends. Yet, coinage is a deeply conservative medium, valuing trust and familiarity above novelty and variety. Coins needed not only to feel right and weigh right, but also to look right. Anything beyond this—comprehension of the words on the coin or the implications of the images depicted—would be, perhaps, an optional extra, not automatically expected from the consumers of coins, many of whom would be illiterate.

Nevertheless, all coin designs had an audience who were expected to understand and to react appropriately with interest, trust, or admiration. Any given design was a means of communication between issuer and user, employing

FIGURE 5.1: Gold sovereign, James I, First coinage, 1603–4. © The Trustees of the British Museum. All rights reserved.

the only certain mass medium available well into the seventeenth century. While the issuer overtly controlled the form of the design, it was thus created with the intention of impacting the user. Furthermore, individual coin designs were also almost always in dialogue with others: most areas issued coins of different values and often different metals, and it was unusual for common designs to feature across the denominational range. New coin would also mix with older coin, issued by the existing or previous regimes. Coins from different contemporary issuers might also mix together, sometimes with, but often without, permission from the local authorities. Currencies were often complex and coins could be preferred, hoarded, exported, rejected, mutilated, or melted down. While coin design was not the sole consideration in this endless process of evaluation and selection, it was always a part of it.

In the late medieval and early modern world, there were four main coinage traditions, each with a shared legacy and a body of characteristics that gave the diverse coinages within them a family resemblance across wide areas: the Chinese, Indian, Islamic, and European worlds. There have usually been three main focuses for coin design: political authority, religious affiliation, and artistic expression. Two main approaches to these have dominated: a reliance principally on text; or, alternatively, a combination of text and image. In 1400, there were long-standing text-based traditions in the Islamic and Chinese worlds, while a mixture of text and image was the hallmark of most European and many South Asian traditions.

THE TEXT TRADITION

In 1400, the text-based traditions of coin design in the Middle East and Asia were ancient and deeply embedded. The proportion of coin users in the major Islamic and Chinese states who could actively interrogate such designs was likely to have been small, but they did exist and they were influential. The artistic dimension of coin production was overwhelmingly based on calligraphy as one of the highest forms of art; a form in which lettering is designed and executed to emphasize harmony, balance, and skill. The absorption and application of this approach by metal engravers was well established in this period, but it remained an area where it was possible for standards to fall and skills fail.

China and its Neighbors

The coinage of China was ancient, of widespread influence, and extremely conservative in design, an approach dominated by the need to honor tradition (Figure 5.2). It was based on a coin known in Chinese as *qian* (coin), *tongqian* (copper coin) or *wen* (literally, writing). This was of copper, small and round,

FIGURE 5.2: Bronze coin, Emperor Xuanzong (1426–35). © The Trustees of the British Museum. All rights reserved.

with a square central opening which permitted the coins to be strung into groups of 1000 for ease of carriage and storage. The coin had letters arranged in a well-established form.

Under the native Ming, who displaced the Mongol Yuan dynasty in 1368, this ancient form was preserved. The inscription was arranged in a form established in the seventh century, reading above-below-right-left of the hole. The first two characters named the reign period, and the second two stated it was a "circulating treasure" or coin (*tong bao*). To all users, such pieces were immediately recognizable as coins, whether or not they could read Chinese. Symbolically, the round coin with the square hole harked back to the coins of the "First Emperor" Qin Shihuang, who unified the Warring States and standardized the currency in the third century BC. Through being so conservative in design, these coins were loaded with tradition and symbolism. The first Ming coins were issued within months of the founding of the dynasty and were generally well made, but they were inconsistently issued and counterfeiting was a problem. Key developments included a change in alloy to brass in *c.* 1503–5.[1] Ming paper money was promoted from 1375, denominated in strings of coins also depicted on the notes, but the system was not well managed, and it was effectively abandoned by the 1430s. Instead, silver became an accepted form of money, but in the shape of stamped silver ingots, not official coins, a development encouraged in the sixteenth century, with the arrival of Spanish-American silver.

The use of state-issued brass cash coins and unofficial silver continued throughout the Manchu Qing dynasty (1644–1911). The first Manchu coins had an inscription solely in the Manchu script. Subsequent issues had a combination of Chinese and Manchu scripts, settling into a formulaic arrangement with the Chinese script on the front (reign period + *tong bao*) and Manchu on the back, naming the mint. Until around 1678, princes in the south of China held out against the invading Manchu and continued to issue coins in Ming style.[2]

The design element of Chinese coinage was thus minimal and highly conservative, though as such it honored ancient tradition. Inscriptions provided basic administrative details of issue: the reign and often the mint. There was no religious or ideological element and no attempt to depict authority through an image. Any messages were instead conveyed by the form of the coin and the inscription. Nevertheless, by virtue of its longevity and reputation, its physical form—cast in bronze, round with a square hole—defined how coinage should look for a vast area well beyond China itself. The design prompted instant recognition that such pieces were coins of the Chinese tradition. When the same design was adopted in neighboring countries, there are clear indications that the issuing authorities sought to reflect this while also moving to proclaim their own identities. So, the kingdom of Koryo, which dominated the Korean peninsula, relied initially on Chinese coin imports before establishing a native coinage in Chinese style in 1625. These had the four-character inscription, *Sang pyong tong bo*, in which *Sang pyong* names the government's Food Supply Stabilization Office (the issuer) and *tong bo* is the Korean reading of the Chinese *tong bao* ("circulating treasure"). Other government offices began to issue coins, identified by the complex system of markings on the reverses.

In Japan, between the thirteenth and seventeenth centuries, the only coins in use were either Chinese or local copies, supplemented by gold and silver ingots. Shortly after it came to power in 1603, the Tokugawa shogunate revived local coin production while still retaining the legacy of Chinese models. As in Korea, the most representative coinage of Japan was first issued in the 1620s and, whilst modeled on Chinese coins, expressed a Japanese identity. The four-character inscription read *Kanei tsuho*, *Kanei* referring to the era name, and *tsuho* being the Japanese reading of *tongbao*, "circulating treasure." Like Chinese and Korean coins, the inscription on the back usually identified the mint. The *Kanei tsuho* coins continued until 1868. In Vietnam, parts of which were periodically under Chinese rule, virtually all the coinage in this period was imported Chinese ones or local issues in Chinese style, but again asserting a local identity through the inscriptions.

Again, in what would become Indonesia, large quantities of Chinese coins were imported, although here they mingled with locally produced gold and tin issues with Arabic inscriptions from the sultanates of Java and Sumatra and a currency mixing these two very different elements continued in the area until the nineteenth century. The sultans of Java and Sumatra also occasionally issued their own copies of Chinese coins, although sometimes inscribed with Javanese or Arabic inscriptions. Chinese coins could be encountered around much of the Indian Ocean, even down the eastern coast of Africa, but mixed with other traditions, particularly the Islamic, and did not generally inspire local coin design.

Chinese coinage in the period 1400–1670 embodied many contradictions, not least of which was its appearance. It did little with the potential of coin design, despite emerging from a culture of advanced administration and a highly developed appreciation of visual forms. However, this apparent limitation was counteracted by the distinctiveness of the shape of Chinese coins—all had the same general look, with little material or denominational variation in form. This was what they had to be. The ideological content of its design was minimal and fairly implicit—an acknowledgment of the current regime with a hint of administrative organization, so it was at least reasonably topical. Despite this minimalist approach, it was evidently viewed as being of political significance, control of coinage being such a fundamental aspect of legitimate government. The response to the invasion of the Manchu bore witness to this. Resistance in the south was manifested in part through the maintenance of Ming-style coinage for as long as possible, while the shifting roles of Chinese and Manchu text on the Manchus' own coinage suggest assessments within the elite on how they viewed their own place in the political and cultural world they ruled. Meanwhile Chinese coinage was used beyond the empire's borders as a manifestation of its power and economic reach.

The Islamic World: Faith and Authority in New Empires

Islamic coinage had a well-established visual vocabulary of authority. Common, though not universal, was the presence of the *shahada* or Profession of Faith: "There is no god but God; Muhammad is the Prophet of God," along with a *hijra* date (for the year of issue, or the ruler's accession year), the mint and the titles of the issuer (see Wasserstein 1993, although it focuses on the classical and medieval period of Islam). By the fifteenth century, the *shahada* was normally placed on the coin reverse in a form known as the *kalima* (the Word or Logos). In the Shi'a tradition a third element was usually added: "Ali is the protector of the realm of God." The language was almost always Arabic, although Persian would become an addition or alternative, and not only in Iran.

Yet, this tradition did not necessarily include overtly religious language, and there were occasions where the religious dimension was largely absent.

Conversely, some dynasties emphasized expressions of faith as a dominant part of their representation of authority. Similarly, while the avoidance of figurative design was widespread, it was not strictly prohibited and was not universal. Whatever the textual content of Islamic coinages, it drew minimal notice from the Europeans who encountered it in this period. They interrogated the coinages of the Ottomans, Safavids, and Mughals with intense interest and in positive terms, but virtually never addressed the messages on them.[3]

The fifteenth century began with one of the most dramatic political shifts in the history of the Islamic world: the impact of Timur and his descendants. In their loose empire centered on Afghanistan and Turkestan between 1405 and 1500, the Timurids issued a coinage which used decorative designs taken from their former overlords the Qarakhanids.[4] Timur himself used a family symbol of three circles arranged in a triangle, along with elaborate frames that surrounded inscriptions giving his name, titles, and a religious proclamation. He also named a member of the Chagatai dynasty, descended from Genghis Khan, into which he had married and whose status allowed him to claim the universal sovereignty of the Mongol khan. Later Timurids, mostly now Chagatai descendants, sometimes employed the three circles, but dispensed with the Chagatai co-ruler. The Timurids perfected the use of decorative frames by adopting an elegant cursive form of Arabic on broad silver coins, though too often the mints undercut the beautifully shaped calligraphy through poor workmanship. Nevertheless, their calligraphic style had a long-lasting influence on their successors the Safavids (1501–1732) and the Mughals (1526–1858).

The three great new Islamic empires of the age, Ottoman, Safavid, and Mughal, interacted with each other and the legacy of Islamic coinage they all shared in quite different ways, in terms of the messages their coin designs carried to their (literate) subjects. In the west, after the disruptions caused by Timur, the Ottoman Turks resumed their expansion relatively quickly. Initially continuity of coin design was maintained, with early rulers copying the style of their regional predecessors by employing the *kalima* and other overtly religious expressions. Ottoman coins normally gave a title, named the ruler and his father and included an exhortation supporting the ruler. So, silver coins of Mehmed I (1413–21) read on the obverse in four lines: "Protector of Religion, Mehmed, Son of Bayezid. Perpetuate his Kingdom" (Sultan 1977: 52). The reverse design was the *kalima* text. From the 1480s, the title sultan was usually included, while the *kalima* was thereafter absent and the promotion of the sultan increased with such phrases as "May his victory be glorious" or "May his kingdom endure" featuring regularly, and these implicit exhortations to God became the only religious element on Ottoman coinage from that point. Meanwhile, from the time of Suleiman the Magnificent (1520–66; Figure 5.3), the sultan's titles began to expand, with the Persian title "Shah" (king) added along with the phrase "Master of the Two Lands and Two Seas." "Striker of the Glittering," "Master of

FIGURE 5.3: Gold coin of Suleiman I. © The Trustees of the British Museum. All rights reserved.

Might," and "Victorious of Land and Sea" also joined the repertoire of Ottoman titles, a selection of which was subsequently used on most coins. Perhaps the most distinctive and defining Ottoman symbol was the *tughra*, the ruler's official signature in Arabic cursive. Despite its long-term significance in the representation of Ottoman authority, the *tughra* was initially used only on the silver and copper coinage, and not until the seventeenth century was it added to the gold. This did mean, however, that it dominated on the money of daily life.

As Ottoman power expanded, it affected the wider Islamic coinage tradition. It replaced many existing coinages, though sometimes retaining local elements. So, in fifteenth-century Syria, Mamluk copper coins with framed and pictorial designs were succeeded by Ottoman coins which retained these local types. Moving east in 1514, the Ottomans activated mints at Baghdad and Mosul, though again retaining a local dimension, with the production of relatively large silver coins. The *tughra* was not employed here until the seventeenth century. In Yemen, the Rasulids of Zabid (to 1454) operated a mint at 'Adan, which included pictorial elements: the reverses of their fifteenth-century coins featured an animal motif—fish, lion, peacock—as a mint mark. Their successors in southern Yemen, the Tahirids (1454–1517), only used inscriptional designs. After the Ottomans conquered Yemen by 1538, their governors issued Turkish-style inscriptional coins, and when they took Egypt in 1517, their style arrived at the Cairo mint. Religious statements here ceased also, while the sultan was exalted: "Sultan Selim Khan, Son of Bayazid Khan, His Victory Will Be Glorious, Maker of Bright Coins, Lord of Power, Mighty on Land and Sea" (on a coin of 1517).

The Ottomans took over Algeria in 1529, and the region thereafter used gold coins in Turkish style; indeed, the Algiers mint often produced more gold than Constantinople, thanks to its access to African gold. Further west, the coinage of the Hafsid rulers of Tunisia (1237–1551) always placed great emphasis on their devoutness on broad gold coins in a very elegant style with lengthy religious inscriptions in praise of God, his Prophet and his chosen one, the Mahdi. In 1534, the Turkish admiral Barbarossa captured Tunis and the region became a Turkish/Spanish battleground, until 1574 when it became a full province of the Ottoman Empire, with a mint set up to issue gold and silver in secularized Ottoman style.

The Ottomans' great rivals, the Safavids, dominated Iran from 1501, adapting the style of Timurid coinage, with its elegant cursive script ornamented by long uprights and interwoven strokes in inscriptions that were both intricate and lengthy. What these inscriptions said was vastly different from the secularizing trajectory of Ottoman coinage. As committed Twelver Shi'ites, explicitly Shi'ite acclamations appeared on the coins from the time of the first shah, Isma'il I (1501–24), along with the names of the twelve imams. The Shi'a version of the *kalima,* naming both the Prophet and 'Ali, occupied the obverse center within a decorative frame. The names of the other imams appeared in the margins outside, in chronological order or in groups of two or three in cartouches or grouped ovals. The names and titles of the rulers, describing themselves as subordinate to Imam 'Ali, featured on the reverse. From the 1570s, Persian text, sometimes in verse form, displaced Arabic, presumably further to stress the Safavids' authority and beliefs. They developed the habit of including a distinguishing mint epithet: Tabriz, Isfahan, and others were the "Seat of Monarchy," Tehran and Shah Jahan Abad was "Seat of the Caliphate," Basra the "Mother of Cities," Yazd the "City of Science," and so on. Safavid coinage was mostly in silver, though there were also abundant local coppers issued in the name of the cities, not the shah, which often carried designs of animals and plants. The engraving of high-quality Persian calligraphy that was a hallmark of Iranian coins from the sixteenth century onwards was assisted by the large size of many Safavid coins.

By the fifteenth century, Islamic coinage with Arabic inscriptions already dominated the Northern Indian world. The Delhi sultanate made distinctive and prominent use of square frames around inscriptions. Its coins were imitated by the other northern sultanates, with a few local adaptations. The Bengal sultans issued large silver coins with decoratively arranged inscriptions that proclaimed both their faith and their titles ("Father of the Victorious, Glory of the World and the Faith, Fighter of Infidels, May God Perpetuate His Kingdom"). They also occasionally incorporated short Bengali inscriptions. The Qutb Shahi sultans of Golconda had a distinctive threatening inscription in Persian: "God curse anyone who changes the king's coin."

From 1526, however, the coinage of the Mughals spread along with their power, to become dominant across much of the Indian world. Descended from the Timurids, the Mughals began issuing coinage that used the Timurid/Shaybanid style.[5] From Lahore, the first emperor Babur (1526–30) issued such silver coins with Arabic inscriptions. Over time, the Mughals gradually adapted the Afghan style to their new lands, and their coinage could differ significantly in details from reign to reign, sometimes seeming to reflect attitudes and approaches that verged on the unorthodox. Akbar's coinage (1556–1605) had inscriptions in Persian and Arabic, and the *kalima* replaced by a new text, part of a controversial attempt to reconcile religious opinions, which read *Allahu Akbar jalla jalaluhu*, "God is Great, Glorified be His Glory," as wordplay on his own name. Under his successor, Jahangir, a florid statement indicated the mint, such as "City of the Caliphate" for Agrah, "City of the Holy War" for Hyderabad, and "Harbour of Blessings" for Surat.

The Mughals also made several departures from the inscriptional tradition with some portrait types and, most famously, from 1619 the zodiac series, coins with designs taken from the signs of the zodiac to indicate the month of issue, an eccentric initiative of Jahangir himself that faltered in the face of the practicalities of coin production (Liddle 2013; Figure 5.4). The Mughal engravers used an elegant script and also incorporated Persian verses into the text, often ones that explicitly linked the ruler's power with his coinage. This was something encountered throughout the Islamic tradition, but it became particularly common in India where it was employed by the Mughals' regional predecessors. "By Akbar's seal this gold becomes bright/His name on this gold is light upon light" appeared on a gold mohur of Akbar;[6] "The face of this gold was decorated at Agrah/By Akbar's son Jahangir Shah" on a mohur of Jahangir, "While the heavens still turn, let this current be/in the name of Jahangir Shah, this Lahore money" on a silver rupee, and "Shah Aurangzib Alamgir struck coin in the world like the shining full moon." The Mughals also issued a range of ceremonial coins, from the tiny nisar ("scattering") for throwing into crowds, to giant coins presented to princes and foreign guests. The spectacular

FIGURE 5.4: Gold mohur of Emperor Jahangir, Agra mint, Taurus. © The Trustees of the British Museum. All rights reserved.

traditions of large and pictorial coins had ceased by the end of the seventeenth century. From the time of Aurangzib (1658–1705), religious inscriptions also disappeared, as the emperor was said to believe that sacred words would be defiled by contact with unbelieving Hindu subjects.

The Islamic World: Beyond the Empires

Beyond effective Ottoman reach, independent Islamic states would survive in western North Africa. In Morocco, the power of the fundamentalist Muwahhids had begun to wane from the thirteenth century, but whatever the shifting political fortunes, all rivals issued Muwahhid-type coins with a strong religious emphasis (Figure 5.5). In the fifteenth century, the Sa'adi Sharifs in the south joined the fray. Emerging regionally victorious, they began to develop their own coinage style from their capital at Marrakesh. They maintained the local tradition of a prominent religious element in their coinage inscriptions, perhaps in opposition to the rival Ottomans.[7] The coins of the great Sharif Ahmad al-Mansur (1578–1603) were issued "In the name of God, the merciful, the compassionate" and describe him as *Amir al-Mu'minin* (Commander of the Faithful), an echo of his controversial claim to the caliphate. In contrast, the Sa'adi's successors the Filali Sharifs eliminated religious inscriptions altogether and dated using Western-style numerals.

FIGURE 5.5: Morocco, Muhammad al-Walid ibn Zaydan al-Nasir, 1631–3. © The Trustees of the British Museum. All rights reserved.

The Indian Ocean area at this time saw the first introduction of Islamic coins, spreading only slightly ahead of European coinage. As so often, the early issues were derivative of a more established coinage. The earliest of the Islamic sultanates of Malaysia to issue coins was Malacca, where Sultan Muzaffar Shah (1446–59) produced small tin coins inscribed in Arabic with his name and titles in a design betraying the influence of the sultanate of Bengal, before Malacca was captured by the Portuguese in 1511. Meanwhile, the sultans of Johore issued Islamic coins from the reign of Ala'al-din (1527–64), with designs derived from those of the sultanates of northern Sumatra, a tradition which continued to the mid-eighteenth century. These were mostly octagonal, a local feature of other Malay sultanates. Gold and tin coins were produced in the sultanates of Kedah, Patani, Kelantan, and Trengganu from the seventeenth to the nineteenth centuries; only Kedah had silver, silver coins elsewhere were provided by Spanish pieces of eight. The coinage of the sultanate of Brunei similarly began in the sixteenth century, with cast-tin coins with decorative Arabic titles for the sultans: "The Just Sultan," "The Acknowledged King" on one side and formal patterns or animal designs on the other, a general type borrowed from Sumatra, but with the animal element as distinctly local (Barrett 1988: 9–12, 20–40). Closely datable coins with the names of specific rulers only began with Nasir al-Din (1690–1710).

IMAGE AND TEXT: INDEPENDENT TRADITIONS IN ASIA

Between the areas dominated by the Islamic and Chinese coinage traditions lay other Asian cultures with long-established forms of coinage, and others where coinage was still barely known. In some places, coins took highly distinctive shapes. Around the Persian Gulf and Indian Ocean, there were the silver wire coins, known as larins (Allan 1912). As Safavid power expanded in the seventeenth century, they adopted larins in the name of the shahs (Figure 5.6). Similar larins were also used in the Maldives in the seventeenth century by the local sultans, the first recorded being Ibrahim Sikandar (1648–87), who named himself and gave his title, Sultan of Land and Sea, in Arabic.

In the kingdoms of Thailand from the thirteenth century onwards, coinage was based on silver rings (Figure 5.7). In the northern kingdom of Chiengmai, the rings were made from silver bars with square sections, stamped in Thai script with the name of the city and their weight, then bent into a ring, cut halfway through and bent again to open the cut to show it was solid silver. In the southern kingdoms of Sukhotai and Ayuthia, the rings were made from rounded bars, bent, and then cut and stamped with small symbols, such as flowers, conch shells, and elephants, the significance of which is not well understood, though some are also found in temple decoration (Krisadaolarn

MONEY, ART, AND REPRESENTATION 111

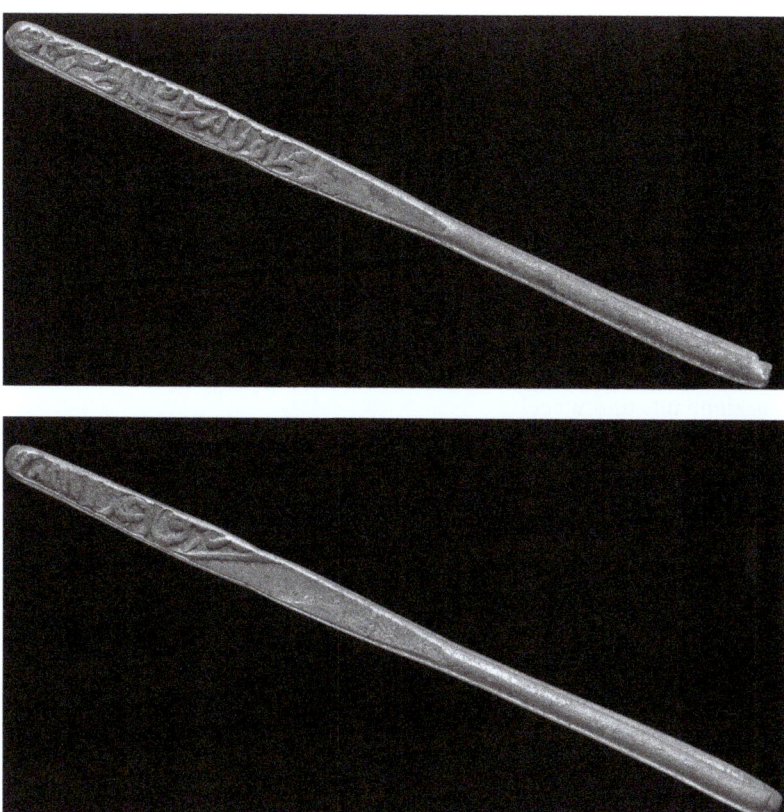

FIGURE 5.6: Silver larin of the Safavid Shah Tahmasp I (1524–76), Shiraz mint.
© The Trustees of the British Museum. All rights reserved.

FIGURE 5.7: Thai ring money, 15th–17th century. © The Trustees of the British Museum. All rights reserved.

and Mihailovs 2012: 83). After the fifteenth century, these rings were hammered into a tight ball—*potduang* ("tied-up worms"), often known as "bullet coins." Despite huge political changes, the tradition of bullet coins survived into the nineteenth century.

In the kingdom of Ankor in Kampuchea, European visitors in the sixteenth century recorded small, silver coins with a variety of designs on one side only: real or mythical animals and plants, but no inscriptions. This type, with a stylized cockerel design, continued into the nineteenth century. In the seventeenth century, European visitors to the Laotian kingdoms of Luang Prabang and Vien Chang (Vientiane), similarly reported on local coinage traditions derived from the Thai tradition, silver bars stamped with symbols such as elephants and wheels.

In southern India, a new Hindi kingdom, Vijayanagar, maintained the established South Indian practice of issuing coins with an animal or deity on the front and an Indian inscription naming the king filling the back, a balance of political authority and religious affiliation manifested by skillful engravers working within a long tradition. The inscriptions were normally in Nagara script. King Harihara's coins depicted Hanuman, the monkey-god; later Vijayanagar coins had Garuda the eagle or Rama and Varaha, all incarnations of Vishnu (for example, Dhopate 2002). Goddesses associated with plenty and good fortune also appeared: Lakshmi, Parvati and Sarasvati (Murthy 2002). In 1565, Vijayanagar suffered a heavy defeat by the Mughals and it fragmented, after which other local rulers issued coins in Vijayanagar style, but without royal names. This tradition of coins with animals and gods on the front and inscriptions on the back continued in the far south of India until the twentieth century. In Sri Lanka, the long-standing medieval design of a standing king on one side and a seated goddess on the other was altered by the latter being replaced by a reclining bull in the fourteenth century.

In western India, the Rajput rulers of Kuth, Nawanagar, and Porbandar followed designs used by the Gujerat sultans, while the northwestern mountain kingdoms (Cooch Behar, Assam, Tripura, Manipur, and Cachar) issued coins with Bengali or other local Indian inscriptions. Assam used octagonal and Manipur square coins. Inscriptional types dominated, however, and only Tripura had pictorial types, of mythical animals or deities. In central India in the seventeenth century, the Marathras, based in Bijapur, rebelled against the Mughals. Their coinage, however, imitated Mughal silver and copper issues, though in southern areas of their control there were coins with Nagari inscriptions which named Sivaji, the Marathra leader (1664–80).

In Nepal, the first significant coinage appeared in the mid-sixteenth century in the three Malla kingdoms of Kathmandu, Patan, and Bhatgaon: silver tankas with designs modified from the Bengali sultanate. Garbled Arabic inscriptions were an important element, though it is unclear if this was accidental or deliberate to mark them out (Rhodes, Gabrisch, and della Rocchetta 1989: 56–8). In the 1650s and 1660s, distinctive designs were introduced: a "star" at Patan, a triangle at Bhatgaon, and curved lines at Kathmandu (borrowed from Mughal design), all framing or separating the inscriptional designs which now named the king in Nepali. Exceptionally, queens were sometimes named, attesting to their important political role, both spouses, and mothers and grandmothers serving as regents, usually named with the kings, but occasionally alone (Rhodes et al. 1989: 136–7). In Burma, there was no local coinage before the late sixteenth century, when the kingdom of Arakan began the issue of Bengali-style silver coins, initially with Persian and Bengali inscriptions, but increasingly with local script. These coins often carried the titles of the kings: Lord of the White Elephant, Lord of the Golden Palace or King of Righteousness.

IMAGE AND TEXT: THE EUROPEAN TRADITION

Late Medieval Coinage

In 1400, most European coinages were multi-denominational and multi-metallic, incorporating gold, silver, and base-silver elements, the latter to shift gradually into a copper element that was still not universal by 1700 (Grierson 1991: 139–45). Practically all designs utilized the conjoined image and text tradition, with the latter in Latin and usually with a religious element, if only through the phrase *Dei gratia* or *DG*, but often more developed, especially on reverses. Exceptions to the use of Latin were rare, apart from Russia, where coinage was revived in the fifteenth century and employed a Cyrillic script consistently. Designs were widely based on civic or dynastic badges—plants, animals, letters, weapons, and architectural features. Alternatively, some states employed stylized representations of the ruler, occasionally full figure or equestrian, but usually busts, profile or full face. Patron saints were an alternate form of human representation and dominated some of Europe's most familiar coins: St John the Baptist in Florence along with its lily badge, St Mark and Christ in Venice, the Virgin Mary in Hungary, St Peter at an array of German ecclesiastical states. It was unusual for the reverse of a coin not to depict a cross, elaborated with decoration and additional features within its arms. Framing devices such as quatrilobes or linked arches could surround the design on either side.

Fifteenth-century Europe produced some of the first literary reactions to coin designs. The English noble, with its design of the king mailed, holding sword and shield, and standing in a ship, first appeared in 1344, but how the design was devised and received remains obscure. A century later, however, an anonymous poet provided an interpretation:

> For foure things our noble sheweth to mee—
> King, ship, and sword and power of the sea,
> —But King Edward made a siege royall
> —And wann the town and in special
> The sea was kept, and thereof he was lord,
> Thus made he nobles coined of record.
>
> —Quoted in Baker (1961: 285)

Nonetheless, the purpose of most designs has still to be inferred from them. Given this, there seem to be clear cases where new political circumstances were reflected in this medium. After Henry V of England was established as heir to Charles VI of France, a design appeared featuring the Annunciation scene on the new salut, a new dispensation for the forthcoming Lancastrian regime in France. A similar intent may be seen on the English angel, introduced in 1464, with its design of the Archangel Michael defeating the dragon, from the Book of Revelation—another equation of regime change with a biblical parallel. Some issuers maintained largely stable designs while others did not. Scotland, while maintaining consistency on its silver, employed a range of means to represent authority on its gold: a heraldic shield, the king on horseback, St Andrew, the unicorn (Bateson 1997: 97–111). In 1434, the Duke of Burgundy organized a common coinage for his principalities in the Low Countries, a single design to represent a new political unity. However, three different designs represented the duke's authority in succession: an equestrian image in 1434, a heraldic lion in 1454, and St Andrew in 1466 (van Gelder and Hoc 1960: 9–17). In other cases, coinage designs reinforced purely monetary unions, as in the Rhineland, where the four Rhenish electors issued aligned issues, often indicated by the linked arrangement of their coats of arms on the reverses.[8]

Alongside evolving medieval traditions, European coinage around 1500 saw a further shift in how authority was manifested. Classically inspired realistic portraiture returned to the medium and heraldry became an even more dominant form, trends which gave an unusual degree of artistic richness to the resultant currencies. The tradition was one of great complexity and variety, with coin-issuers ranging from relatively centralized kingdoms, to highly decentralized polities with many different coin issuers: princes, ecclesiastical lords, provinces, and cities, each with their own mode of self-presentation. Heraldry came to be almost universally employed, with traditional badges placed in heraldic shields. In some important traditions, the shield became the dominant form of representing authority, for example, on France's gold coinage well into the seventeenth century and on most Spanish coinage from the 1520s. Otherwise, heraldic shields often displaced the medieval reverse cross, wholly or else by overlaying it.

A further factor was the advent of mechanized techniques of coin striking, pioneered in several mints in the sixteenth century and spreading more widely through the seventeenth (Adams 1978). Much of the attraction of the screw press and its rivals was the improved appearance of coinage. Early mechanized processes were rarely cheaper or more efficient than traditional methods, as mint workers consistently noted (for example, Sellwood 1986). The appeal was the strongly struck, higher-relief designs, especially princely portraits. Samuel Pepys summed things up as full mechanization came to England in 1662–3: "They say that this way is more charge to the King than the old way. But it is neater" (Pepys 1971: 147).

Representing the Prince

Many of these design changes brought to the coinage aspects of the phenomenon known as "the Renaissance." At its heart was the revival of classical approaches to learning and among the most accessible of ancient products were coins, providing images of rulers executed with a realism and skill that were a model and a challenge to artists of the Renaissance and alluring to their patrons. The revival of the antique could be in terms of classical symbolism, ornament, and costume. The essential change, however, was the development of naturalism, or realism, as one of the main aims of artistic skill, a realism to match the coinage of the ancient world. While naturalism did not preclude idealizing, it nonetheless provided a new conceptual framework for representing personalized authority. And with all this there came a shift in the position of the coin engraver, from being an anonymous artisan, to a valued artistic practitioner.

Two further factors also contributed to changes in coin design around 1500. One was an increase in the supply of bullion, which brought with it an increase in the size of coinage. While these new coins did not *necessarily* demand the application of Renaissance design features, they did give engravers much more scope, obviously in terms of sheer size, but also in the higher relief that benefited portraiture. The second phenomenon, initially peculiar to Italy, was a shift in the nature of many of the coin-issuing authorities. Most medieval Italian coinage had been communal issues with designs based on established civic badges. However, in the late fourteenth and fifteenth centuries, powerful families established control of the leading cities and built up their own statelets. The arts were called in to support this upstart dynasticism, and a vocabulary of coin design was needed to represent the new political order (Grierson 1971).

Among these were the Sforza dukes of Milan and the first duke, Francesco Sforza, introduced the naturalistic coin portrait in Italy in 1462 (Crippa 1990: 35), a move allegedly inspired by his humanist adviser Constantino Lascaris explicitly to follow the example of the ancients. Venice also became, briefly, a pioneer in the field. The leaders of the Venetian republic kept a close watch on the pretensions of their elected doge, and it was apparently only through subterfuge that Niccolo Tron arranged the issue of his portrait lira, the work and possibly the idea of the medallist and Mint Superintendent, Antonello della Moneta (Stahl 2001). On Tron's death, the senate altered the doge's oath to prevent such a thing recurring. A later Venetian author commented: "I signori tiranni si mettono in medalia, ma non i cavi (capi) di repubblica" ("Tyrant lords may put themselves on the coinage, but not the head of a republic"). In Florence, Alessandro de Medici, the first duke, issued coins designed by Benvenuto Cellini, their reverses showing Saints Cosmas and Damian, personal patrons of the Medici, instead of St John, patron of the city (Hipkiss 1937). Meanwhile, the defining coin of medieval republican Florence, the gold florin, vanished, never to return.

The vicissitudes of the Italian Wars eventually incorporated Milan into the Habsburg lands, and its coinage received the full imprint of classical style and imagery, courtesy of Leone Leoni, who depicted the Emperor Charles V as a completely Roman figure with cuirass and laurel crown (Leydi 2012). His most dramatic coin design was a silver ducatone of 1551, with a reverse depicting Jupiter striking down the Titans, a reference to Charles' victory over the German Protestant princes at the battle of Mühlberg (Figure 5.8). This coin was the first coin of its size in Italy, and in its magnificence set the trend for the Italian princes (mostly Habsburg satellites) of the Baroque age.

By definition, the papacy could not become a dynastic state, and individual popes had to make their own mark. Reinforcing their authority after the Great Schism, the popes eliminated the communal element in Roman coinage and introduced, for the first time, a coinage solely in their own names. Sixtus IV (1471–84) introduced portraiture to papal coinage, the work of the outstanding engraver, Emiliano Orfini (Hill 1930: 202). Subsequently, Julius II (1503–13) revived the thereafter continuous tradition of papal portraiture. A new aspect was added to papal, and indeed European, coinage by his successor Leo X,

FIGURE 5.8: Silver ducatone, Emperor Charles V, Milan. © The Trustees of the British Museum. All rights reserved.

Giovanni de Medici (1513–21). He explicitly wished his coinage to be as fine as possible ("pulchriori modo quam sit possibile"), although this concern for appearance was matched by strong administrative controls that spread the papal visage across the increasingly well-organized Papal States. His innovation was the use of coinage for specific and topical messages for the first time since the Roman Empire. Examples included probably his proudest achievement, the rebuilding of St Peter's Basilica (Muntoni 1972: 1: 118–20). The second Medici pope Clement VII (1523–34) continued this tradition. Leading artists were brought into service to embellish the coinage; Pier Maria Serbaldi (Hill 1930: 225–6), Valeriano Belli (Attwood 2003: 210–24), and Benvenuto Cellini were among them. "Your Holiness may boast a coinage more perfect than that of the ancients," declared the papal secretary when Cellini presented a set of dies for Clement's approval, according to Cellini (quoted in Attwood 2004). These papal coins belonged to issues of workaday denominations, often the silver giulio, instead of figuring on just the larger testone or the gold. This was presumably a matter of economy of scale—the papal mints operated on a much larger scale than even Ferrara (Manca 1989) or Mantua, let alone Messerano or Carmagnola, and could afford a pool of skilled engravers producing quantities of finely wrought dies.

The influence of the Milan silver testone and its successors swiftly spread beyond Italy, and in the Alpine region a new, even larger coin also emerged, produced by rulers with their own silver mines. The Habsburgs, rulers of Tyrol, had direct access to the mines of the Schwaz mountains, near which they opened the Hall mint. They struck a coin, equal in value to their old gold coin, the gulden, but of silver and thus much larger: guldiners or guldengroschen. The guldengroschen of the mine and mint at St Joachimsthal (Jachymov) in Bohemia earned this new coin its more familiar name Joachimsthaler, or thaler/dollar. The first silver guldiner was issued in 1486 from Hall by Sigismund of Tyrol, a coin weighing 32 grams (Moser and Tursky 1977). Depicting Sigismund as a standing, mailed figure, it was not obviously classical in style. However, other silver sources were discovered in the lands of the electors of Saxony, and their mints produced guldengroschen with portraits in the Italian testone style, in profile and in modern dress, reputedly the work of the engraver Adriano Fiorentino, who moved to the Saxon Court from Naples and Urbino (Hill 1930: 84–5). In 1497, the main line of the Habsburgs inherited Tyrol, and thus Emperor Maximilian I (1486–1519) was given a prime coinage medium to express his ambitious self-projection. Under him, the Hall mint began a spectacular tradition of prestige coins (show-coins), principally the work of his great engraver, Ulrich Ursentaler the Elder (1482–1562; Silver 2008: 100–1, 199–200). In this work, the lessons of the Italian renaissance were absorbed in monarchical transalpine Europe. Meanwhile, as its role expanded in the 1530s and 1540s, the ordinary currency thaler remained an ideal vehicle for portraiture and set the pattern for the spread of coin portraiture through northern Europe in the mid-sixteenth century.

Representing the Queen

While female rule was not unknown in medieval Europe, it was only occasionally represented in gendered terms on coinage (Stahl 1990; also Monter 2013). This was to change under the impact of a number of long-lasting queens and the spread of portraiture. The first was Isabella of Castile. Her marriage to Ferdinand of Aragon in 1469 united most of the Iberian kingdoms and the coinage of her kingdom of Castile became the dominant one for Spain as a whole. A reform in 1497 produced a highly influential design, the excelente and its multiples (Crusafont, Balaguer, and Grierson 2013: 409–15). These coins engaged with the issue of sovereignty and power under a ruling queen whose husband was given the title of king, a situation complicated by Ferdinand having a royal title in his own right. Ferdinand and Isabella were depicted facing each other, the king in the place of honor on the left and with his name first on the inscription, although the sovereignty of Castile remained vested in the queen (Figure 5.9). Medieval Castilian coinage had commonly featured a stylized profile-bust design, and the excelentes thus maintained an established tradition, since they do not present a consistent treatment of individual features: that is, they do not appear to be genuine portraits in the new Renaissance style. This design was to be a major influence in the course of the century, and was employed whenever Isabella's situation was replicated, although, thereafter, the individualized portrait style was adopted: Mary Tudor and Philip of Spain in England (Cook 2017), Mary Stuart and Francis II and Henry, Lord Darnley in Scotland, Jeanne d'Albret and Antoine de Bourbon in Navarre.

FIGURE 5.9: Gold 4-excelentes, Ferdinand and Isabella, Seville mint. © The Trustees of the British Museum. All rights reserved.

The rule of an unmarried queen was easier to indicate, through a single portrait, although it was also a rarer situation. Mary Stuart used one at various times from 1553; Mary Tudor established an English precedent that, as so often, was maintained by Elizabeth I, whose over forty years of rule and coinage output created a lasting numismatic legacy for female rule that persisted as late as the 1690s, when the Great Recoinage finally removed the old hand-struck issues from currency. Both queens were clearly involved in their coinage designs and Elizabeth is the first English ruler who is recorded as giving sittings to her coin engravers (Challis 1978: 18; Symonds 1910: 89).

In the seventeenth century, with the exception of Christina in Sweden, the major female rulers formally shared sovereignty and a different way of expressing this through coin design was adopted by Albert and Isabella in the Spanish Netherlands and William and Mary in Britain.[9] In both of these cases there was the same scenario of sovereignty shared but with the male holding executive power. The model adopted by both pairs was the jugate portrait, two portraits facing the same way, the junior figure further back. The jugate style originated in the Hellenistic kingdoms, but was most familiar as a feature of imperial Roman coinage, associated with collegiate imperial power. By the time of William and Mary, the Roman imperial style was thoroughly embedded in many European monarchies, making this mode of representation even more apposite. By the end of the seventeenth century, there was an established visual language for depicting subsequent queens whether as sole monarchs or in shared sovereignty status, assisted immeasurably by the move to realistic portraiture as a default format for monarchies. The only limitation was the lack of an option to use military imagery, whether contemporary or classical, which was open to male non-ecclesiastical rulers.

Representing the City

There were some scenarios where the royal portrait was not appropriate. A new polity such as the Dutch Republic had to find its own visual language, incorporating quasi-portrait styles and heraldry in a style that focused much more on balancing provincial identity in its detail against a common overall design used across the provinces. Established republics such as Genoa and Venice had an existing repertoire to continue. The self-governing cities of Central Europe could similarly call upon long-established civic and regional badges, especially in developed heraldic forms and the cities in the Holy Roman Empire and Polish Prussia had no problem additionally depicting, naming, or otherwise referencing the emperor or king who guaranteed their status against the powerful princes around them. Yet, some of them added a new element to coin design, the city panorama.

Thus, from the mid-sixteenth to the early nineteenth century, some of the great cities of Europe applied the artistic tradition of the city view to their coins.[10] These gave physical expression in silver and gold to urban pride and civic power. The city view itself emerged as an artistic genre in the early sixteenth century. By the seventeenth century, few significant cities lacked a portfolio of topographic views. The numismatic cityscape was pioneered on the medal, made in smaller quantities and often topical in intent. Several things were necessary for the cityscape to shift from graphic media first to medals and then to coins. One was the existence of large coins. They also required engraving skills sufficient to create a city image in miniature. Most importantly, institutions were needed to commission them.

The medallic cityscape originated in the sixteenth century in Italy, but the real stimulus for its development came elsewhere. In the 1570s, the Dutch broke away from the king of Spain and produced medals commemorating their successes—often cities withstanding sieges or recovered from Spain. The cityscape design was thus born out of a sense of communal pride and civic self-awareness at a time of crisis. When the Thirty Years' War erupted in 1618, the cityscape design made its transition from medal to coin, on special issues made by cities in the Holy Roman Empire to present to their troops, or by conquerors of cities to celebrate their successes. Usually, the dominant aspect was celebratory: self-governing cities emphasizing their autonomy under the legitimate authority of the emperor. The great days of the cityscape were the later seventeenth and early eighteenth centuries. The cities which made the most impressive use of the design on both coins and medals did so during the peace that followed the Thirty Years' War (Figure 5.10).

FIGURE 5.10: Gold 10-ducats, Hamburg, 1675. © The Trustees of the British Museum. All rights reserved.

There were many ways of depicting a city on coins. A city could be shown from the sea, the river, or the landward side. The height of its buildings could be exaggerated to give a compact, bristling appearance, or the view might be spread out, as though from further away, expansively emphasizing the city's breadth. These city portraits were always highly subjective, emphasizing some aspects, and downplaying others. The city's fleet, its agriculture, its fortifications, its churches—all might be emphasized to indicate a particular message: military or commercial power, wealth, strength and above all divine protection and favor.

Limits and Legacy of the Renaissance

The impact of Renaissance coinage in Europe was highly variable and indicates the link between new designs and new types of coin. Henry VII of England's testoon was the first coin worth a shilling and carried an excellent portrait (Grierson 1972), which was also used on the common smaller denominations of groat and half-groat. The portrait expresses so much individual personality that it is a surprise to realize that on Henry VII's death in 1509, it remained on the coinage of his son, Henry VIII, for another seventeen years. The implication may simply be that no one particularly cared so long as standards of weight and fineness were maintained, or else that the quality of the workmanship displayed, and perhaps its radical style was more important than its nature as an individual portrait. In contemporary Spain, a similar phenomenon is observable in the retention of the Ferdinand and Isabella coinage into the reign of Charles V, until *c.* 1520. In England, a few years before the testoon, a second new denomination was added to the English coinage in the shape of the sovereign, the first pound coin, which is about as Gothic a piece as one might meet: old-fashioned and hieratic, the image of royalty rather than the person of the king (Grierson 1964; Challis 1978: 47–9). So, coinage did not necessarily present a clear and coherent image of kingship, or at least it seems that virtually any powerful image of regality and authority would pass muster.

The French coinage also manifested this approach, preserving its own traditions while incorporating new developments. French involvement in Italy gave them the direct experience of Renaissance coinage and Louis XII took his lessons home, though it was only in 1514, shortly before his death, that he introduced a portrait teston, an innovation maintained by Francis I (Drappier 1978). A succession of portraits record the aging of Francis on this denomination, but they were produced with a varying degree of skill in the decentralized French mints, some verging on caricature (by the seventeenth century, the techniques of die production had evolved to protect such elements as finely worked portrait punches and this limitation disappeared). Otherwise, in the first half of the sixteenth century, the remainder of the French coinage altered little. The system rested on the long-established gold écu, with its coat of arms design; only in 1548 did Henri II add portraiture to the gold. However, his successors reverted to the old shield design, and portraiture on gold coinage did not become continuous until the seventeenth century.

Virtually everywhere the influence of the Renaissance has to be qualified. Old-established, trusted coinages were not easily to be changed to respond to the dictates of artistic fashion, although their designs might be rendered with an increased naturalism, as the skills of the leading coin engravers received recognition and they became part of the repertoire of many leading artists. The greatest artistic products of this trend, like Leoni's Milanese coins and Cellini's commissions, were often prestige productions with limited currency, but the attitudes that secured their involvement also ensured the regular employ of lesser, but still skillful engravers who could combine aesthetic quality sufficiently with the practical requirements of mass production. Even in Italy, full Renaissance-style coinage was often essentially a prestige coinage, a brief moment when fashions and skills joined with the appearance of new coins to enable the *signori tiranni* to give expression to their personalities and ambitions before succumbing to the hegemony of powerful neighbors. Another limited phenomenon was the coin with a message, the propaganda coin, which remained restricted to a few issuers, particularly the popes, who elevated it to a high level in the later seventeenth century, with exquisite commemorations of civic improvements and papal political initiatives. The economic arguments against topical coinage were strong: the costs of die production for large-scale coinages inevitable with frequent changes in design would be a major disincentive.

The great success of the age was naturalistic portraiture, which firmly established itself as an appropriate expression of monarchical and princely power and personal sovereignty. Even the ecclesiastical states of the Holy Roman Empire shifted to portraiture for its archbishops and bishops, sometimes relegating patron saints to the reverse. Coin portraiture in the later sixteenth and seventeenth centuries, in the Habsburg ambit especially, attained a level of cold-eyed realism, unmatched since the early Roman Empire. The mid to late seventeenth century was also a great age of overt classicizing in portraiture: cuirasses, laurel wreaths, diadems, military cloaks, and antique drapery earned a lasting place in the medium, while contemporary costume, usual in the sixteenth and early seventeenth centuries, often vanished from use. Of huge significance was the international standing of Louis XIV, whose coinage inspired this approach in many other kingdoms. Scandinavian kings and princes of the Empire adopted the style, as did Charles II in 1662 and British rulers retained it well into Victoria's reign (Cook 2019).

This change in attitude to the appearance of a coin, viewing it self-consciously as an artistic medium and giving as much weight to the execution of a coin design as to the message encapsulated by that design, is perhaps best indicated by the development of traditions of prestige coins, pieces for display and presentation by a ruler to favored subjects, of minimal significance in currency, but, nevertheless, a potent reflection of how a coin was increasingly a thing to be looked at as well as to be used (Cook 1995).

New Worlds

In the course of the sixteenth century, while in Europe itself major areas of the existing coinage tradition were absorbed into the Islamic world following Ottoman conquests, elsewhere a new world was literally opened up to coinage for the first time. Spanish colonial expansion in the Caribbean, Mexico, Central and South America was followed and accompanied by the discovery of immense new sources of silver and mints opened there to coin it. Mexico City received the output of the Mexican silver mines and much of the great deposits at Potosi in Bolivia, the "Silver Mountain," discovered in 1545, passed through the Potosi mint opened in 1573–5, its output consisting of macuquinas, or cobs: relatively crudely struck pieces, most of which were shipped to Europe for reminting.

While much American silver was exported to both Europe and Asia, with profound influences on both continents, much remained to form the first coinages of the Americas. The designs of this coinage did not, however, have anything distinctive about them before the eighteenth century. The current forms of Spanish coins were transplanted in appearance as well as denominations: the Habsburg coat of arms and the lions and castles of the Castilian kings. Spanish-American coins dominated the coin-using colonies of the Americas, well beyond the area of direct Spanish power. The nascent French and British colonies to the north had no local bullion supplies on which to draw and little useable money was ever transferred from the home countries. However, in the seventeenth century, a few cases of locally minted coins represented the only locally derived designs of the period. The most notable was the Massachusetts series of silver coins, which initially used the initials NE for New England and then a succession of tree types—Willow, Oak and Pine—struck from 1652 until 1682, though most carry the date 1652 (Mossman 1993: 79–90; Salmon 2010). Even earlier was the Bermuda or Sommers Island "Hogg Money" coinage of 1616—probably the first coinage made in North America outside Spanish Mexico—which carried the design of a pig (Figure 5.11).

From the mid-fifteenth century, direct Portuguese access to African gold greatly affected its own coinage. This changed from base-silver reals to a range including plentiful gold coins: the cruzado, and larger multiples which carried a new title for the king: "King of Guinea."

The Portuguese were the first Europeans to settle in India, Sri Lanka, and in Malaysia to advance their trade, and to produce coinage for their settlers and traders. Malacca (captured in 1511) was the site of the first of these coinages, using tin as had their predecessors, the sultans of Malacca, with a globe and

FIGURE 5.11: Bermudan hogg coin. © The Trustees of the British Museum. All rights reserved.

cross design in the name of Manuel I (1495–1521), subsequently adding the arms of Portugal. Similar coins, with silver added, continued to 1641, when the Dutch seized Malacca. Goa was the main Portuguese settlement in India, and its coins sometimes showed St Thomas, Apostle of India. In Sri Lanka, the Portuguese briefly began their own issues in the early seventeenth century, with silver and copper coins similar to their Goan issues, although after 1649 Goan imports were used instead (Cook 1998).

The Dutch East India Company (incorporated in 1602) was Portugal's rival in the Indian Ocean. They followed Portugal's example by producing local coinage, though in the Company's name rather than that of the home government. The early coinages they produced echoed the traditions of the region, though with the Company's VOC monogram often in evidence. In Sri Lanka, the Dutch and the king of Kandy united to expel the Portuguese in the later seventeenth century, and Dutch-influenced coinage appeared: initially the Dutch counter marked local currency with the VOC monogram. But from 1660 onwards, they struck their own coins, with a denominational mark on both sides: the VOC monogram and date were only added in the late eighteenth century.

New World silver crossed the Pacific to the Spanish colony of the Philippines. The first "Manila Galleon" crossed in 1565, to be followed by an annual shipment. Many Spanish coins entered China, where they could receive local merchants' stamps. Attempts by the English and Dutch to create rivals to the great Spanish eight-reales foundered in the face of its embedded familiarity. At the same time as Henry Middleton was using English coin to reassure Spanish subjects in Asia, the English were abandoning an attempt to rival the Spanish coinage in the East, one source claiming "because the Spanish piece of eight royals had been before that time much counterfeited by other nations which made the East Indies to doubt of our coin, although without cause" (Wodak and Pridmore 1957). This claim was disingenuous: rivals failed not because Spanish coin was doubted, but because it was accepted. Across Southern Asia and around the Indian Ocean Spanish, pieces of eight, like the Islamic and Chinese coinage it often circulated alongside, had become what a coin looked like, even if the users had no clue about what the details of its design actually meant.

Coinage design in the period 1400–1680 experienced a range of transformations, in response to geopolitical, religious, commercial, and technological developments—though in this perhaps no more so than in any other period of monetary history. What was new was the range of encounters between different traditions, of increasing awareness of these differing traditions, and of the spread of coined money into completely new areas of the world. The full consequences of these developments were in the (near) future, but the scene had been set.

CHAPTER SIX

Money and its Interpretation

Two Early Modern Transactions

DAVID J. BAKER

The single most important fact about early modern England's money, the fact that had the greatest bearing on how it was understood, was how little there was of it. There were, of course, English coins in circulation, the pennies, shillings, sovereigns, and angels that were issued by the Royal Mint, each compounded of some admixture of gold or silver and alloyed with base metal (often copper), according to the current official standard. And, by the 1540s, the gold and silver that was being imported into Europe from the Spanish-controlled mines in the Americas had begun to make its way to England in significant quantities. Under Elizabeth I, the Royal Mint was able to boost its output considerably. But it was not enough. The same period that saw an influx of foreign metals and a surge in the supply of coins also saw a severe coin shortage. The culprit, somewhat paradoxically, was economic growth, urged along, after the 1520s, by population growth. These twin pressures drove up buying and selling (and also prices, thus the spiraling inflation of the time), and so much so that, by the end of Elizabeth's reign, the number of transactions among her English subjects was double what it had been when she first ascended. As Craig Muldrew, an economic historian, tells us, "by the end of the sixteenth century the demand for money had probably increased by something like 500 percent, while the supply had expanded by only 63 percent" (1998: 100). Between the coins that the English had and the coins they needed, there was an astounding gap. After 1600, the flow of precious metals into England picked up somewhat, but still not enough to offset the shortfall. Well into the seventeenth century, cash in hand, according to one estimate, made up only about half of the means of payment in the kingdom (Mayhew 2013: 26). During this time, coins were certainly not absent from the economic affairs of the English, but neither were they a persistent presence. For the most part, such tokens were something they managed to do without.

This shortage had two larger results. First, it drove the English people, and their rulers, to many expediencies to adjust the value of the coins that they did have. Today, coin and notes are often the first thing that comes to mind when we talk of "money," but, in fact, money can assume many forms. At present, we take something to be money if it satisfies three main criteria: it circulates as a medium of exchange, it serves as a store of value, and it serves also as a "unit of account" (that is, it can be used to measure value). In this period, English coinage did all of this, but not with the consistency and predictability that we have now come to expect. Many of the coins that passed among the English from hand to hand were issued by the royal government, and these came in various denominations. (There was no official paper money in the kingdom. It was not until 1694 that the Bank of England was founded, and not until 1833 that its notes—handwritten at first, and printed later—became legal tender.) These coins were backed up by the sovereign authority of the Crown, but, at times, it was the Crown itself that was responsible for their fluctuating value. Between 1541 and 1562, Henry VIII enacted monetary policies that have come to be known as the Great Debasement. He had the officials at the Mint cut down on the proportion of precious metals in the coin of the realm, while still stamping them with his royal visage. (Since the silver on the outside of these coins often wore off, revealing the base metal within, he became known as "Old Coppernose.") Subjects who brought in silver were reimbursed in coins of less and less intrinsic value, and all to the betterment of the royal coffers. The inflationary shock of successive debasements drove England into a mid-century recession and devastated England's financial reputation overseas. These policies continued after his death, and, by the time they were concluded, "the fineness of the coins had declined from the sterling silver standard of 11.1 ounces silver (out of twelve) to three ounces" (Landreth 2012: 20). Some of the lower denomination coins, the groats, were being rejected as legal tender. When she came to the throne, Elizabeth I made it one of her first priorities to rescue English coinage from the debasement imposed on it by her father, and doing so successfully was one of the proudest accomplishments of her reign. To accomplish this, however, she not only had to restore the silver content of English coinage to what it had been, she also had to counteract some of the means by which her own subjects were also altering the value of coins (in their own favor, of course). Counterfeiting was rampant, and false coins were hard to spot, especially given

FIGURE 6.1: Post-medieval clipped silver coin, probably a shilling of Elizabeth I. Photographed by Tom Brindle, Birmingham Museums Trust, courtesy of The Portable Antiquities Scheme/The Trustees of the British Museum, via Wikimedia Commons.

the poor condition of many of the official coins they mimicked. Even more ubiquitous was the practice of "clipping," cutting or filing off a small amount of precious metal from coins, collecting the shavings and melting them down, to be cast either as counterfeit coins or bars (Figure 6.1). The offence was punishable by the death penalty, though this did little to restrain it.

Moreover, English coins, shoddy and of uncertain value, were not the only ones circulating within the English kingdom. As Stephen Deng notes, this was a period before the notion of "*monetary* sovereignty" (original emphasis) was in place. Nations, that is, still allowed the coins of other nations to pass current within their borders, as they would until the nineteenth century. According to one source, in 1614, "400 different coins circulated in the Low Countries while 82 types of coins circulated in France" (Deng 2009: 19). In England, besides the domestic coins, to be had there were Venetian ducats, German thalers, French crowns, and Spanish pieces of eight, and these also were an accepted medium of exchange. English money served as a store of value, certainly, but that value was fluctuating, dependent on contingencies that were mostly beyond the control of the English and, perhaps, their entire understanding.

And the lack of coin had another consequence, as well. What took up the slack of the missing coinage? In a word: credit. With so few coins to be had, as Muldrew has also shown, the early modern English developed an economy that mingled cash and credit, but in unequal proportions. Coins were used for "very small transactions between strangers . . . market sales between sellers and purchasers who might see each other only irregularly." And, on a "much larger scale," coins were employed by "landowners to pay bills drawn on the London market . . . by merchants who needed it for overseas exchanges . . . it was also collected by the

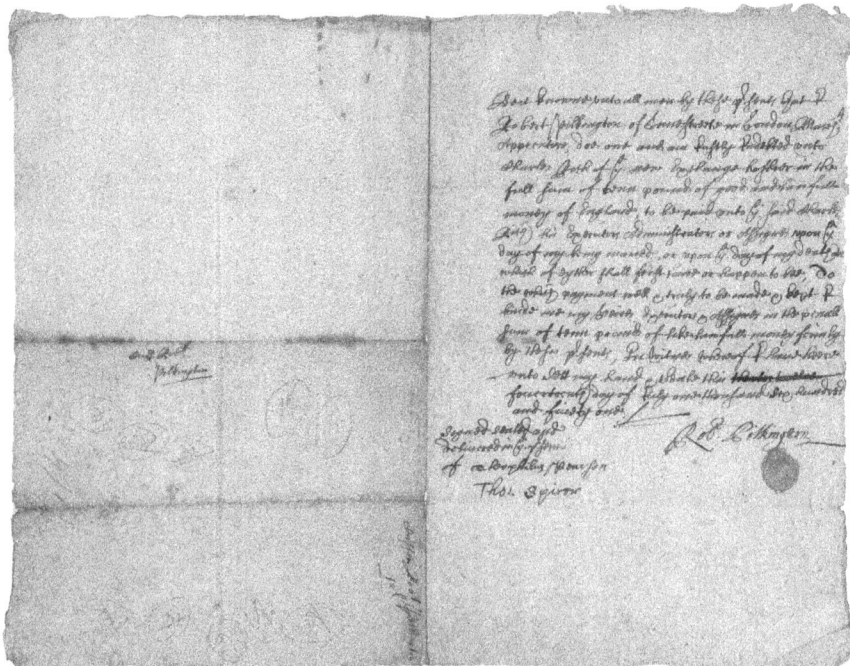

FIGURE 6.2: Promissory note for £10 from Robert Pilkington of Limestreet, London, to Charles Rich of the New Exchange. Courtesy of the Folger Shakespeare Library.

government in the form of taxes" (Muldrew 1998: 101). Sometimes they relied on coin substitutes, such as trade tokens issued by shopkeepers for use on their own premises. "Between 1649 and 1675, more than 6,000 shopkeepers in some 1,500 locations" made them available "in lieu of the small change needed for minor purchases by their customers" (Wrightson 2000: 248). Deals might be sealed with formal instruments—bills, bonds, receipts, and the like (Figure 6.2).

Many were not, however, and, in any case, it was held that the true guarantor of good faith in transactions was *trust*. In theory and in practice, English transactions were underwritten by bonds of mutual and reciprocal obligation, or what Muldrew terms the "currency of reputation" (1998: 3). As he stresses, this was largely a social economy. Many exchanges were face-to-face, and the questions that mattered to buyers and sellers went to the character of the other parties involved. Was his word his bond? Was she the sort to repay her debts? What did his creditors think of him? And her debtors? Because most of the participants in a deal would have owed money to some, and be owed money by others, reputation—the communal verdict on a person's trustworthiness, neighborliness, and even godliness—was crucial. It was this social index that allowed the early modern English to calculate one another's probable economic behavior, and it was this calculation that came first, before the more abstract estimation of profit and loss that we think of as accounting. The prime "interpretive" problem for the English, as they went about their everyday business, was other people, their motives, loyalties, and inclinations.

It is tempting to conclude that, because the early modern English relied on credit for most of their transactions—and thus the bonds that joined them one to another—their everyday dealings were free from obfuscation and uncertainty. But, unfortunately for them, the opposite was true. As I have shown elsewhere, problems of violated trust and financial malfeasance were endemic in England's credit economy, and just because it *did* rely so heavily on credit (see Baker 2009). To take part in the market dealings of the kingdom was to link yourself to a network of commitments, of money owed, goods promised, and payment postponed. But just because that network was so extended, and because, at every point in the network, buyers and sellers were held together by little more than trust, deals could easily fall apart or fall prey to unexpected complications: "many bargains . . . were remembered differently by the parties involved and payments to third parties could also be communicated badly," Muldrew says. "Notes were also lost and payments were forgotten. Arguments over the nature of contracts took place, as did disputes over damaged or poor quality goods" (1998: 199). The result, as he shows, was surging litigation over business deals gone bad throughout this period. The credit economy, that is to say, was just as difficult to construe as the coin economy to which it owed its existence. The economic "interpretive" problems that plagued the early modern English began with coins themselves, but by no means did they end there.

To say that the early modern English, taken altogether, did not have the coinage that they needed to conduct their affairs is to say that, for them, coins were *scarce*, and scarcity, as is well known, is the fundamental problem of economics. Then as now, it is because resources are limited, but wants and needs are not, that people are compelled to make choices, to decide where and how to allocate the resources they have to get the outcome they desire. And coinage is one such resource, as is credit. It follows, then, that how the early modern English put both to use has something crucial to tell us about what they valued and about how they understood the economic world that they inhabited—or, to put it another way, how they interpreted it. In this essay, I consider the paucity of English coins and the consequences it had for the daily economic lives of the English, as well as for some of the literary texts in which those lives are depicted. Recently, there have been several fine studies of the role that coins played in the literature of the period. As David Landreth, for instance, frames his project, he is "concerned . . . with the discursive effects of the presence or absence of coin"; "cash up front," he says, is what he insists on (2012: 36; also see Deng 2011). Notably, though, in practice these studies usually make it their concern to investigate the *presence* of coins and the "discursive effects" that they have, and not the absence.

Here, I would like to think about what "discursive effects" are generated when coins are subtracted from the equation, when they do *not* circulate, or circulate only partially, within an early modern text's economy. To underscore this absence, I will take a look at a particular transaction, an episode of buying and selling. It shows up first in Thomas Deloney's early modern novel, *The Gentle Craft, Part I* (1597), where he details the rise of Simon Eyre, a humble shoemaker, who, after he turns a cargo of cloth into riches, rises to become the Lord Mayor of London. We have good reason to think that this episode resonated with the early modern English, and intrigued them, because it appears again in another medium. Thomas Dekker lifted it from *The Gentle Craft, Part I* and fashioned a popular play around it, *The Shoemaker's Holiday* (1600). These works, I argue, speak to the monetary problems of the period not so much because they demonstrate the effects of coinage, pernicious or otherwise, but because they incorporate the problems of the both/and economy—coins and then also credit—that their audiences encountered daily, problems that they spent more than a little time trying to untangle (thus, we may assume, the popularity of these works). If what we're interested in is "money and its interpretation" in this period, then it is here, I suggest, at the intersection between coins and credit that we should locate our own interpretations.

The episode in question concerns Simon Eyre, a figure based loosely on a fifteenth-century merchant of that name (in both Deloney's and Dekker's version, he has become a shoemaker, "and none of the best sort, neither" [Deloney 1961: 148]). He has learned through a journeyman that there is a cargo of cloth to be had, "Lawnes and Cambrickes, and other linen," and he knows besides that these "commodities at that time [are] in London very scant." But he needs "3000. pounds ready money" to purchase them (a large sum, then as now) before he can sell them on. Where to get it? He paces his room, "hammering still this matter in his head," until his wife comes in. What's on his mind? When he tells her, Mistress Eyre suggests that he "giue [the owner] halfe a dozen Angells," each worth ten shillings, and promise "eight and twenty dayes after the delivery of the goods . . . to deliuer him the rest of his money." Eyre is astounded. "But woman (quoth hee) doest thou imagine that he would take vpon my word for so weighty a masse of money, and to deliuer his goods vpon no better security?" (Deloney 1961: 142, 143, 144). Why would a man of moderate means be trusted with a fortune in merchandise upon no more than his say so? Why, indeed? And, yet, he is. His wife's plan, which involves costume changes, impersonation, and willful deceit, works, and on the strength of this scam Eyre becomes a rich merchant and, eventually, Lord Mayor of London.

Now, the first thing to acknowledge is that, if we try to track just the flow of coins through this episode, either in *The Gentle Craft, Part I* or *The Shoemaker's Holiday*, we do not get very far. Try it. It's confusing. In the first, Eyre and his wife are flummoxed by the enormity of the sum they must raise. Mistress Eyre offers to borrow forty shillings from a friend, and then there are also a "couple of crowns that saw no sun since we were first married." But her husband, as I noted, says he needs "3000. pounds ready money." From this, he expects to get "three and three thousand pounds profit"; that is, he expects to double his investment, though, at the moment, he cannot "lay downe three thousand pence" (Deloney 1961: 143, 144). Mistress Eyre, though, comes up with her plan to bilk the sea captain and to pay him on the installment plan—and suddenly, it seems, they're rich. Just a little time later ("Anon after"), he is being praised as someone who is "able to deale for a bargaine of fiue thousand pounds at a clap" (Deloney 1961: 147, 148). At the very least, a great deal of complicated economic activity has been squeezed into a very small compass.

What seems to matter most in the story—and thus, assumedly, what mattered most to early modern readers—is how well liked Eyre is, and how rapidly he is able to parlay his windfall into social standing. Eyre becomes wealthy, but by following the shrewd advice of others, and not because he himself is a canny market actor. Money, you could almost say, is something that happens to him. Shortly after he closes the deal, he is invited to dine at the home of the current Lord Mayor, and this occasion Deloney gives us in richly rendered detail: who is invited to sit where, the talk around the table, who eavesdrops on whom. The transaction that has made possible Eyre's sudden alteration from uncouth shoemaker to well-respected merchant, his purchase of the cargo of cloth, is not even described. It takes place somewhere in the background of the anecdote, while the social give and take that it has bankrolled is placed firmly front and center. For Deloney and his readers, clearly, it is very much reputation that counts—that, of course, and the ability to manipulate people and their expectations for your own profit. What we have here, perhaps, is a literary glimpse into a bygone market-world, one in which the "money medium" is not yet the "most critical," in which, as Jean-Christophe Agnew puts it, the pursuit of gain is "constrained by other cognitive and affective priorities" (1986: 27).

In *The Shoemaker's Holiday*, the means by which Eyre succeeds are even more opaque. Not only does money move about in mysterious ways, its wonders to perform, but it puts in its appearance in bewildering amounts and in a variety of forms. This time, the owner of the goods, a Dutch ship captain who has come to grief on England's coast, simply hands the bills of lading to Lacy, one of Eyre's employees. (He is under the impression that Lacy is a fellow countryman. Appropriately for a scene in which there is so much identity confusion, Lacy is, in fact, an English aristocrat in disguise.) Standing by, Firk, another of Eyre's men, adds up the value of the cargo: "two or three hundred thousand pounds," he estimates, which he then dismisses (ironically?) as "a trifle, a bauble" (Dekker 1990: 34, vii, 14–15; Figure 6.3). In fact, however, this was a "colossal figure at time," so unthinkably vast, an editor speculates,

FIGURE 6.3: Fitting out a hull [graphic]/W. Hollar, fecit. Courtesy of the Folger Shakespeare Library.

that "Dekker may have written 'two or three hundred' and revised the last word to 'thousand', with the printer missing the deletion" (Dekker 1990: 34).

And the coins that Eyre will need for a down payment? Hodge, another workman, has them, even though the last time we saw them they were being given to Lacy by his uncle. "Hark," says Hodge, "they jingle in my pocket like Saint Mary Overy's bells." How did they get from pocket to pocket? It's unclear, and even Firk seems confused by the money involved. He calls the coins "porpentines," when what they are is "portagues" (Dekker 1990: 35, vii, 23–25, 23), "Portuguese gold coins also known as 'cruzadoes'" (Deng 2009: 270). The slip in nomenclature matters. As Deng observes, it reveals the "commoner Firk's ignorance of foreign coins" (2009: 271). But ignorance, whether real or assumed, is not limited to Firk's confusions over coin in this scene. It pervades the narrative. "Here be the portagues to give earnest," says Hodge as he hands his boss the coins he'll need for a down payment. "If you go through" with the deal, he prophesizes, "you cannot choose but be a lord at least." In this play, Eyre, like his namesake in the novel, seems almost to fall into wealth. Hardly has Hodge spoken, and *before* any transaction has taken place, a boy shows up onstage with *"a velvet coat and an alderman's gown"* for him. Eyre is a made man, but, again, hardly of his own making (Figure 6.4). Everyone around him conspires to make him rich, and mostly, it seems, because they admire him and appreciate his good cheer and guileless ways. Just as his workman says, Eyre does not "choose" to operate in the market, nor to become a "huge gainer."

FIGURE 6.4: Portrait of a Man, Maarten van Heemskerck, 1529. Public domain, via Wikimedia Commons.

Money is the mark of his success, but it seems almost incidental to the process that gets him there; no actual buying and selling needs to occur. "Why, now you look like yourself, master!" cries his foreman as Eyre puts on his "silk and satin" robe (Dekker 1990: 38, vi, 94–6, 21, 114, 108). Getting money allows him to become the rich man that, somehow, he always was.

Of course, neither of these episodes are meant to be precise case studies in early modern financial transactions; they are meant to entertain. Still, we can hardly ignore the oddly meandering track that cash money leaves through them. Large sums of coin seem to appear, and then to disappear, to shrink, then bloat unaccountably. Indeed, when it comes to coin, there is a rather delirious quality to both works. The general impression that we get is that coinage, its relative values, and the manner in which it circulates, is not something that the early modern English feel the need to imagine with much precision, especially when it comes in very large amounts or in unfamiliar denominations. In financial terms, the transactions that we see in Deloney and Dekker just don't add up.

What happens, though, if we approach this episode not as a chapter in the literary history of coin, but as an index of the bifold coin and credit economy that the paucity of specie had created? One such approach has been suggested recently by an historian, Carl Wennerlind. In his cogent book, *Casualties of Credit*, he picks up on a well-known claim that was first put forward by Karl Marx, and then modifies it to account for, not just the effects of cash in an economy, but credit, too. Like Marx, what interests him is the relation between the medium in which most transactions occur and then also the sort of awareness that this medium promotes—or disables. And, like Marx, he argues that the prevalent medium can give rise to a certain "unknowingness," to a refusal (perhaps unconscious) to acknowledge some of the basic facts about how an economy is operating. Marx famously said that a cash-oriented economy brings with it a specific kind of obscurantism. When most exchanges are mediated by money, he claimed, useful things ("commodities," as he called them) appear to have value in and of themselves, and not because someone's labor gave them that value. In such an economy, (some) people are allowed to "forget" that (other) people have worked, often onerously and unprofitably, to produce what they consume, and so "a definite social relation between men . . . assumes . . ., for them, the fantastic form of a relation between things" (he called this "commodity fetishism"). When money is the measure of all things, then it is the mesmerizing play of these things, these seemingly "independent beings endowed with life," that is most visible, while the realities of toil and exploitation are obscured (Marx 1906: 83).

Now, the relevance of Marx's dicta to the economy of early modern England is questionable. As we have seen, the English of this time did have something of a cash economy, but it was not their only economy, and, among them, cash did not reach the degree of saturation in marketplace dealings that Marx assumed. That is, buying and selling in the kingdom was not "monetized" to the point where money crowded out other media of exchange and reduced most social relations to merely fiscal ones. This, again, was a direct result of the scarcity of coins. As Muldrew insists, money in early modern England was "never used on a large enough scale to alienate economic exchange from social exchanges in the Marxist sense of a 'cash nexus.'" Money was employed as the "measure of economic transactions," but in its "actual use it was only the grease which oiled the much larger machinery of credit" (Muldrew 1998: 101). Marx's notion of "commodity fetishism" might apply to the early modern English to some extent—perhaps precisely to the extent that they really did have a monetized economy—but it cannot speak to the mentality that must have prevailed among them, because the economy that it presupposes was not theirs. Their lives were dominated by the intricacies of cash and credit, and, whatever we want to say about the amalgam of blindness and insight that they brought to their commercial affairs, it has to be traced back to both.

This Wennerlind tries to do. In economies like early modern England's, he posits, acting alongside commodity fetishism there is another mode of perception, or what he calls "credit fetishism." Commodity fetishism, he says, "allowed seventeenth-century Londoners to purchase a cup of sweetened coffee for a silver coin without ever considering the social conditions within which silver, porcelain, coffee, and sugar were produced." And credit fetishism, like its monetary counterpart, also entails the "careful construction of a social imaginary," not as a "conscious or conspiratorial attempt to conceal important facts," but more as a "form of unwilled or built-in blindness grounded in a particular understanding of the world." For those who deal primarily in credit, as in cash, some things just cannot be seen, "even after careful deliberation." Where the two fetishisms diverge, though, is at the axis of *time*. Commodity fetishism is backward looking: it "frees people from thinking about the past conditions of production." Credit fetishism, by contrast, is forward looking: "it necessitates that the future conditions are carefully considered and vividly imagined" (Wennerlind 2011: 230).

Wennerlind's remarks on these fetishisms are brief, but we can unpack them here. When money has become the foremost medium of exchange, and the structures that allow some to appropriate the labor of others are firmly in place, then it is in the interests of those who benefit to "forget" the people they are benefiting from, and to imagine the market solely as a "mass of commodities mediated by money" (Wennerlind 2011: 229). By the time the sugar arrives on your table, you have little inclination to think about where it came from, and, in particular, not the plantation on which it was produced. But in a credit economy, as we saw, things are different: thinking about other people is exactly what you are required to do to get ahead, and to do this you must extrapolate from what you know of them now to their probable behavior in the future. That is to say, to succeed you must summon up what you believe, or can infer, about the chain of buyers and sellers of which you are a part and consider carefully the dispositions of each person in it. And then you have to run a scenario in your mind: what will all these people do if I do this? Credit fetishism is oriented toward the future because it relies first of all on social understanding and conceives of the market not as an abstraction but as an assortment of people bound to one another by ties of mutual obligation and dependency.

As to what it "forgets," Wennerlind does not say, but, again, we can speculate. To put it aphoristically: commodity fetishism enables us to forget the other people that we are exploiting. Credit fetishism enables us to forget that *we* are exploiting other people. In credit-driven economies, as we have noted, what matters most is good faith and reputation, and precisely because these are often contested. In the social imaginary that you inhabit when you depend on credit, comity and fidelity are paramount, the *sine qua non* of economic relations.

This was certainly the case in early modern England, where, as Muldrew reminds us, "[m]arket relations ... were interpreted in a way which stressed the importance of trust and the maintenance of human obligation in a world where the complexity of bargaining and competing desires was causing many contradictions" (1998: 125). In the credit fetishist's imaginations, it will be these competing desires that are pushed into the background, while meticulously contrived scenes of good friends brought together for their joint profit will be ushered to the front. This is one reason that money and credit, as economies, are different: they "enable different practices of abstraction and different kinds of fetishism" (Wennerlind 2011: 230).

Now, as it happens, this mix of sharply observed social relations and oddly blinkered perspectives is just what we do find in much of the literature in which the early modern English told themselves the story of their economic lives, and, in particular, in *The Gentle Craft, Part I* and *The Shoemaker's Holiday*. When we tried to follow the track of cash through these fictions, we did not get very far. If we look at these texts with Wennerlind's remarks on "credit fetishism" in mind, we get much further. Both works implicitly pose a question: how can a man of some social standing, and with some few coins at his disposal, become rich? But the way this question is posed, and the answer it receives, varies considerably between the two, and not just because one is a novel and the other a play. In *The Gentle Craft, Part I*, the characters of Eyre and those around him are rendered with nice precision, as is the interplay among them. This nuanced give and take allows Deloney to present in their dialogue the sort of "interpretation" that typifies the marketplace familiar to his readers, one that combines both credit and cash economies. And his approach to those readers is subtle. What they know or don't know (or choose not to know) of such a marketplace is mirrored in the text itself. As a result, even today, we can follow the operations of credit fetishism as they are enacted before us. In both works, Eyre plays the naïf, the one who doesn't get it. In *The Gentle Craft, Part I*, he learns eventually, thanks largely to his wife, who leads him through a tutorial in acquiring wealth by exploiting social credit. In *The Shoemaker's Holiday*, by contrast, Mistress Eyre is cast in an opposite role: she is the one who doesn't get it and who has to be set straight by those around her, often her husband's employees. Of the two authors, it is Deloney who offers us, if not an "analysis" of early modern credit fetishism, then a knowing demonstration of it. He encourages us, as readers, to participate in the "careful construction of a social imaginary." It would be hard to describe Dekker's adaptation of Deloney as careful, though. His credit fetishism is supercharged: a celebration of spontaneous wealth, of affluence generated out of nothing but good will and sustained by nothing but mutual amity.

Keep in mind the ways in which credit fetishism does its work. On the one hand, it downplays the role of money in financial affairs. On the other, it plays up the role of credit, and especially the role credit will have in the *future*, when the social fancies with which this fetishism entertains itself have come to pass. We can see both of these affordances in *The Gentle Craft, Part I*. When Eyre begins his cogitations, he has nothing on his mind but coin. He knows that he needs "3000. pounds ready money," but he doesn't have near enough, and all he can think about is that he needs more. At first, his wife joins him in pursuing this line of economic thought. As we saw, she offers to "procure friends to borrow one forty shillings," and to throw in two crowns of her own (Deloney 1961: 143; Figure 6.5). Even here, notice, the emphasis is on sociability, just as an early modern reader would expect and credit fetishism demands. Mistress Eyre thinks first of *friends* who will lend her the money, and not because they see a good investment, but because they trust her. When we drill down to the economy that Deloney is presupposing in this episode, we arrive where the English of this time always started: with other people, and with coin as an earnest of the good faith among them. When they think about coins, as in this episode, what they must inevitably consider is their own credit, and how much they can leverage that credit to get cash in hand.

FIGURE 6.5: 7 gold coins. Courtesy of the Folger Shakespeare Library.

At the same time, though, the episode allows us to see that cash in hand will not suffice. If Eyre and his wife remain within the economy defined by the circulation of coins among them and their acquaintances, he will never become Lord Mayor of London. To make that happen, they must ramp up their *speculation*, a word that has a useful double sense: both to formulate a hypothesis without much in the way of hard evidence and also to invest without much in the way of certain reward. The speculative mind they must adopt now is different from the one that calculates the credits and debts they have accumulated among their neighbors. They must operate, not "outside" the credit economy that the English understand—how could they?—but within this economy, though conceived on a much larger scale. And you can see this happen. "Now," Mistress Eyre reminds her husband, they are "able to pay euery man his owne," and they "liue out of debt and danger, and driue the woolfe from the doore." She "desire[s] no more." But, he asks, could she "make shift to beare the name of a Lady, if it shold be put vpon" her? "In truth husband (quoth she) ile not dissemble with you, if your wealth were enough to beare it, my mind would beare it well enough." And as for her husband, he would rather one of that "sort . . . whose rents can maintain the greatnes of their minds" (Deloney 1961: 143). Like many an entrepreneur before and after them, the Eyres have realized that to become rich they must first change how they think.

But what makes *The Gentle Craft, Part I* so characteristically early modern is just how they go about doing that. They put aside any notion of finding the "3000. pounds ready money" that they will need to buy the cargo of "Lawnes and Camrickes." Indeed, they abandon the realm of coin altogether—or, at least, Mistress Eyre does, because in this episode the business of articulating the bottom line has been outsourced to her. For all Eyre's talk of upgrading his mentality, he doesn't know how to do this. His wife, on the other hand, is an astute market operator. When she hears of the sums involved in the transaction, she is "inflamed with desire," since "women are," Deloney lets us know, "(for the most part) very couetous" (1961: 143). This misogyny has a point: it shields her husband from any imputation of avarice and permits him to become rich without wanting to be so: he knows nothing of the greed that cannot speak its name. In fact, this denigration of Mistress Eyre is the pivot on which the credit fetishism of the episode turns. With Eyre himself safely consigned to bewilderment, Mistress Eyre is freed up to engage in the vivid imaginings that fetishism of this sort requires. And, just as Wennerlind might predict, her scheming consists of carefully devised projections into the future. As she plots out the sequence by which her husband will translate a few coins into a fortune, she parses in her mind just what each buyer and seller is likely to believe and to do. She is sure, for example, that the merchant will be satisfied with an initial down payment and the rest a month later, "or three weekes at the least," and she is right, because the merchant is in no position to demand cash up front

(Deloney 1961: 144). She also anticipates that the merchant will not hold Eyre's humble attire against him, but will judge him a "prudent discreet man, that will not make a shew of that you are not, but go in your attire agreeable to your trade," just as she expects that when Eyre shows up later in the garb of an alderman, the merchant will accept that he is one (Deloney 1961: 145). She knows this, she says, because she can literally picture it. "[M]e seemes in my mind," she tells Eyre, "I see you . . . already, and how like an Alderman you will looke, when you are in this costly array" (Deloney 1961: 146).

It is Mistress Eyre who fetishizes credit in this episode, then, extracting the monetary profits of the future from the social possibilities of the moment. But, once she has done that, it seems, Deloney needs her to do it no longer. When, in fact, all of her predictions come true, and she and Eyre are invited to dine with the Lord Mayor, she is suddenly unsure of her social standing and unequal to the demands of the situation. She is "abashed," and "did eate but little meat at the Table, bearing herselfe at the table with a comely and modest countenance, but what she wanted in outward feeding, her heart yeelded to with inward delight and content" (Deloney 1961: 148). The next day, she can talk of nothing else but who said what to whom, and thereafter Eyre ascends smoothly to the elite without any help from her. Soon, he is worth "12. or 13. thousand pounds" (Deloney 1961: 154). In a later episode, one concerning a cagey bargain Eyre strikes over a "Table in his house" (Deloney 1961: 157), *she* is the one who needs instruction from him. There is a sense, though, in which the sharp-minded Mistress Eyre does not disappear, not at all. Instead, the pleasure that Mistress Eyre feels, as she eats silently but inwardly rejoicing in the success of her maneuvers, is the same pleasure that Deloney offers to early modern readers. She (and they) know how canny one must be to win out in a credit economy, how rigorously committed to the profit motive. But with this motive displaced first onto Mistress Eyre, and then out of the novel altogether, they can enjoy the story of jovial Eyre's rise to prominence, while "forgetting" the woman (and the wiles) that got him there in the first place.

It is not especially surprising that when Mistress Eyre returns in *The Shoemaker's Holiday*—this time named Dame Margery—she seems to have almost no grasp of the economic concerns going on around her (Figure 6.6). In fact, she is a detriment: she hands out bad advice and interferes with the management of her husband's business. She scolds the workmen and demands that they put in a full day's labor, without loitering, drinking, and singing, as they are wont to do, while Eyre is conspicuously easy going. He believes, it appears, that his business will go much more smoothly if his employees think of their work as a lark. "I fear for this singing we shall smart," she tells them. But Eyre intervenes. "Peace, you bombast-cotton-candle quean—away, Queen of Clubs," he orders in his colorful way, "quarrel not with me and my men . . . drink and to work" (Dekker 1990: 35, 36, 37, vii, 30, 38–40, 80). Today, we

FIGURE 6.6: *The Shomakers Holiday. Or The Gentle Craft*. Courtesy of the Folger Shakespeare Library.

might think that Margery is onto something: Eyre's profits will be directly linked to the efforts that his employees put in. In Deloney's *The Gentle Craft, Part I*, as we saw, a knack for economic forecasting is the mark of a shrewd dealer. Mistress Eyre becomes the lady that she wants to be because she can think ahead and fashion success out of futurity.

But, something interesting has happened to credit fetishism in the transition from page to stage. In Dekker's version of the story, this same prescience signals someone who is out of step with the market. Simply put, there is no economic futurity in *The Shoemaker's Holiday*, at least for those who are in the know, and the success that, in Deloney, is projected forward into the future and then later realized is, in Dekker, what is always happening right *now*. Look again at the passage where Firk rejoices in the deal that will "bring my master to buy a ship worth the lading of two or three hundred thousand pounds." "The truth is, Firk," Hodge narrates back to him:

> that the merchant owner of the ship dares not show his head,
> and therefore this skipper, that deals for him, for the love he bears
> to Hans offers my master Eyre a bargain in the commodities.
> He shall have a reasonable day of payment; he may sell the
> wares by that time, and be an huge gainer himself.
> —Dekker 1990: 34, vii, 13–21

Note first the social convolutions of this. For no obvious reason, Dekker has added a character to the ensemble, the "skipper" who goes between the merchant and Eyre. And then, to ratchet up the degree of social complexity, another relation, that of Hans and the skipper. But note as well the temporal sliding of the dialogue. In the present, these workmen are bringing Eyre a cargo worth a fortune. Simultaneously, the skipper is offering "Eyre a bargain." Hodge knows already, before any deal is made, that it will be concluded and that Eyre "shall have" a "reasonable" period to pay, and also that by this time he will have sold all the goods for a mark up. Syntactically speaking, Eyre is a "huge gainer" at this present instant, as the lines collapse tomorrow back into today. Against this kind of felicitous time-twisting, Margery, with her linear insistence on connecting bigger costs to smaller profits, cannot compete. When Eyre's workers want to hire Hans, since he will keep them amused with his foreign "gibble-gabble," Margery worries that they have "men enough"; no need to hire more. But Firk and Hodge set her straight. "Dame, 'for God, if my master follow your counsel he'll consume little beef.'" Having Hans around "'twill make us work the faster" (Deloney 1990: 25, iv, 53, 55–6, 48–9). That this does not really make sense in accounting terms is exactly the point. Profit, and the motives that go with it, are what's being "forgotten" in this "social imaginary" of a marketplace that runs purely on good will, a frictionless economy powered by endless faith. In *The Shoemaker's Holiday*, then, we see an intensification, a doubling down, of the logic of credit fetishism that distinguished *The Gentle Craft, Part I*. While the novel is able, intermittently, to acknowledge the drives that make for economic success—"all the goods of that great Argozy are my owne," boasts Eyre when he dines with the Lord Mayor (Deloney 1961: 147)—and to put on display the machinations it requires, this is obliterated in the play. But, of course, Dekker learned this from Deloney. In a sense, *The Shoemaker's Holiday* is a reading, and a perceptive one, of *The Gentle Craft, Part I*. When he transforms Mistress Eyre, the shrewd market analyst, to Dame Margery, the penny-pinching scold, the playwright is doing what the novelist did first: making her the vehicle for a kind of economic thinking that can be articulated only so long as it can be disavowed.

What do these two works suggest about the larger issues of money and its interpretation in early modern England? A first—and obvious—point to keep in mind is that, when we read such works and consider the economic behavior they depict, it is *we* who are doing the reading. And, as Muldrew has pointed out, we live in a "utilitarian world in which a massive body of economic knowledge is used to operate systems which seek to reduce economic agency into predictable patterns of behaviour in order to preserve stability and permit the trajectory of utilitarian economic growth" (1998: 6). To some extent, Eyre and his wife are economic actors that we can recognize. Eyre has a shrewd sense of supply and demand (he knows what in London is "very scant"), and his wife is unambiguous about her allegiance to the profit motive. In the end, though, these characters do not behave as we would expect them to, and that is because the market world that is fashioned around them is not ours. In the scheming of the Eyres, we are looking at economic behavior before it has been reduced, almost entirely, to that "particular grammar of motives" that Agnew calls the "hedonistic calculus" of current economic thinking (1986: 5). By contrast, this is a grammar of motives that we find almost ineluctable, and that is because we have displaced the need for social trust onto an array of institutions—centralized banks, credit bureaus, government agencies—that take up the job that reputation used to do. These institutions, in a real sense, constitute us, at least as economic actors. They mediate between ourselves and others and allow us to make mutual sense of one another as we buy and sell. And this commerce proceeds, as it is meant to, without much attention from us. (When you use a credit card or take money from an ATM, how much do you think of the many others involved in the transaction? Our everyday credit fetishism allows us to "forget" them.) Another way to put this is that we, for the most part, subsist in an economic milieu that requires a low degree of "interpretation" when it comes to money.

The early modern English, though, did their buying and selling in an economy that required maximal "interpretation." Much of this thinking about money proceeded, we should say at once, along traditional lines. Recent scholars have shown that money in this period was bound up in several interlocking debates about the inherent value of coins, about the ethics of usury, and about the moral implications of trade and commerce generally (see, for instance, Hawkes 2001, 2010; Landreth 2012; and Deng 2011). On these matters, their counterparts at the time—theologians, moralists, and proto-economists of various stripes—had a good deal to say, and their controversies sent roots back into the medieval period, and even earlier, to Aristotle (see Wood 2002). But here we have been when trying to get closer to the grain of everyday economic experience, and to ask, as one critic does, "what *the market* felt like" (Leinwand 1999: 5, original emphasis). The economic awareness that we detect in *The Gentle Craft, Part I* and *The Shoemaker's Holiday* cannot be reduced to what intellectuals typically said about money. Instead, it's something more nuanced, but also something harder to formulate. Not, as the historian Keith Wrightson points out, that we should expect knowledge of some systematic kind from market participants in the period. Such people, he says, "were not engaged in imagining [their] economic system as a whole, though they were aware enough of the manner in which its dynamics impinged upon their own lives." Rather, they were "preoccupied not so much with the search for meaning in economic affairs as with the more immediate problem of getting a living" (2000: 335). That is true enough. But what Deloney and Dekker have to show us, I would add, is that even the distinction between searching for meaning in economic affairs and making a living is schematic. In their works, we witness English people who are definitely trying to make a living (and more), and who have invested, not just their money, but themselves, in their search for wealth. In the bifurcated economy in which they make their way, the "interpretation" of money as coin will always be contingent upon the "interpretation" of credit, and this, in turn, will always entail a full-orbed analysis of everything that goes into their social being: their sense of themselves, of their aspirations, their outstanding debts (monetary and otherwise), and all the credit, in many different forms, that they can claim.

And even this complex hermeneutic, as we have recognized, had its blind spots, its complicity with a "social imaginary" that promoted some economic realizations and blocked others. If we cannot call the upshot of such economic interpretation "knowledge," then perhaps we should consider another term: "disknowledge." This, Katherine Eggert defines as: "being acquainted with something and being ignorant of it, both at the same time." In her nuanced formulation, early modern disknowledge is an instrumental form of reasoning, a "specialized means of defining what falls within the boundary of 'the known'—and, concomitantly, of defining what counts as 'not known,' 'not knowable,' or 'not worth knowing.'" She attributes this motivated perception, in the period, to "England's learned classes" as they "acknowledged and articulated . . . [the problems of humanism] but at the same time continued to employ it as if there were nothing problematic about it" (Eggert 2015: 3, 40, 17). But, if Deloney and Dekker have anything to show us, it is that these subtle epistemic operations were not confined to the intellectual cadre in the kingdom. They show up in these works of popular literature, too, penned by base-born authors for common audiences (Deloney worked as a silk-weaver and balladeer; Dekker, a hack playwright, was chronically in debt and imprisoned for it.) And, in them, the habits of mind that sort out what can be celebrated, and what ignored, in the economic experience of the day work just as smoothly to push certain contradictions off the page (or the stage) and to demand attention for other, more salutary, fantasies. In fact, it is hard to understand these and other economically inflected works of the period except as imaginations of this very kind. They are knowing constructs that shuttle between that which can be articulated about the market realities of the time and that which cannot be expressed, but can be understood (implicitly) and experienced (vicariously), and no less urgently for all that. Perhaps it is time to move our inquiries into disknowledge, as a "subspecies of strategic ignorance" (Eggert 2015: 42), down the social scale.

Much of this is encapsulated in a joke (of sorts) that appears in another novel of Deloney's, *Thomas of Reading* (1612). In the eleventh century, he recounts, a group of clothiers came before Henry I with complaints, petitioning him for "reformation." The first was that there was no authoritative standard for "Cloth measures," but "euery good towne had a seuerall measure, the difficulty thereof was such, that they could not keep them in memory, nor know how to keepe their reckonings." And the second was that there was far too much "crackt"—broken or damaged—money in circulation, which "the people" would give in payment, but not accept, "though it were neuer so good silver," so that it "lay vpon [the clothiers'] hands without profite or benefit." In response, the king measures out the length of his arm and establishes that "no other measure throughout all the Realme of England shall be vsed, and by this shall men buy and sell." (He calls this a "yard.") And the cracked money? "[N]one shalbe currant but crackt money," he declares. Indeed, "all the money through the land shalbe slit, and so you shall suffer no losse." Gratified by the judgment, the clothiers start planning a banquet at a local inn, the cost of which "we shall recouer in our crackt money"—as much as "forty shillings apiece" (Deloney 1961: 285, 286, 287)!

The joke here, of course, is not so much that the clothiers are overly impressed by the king's largess (even at the turn of the seventeenth century, forty shillings was a respectable sum, though hardly a windfall), but how little has changed in the intervening years. After all, the English of Deloney's day were still using the yard to measure, and, more to the point, they were still bedeviled by a coinage that could not be trusted. In his historical fable, suspect coin is mingled everywhere with sound, and buyers and sellers must exert themselves to distinguish good from bad (Figure 6.7). But different standards of value apply, it seems, and at the same time. The public thinks the physical condition of coins should be determining, and it rejects masses of coins outright just because of some flaw in their appearance. The clothiers uphold content over form; they think that the proportion of silver should be deciding. (This makes them adherents of what has come to be called the "metallist theory" of coin: they believe it has "some inherent value of its own, due to its composition of precious metal.") These tradesmen are left with quantities of currency that they cannot spend.

FIGURE 6.7: Clipped shilling. Photograph by Mike Peel. Available at: http://www.mikepeel.net/ (accessed June 6, 2016). Courtesy of Creative Commons.

Some arbitration by authority is needed, but when it comes, it turns out to be every bit as arbitrary as the economy itself. The happenstance of Henry I's arm length becomes a kingdom-wide measurement, and the king blithely flips the realm's money supply on its head: debased currency shall be honored! And the other way around! Then he offers to call in England's coins and alter them *en masse*. (This makes Henry I a proponent of the "sign theory": coin is "simply an artificial measure of value, given its own validity by the State" [Wood 2002: 72–3, for both theories, see 72–6].) It sounds like a monetary dystopia, despite the wry tone that Deloney adopts. But, for his English readers, some of it was real enough. They, too, had a currency in which coins of many different values (and types) circulated, and they, too, needed considerable acumen to sort them out. They, too, conducted their economic lives in a milieu cross-cut by competing monetary theories and liable to capricious interventions. (Deloney does not mention Henry VIII and the depredations wrought by the Great Debasement, but it is likely it was not far from his readers' minds.) Deloney's anecdote is a parable, I think, a parable about money and how to make sense of it. Coins, he seems to be saying, are things whose value is, above all, contingent. They depend on the vagaries of public opinion, the quarrels of scholars, and the whims of rulers. They can be transformed from something to nothing by a mere edict. Something so nebulous, and yet so consequential, requires "reckoning." It needs interpretation.

CHAPTER SEVEN

Money and the Issues of the Age

Coinage, Sovereignty, and the Liquidity of Imagination

BRIAN SHEERIN

What does it mean for money to be imaginary? And how, if at all, could imaginary money work as such? These questions, as broad as they are, serve to focus some of the most far-reaching theoretical "issues of the age" developing in Renaissance England and Europe. In fact, it is no exaggeration to say that the ontological status of money as "real" or "imaginary" at this time was linked to the very meaning of Truth itself. Michel de Montaigne, in his 1580 essay titled "On Giving the Lie" (translated into English in 1603 by John Florio), makes the connections clear enough:

> *But whom shall we believe speaking of himselfe, in this corrupted age?* since there are few or none, whom we may beleeve speaking of others, where there is lesse interest to lie. . . . Now-adayes, that is not the trueth which is true, but that which is perswaded to others. As we call mony not onely that which is true and good, but also the false; so it be currant.
> —1603: sig. Llr–v

Montaigne's point here is a complex one, for he is not simply chastising the prevalence of liars in the world. Rather, what upsets him is that no one even cares any more to distinguish the true from the false. So long as lies are held "currant" in popular opinion—i.e., used as good currency—they function as well as truth. Such is precisely the problem with money, where debased and counterfeit coins pass for the same value as "true" ones so long as they are accepted as payment. Francis Bacon, drawing on Montaigne's writings, would later make an even more curious point in an essay titled "Of Truth": in matters of civil business, he contends, the "Mixture of Falshood, is like Allay in Coyne of Gold and Silver, which may make the Metall worke the better, but it embaseth it" (1625: sig. B3r). As much as Bacon seeks a clear distinction between truth and falsehood in this essay, his monetary reference cannot but help introduce a disconcerting paradox: what happens when falsehood not only functions *like* truth, but in some ways works even better than the very truth it is corrupting?

As both Montaigne and Bacon imply, discussions of the truth about money are never far removed from the presence of the sovereign; indeed, monarchical experiments with debasing national currencies are what initiated many of the ontological perplexities that came to obsess Renaissance thinkers. It may be one thing to scorn the circulation of counterfeit coin, but what happens when "false" currency becomes institutionalized by the same authority that also guarantees its legitimacy? When "intrinsic" metallic value contradicts "extrinsic" denominational value, which does one decide to credit? Monetary historians have noted that most money relies on both "heads" and "tales" for its social function: that is, coins work "in tale" as a way of calculating or tallying debts, but they are given an authoritative *worth* by means of their "head," or face—usually the face of the sovereign.[1] In this way, then, one can see how thinking about the reality of money has everything to do with evaluating the face of the sovereign; to what extent does that face merely verify the coin's value in tale, and to what extent does it *create* that value to begin with?

In addressing these questions, the purpose of this chapter is to see Renaissance money as a material emblem of abstract and ideological tensions, where boundary lines of reality and fantasy struggled for coherence within a context of monarchical politics. Ultimately, I hope to show how the stakes of "imaginary money" changed in provocative relation to that politics, as the heads of Renaissance coins became increasingly at odds with their tales.

COINAGE AND THE DILEMMA OF CREDENCE

David Landreth has cogently remarked that it is only when coins fail to work that people start to pay attention to *how* they work; their "incompletely material" nature suddenly becomes apparent at moments of transactional friction (2012: 13–15). By this token, one of the best windows into the mysteries of real money was the prevalence of its fake counterpart. Counterfeiting was not a Renaissance invention, of course, but certain other factors in the sixteenth century arguably made it more interesting and complicated than in previous eras. Among these factors was the widespread shortage of currency that could be used for daily transactions. This shortage has been well documented by a number of economic historians; in a study of coinage in Tudor England, C.E. Challis concludes that "in practice the chances of the circulating medium ever containing sufficient small change to meet the nation's needs must have been infinitely remote" (1978: 202). During certain periods of minting, in fact, the amount of silver designated for small coins was as little as 1.2 percent of the entire monetary output. This situation resulted from a complex intersection of population growth, increased global trade, the periodic shortages of precious metals, and a general reluctance from governments to mint small-value coins. Even when gold began flowing into Europe (primarily via Spain) from the conquest of the Americas, much of this new metal either went directly into high-stakes foreign trade and money markets, or into coins whose value was so large as to be impractical for most daily commerce. In this context, counterfeiting occasionally found an odd niche of providing a usable currency when more authentic versions were lacking (see Figure 7.1).

Of course, counterfeit coins had a variety of different origins, motivations, and quality-levels. Often, disks of base metal were simply given a thin coating of silver and then hammered with an imitation stamp. The playwright Christopher Marlowe was once arrested in tandem with a goldsmith for "coining" a very small amount of currency in this way—although as Robert

FIGURE 7.1: Sixpence of Elizabeth I—struck counterfeit, obverse. Photographed by York Museums Trust Staff, courtesy of York Museums Trust Staff, via Wikimedia Commons.

Sidney noted in his report on the matter, "I do not think that they would have uttered many of them, for the metal is plain pewter and with half an eye to be discovered" (quoted in Nicholl 1992: 235). The majority of imitation English currency was done more professionally by overseas craftsmen who would make slightly debased versions of official coins using cheaper metals, then import them for a profit. In either case, although it is difficult to tally how much bad coin comingled with the good, it was certainly thought to be prevalent, and was not always despised for being such. As Glyn Davies notes, "The recurring shortage of coins relative to growing demand . . . was such that the counterfeiter readily stepped in to fill the vacuum, thereby in effect, if not intentionally, performing a public service" (2002: 170). In the same vein, it is also telling that even though coining crimes were considered a form of treason, punishable with death, scholars have noted that juries were often loathe to award capital punishment to offenders.[2] One can understand the intense ambivalence that may have arisen around a practice embodying the propagation of falsehood, yet one that nevertheless facilitated real economic needs among a currency-starved populace.

In a similar way, token money—coins or bills with little or no intrinsic value—could exist in a liminal realm between money and anti-money (see Figure 7.2). Such currency was often made by business owners and circulated in local communities that maintained a relatively small circle of transaction. Among merchants, bills obligatory fulfilled a similar role: although technically they merely "stood in" for currency as notes of credit, they became transferrable to third parties in a way that directly anticipated bank-issued paper money. As one English merchant noted of these bills, "herein we see and may observe that things which be indeed, and things which are not indeed, but taken to be indeed, may produce all one effect" (Malynes 1622: sig. K2^r). Because these token and paper economies could exist entirely outside of sovereign jurisdiction, they were often regarded with scorn or suspicion. A sixteenth-century observer in England could readily criticize the "west parts" of the country:

> both vintners, grocers, chandlers, tipplers and other retailers do coin in their houses several tokens of lead and do cause them to go instead of pence, halfpence and farthings to the great dishonour of the realm, and like hindrance to her majesty's subjects for that the said leaden tokens are current in no place but in the several houses where they are coined.[3]

Even though some relatively successful experiments with token currencies had been conducted in parts of Europe—including Venice, Naples, and the Netherlands—most rulers were wary of openly backing "false" monies. Multiple proposals were made in England, for instance, to produce a national token coinage to assist with small-scale transactions amidst a currency shortage, but

FIGURE 7.2: Lead token decorated with six-petalled flower, with casting sprue attached. Photographed by Derby Museums Trust, Rachel Atherton, courtesy of The Portable Antiquities Scheme/The Trustees of the British Museum, via Wikimedia Commons.

no such plan was ever authorized in the sixteenth century; while Queen Elizabeth tentatively allowed towns such as Bristol to regulate its own token money,[4] she had no ambitions to sanction it on a national scale (see Figure 7.3). On the one hand, of course, it was simply not profitable for the government to make money that was "worth" significantly less than its labor costs. But, on the other hand, she shared a large unease with authorizing money that lacked even a pretense to intrinsic value.

When James I finally sanctioned "farthing tokens" in 1613 (see Figure 7.4), he did not hide his intense ambivalence about the procedure. He begins his proclamation on the issue by acknowledging the "necessitie" of such tokens amidst a dearth of small change, especially for "the poorer sort of people" so that "things vendible ... may be conveniently bought, and sold without enforcing men to buy more ware then will serve for their use" (James I 1613: n.p.). Nevertheless, he spends nearly the remainder of the proclamation documenting his reservations. The problem he faces, it becomes clear, is that token money will circulate with or without his approval: its usage is both too crucial and too widespread to attempt to suppress. For such currency to be used without sovereign approval, however, is a "derogation to Our Prerogative

FIGURE 7.3: Post-medieval trade token: City of Bristol square token. Photographed by Oxfordshire County Council, Anni Byard, courtesy of The Portable Antiquities Scheme/The Trustees of the British Museum, via Wikimedia Commons.

Royall"—as if "any thing whatsoever currant, or not currant, should be made a Measure of Buying and Selling in any manner of similitude to the use of Our Moneys." Like Montaigne, James is appalled that "money" would be determined more by what is "currant" than by what is (legitimized as) true, more by tales than by heads. On the other hand, to authorize the tokens *as* something true seems to make a mockery of sovereign legitimation to begin with. This dilemma results in a fascinating incoherence by the end of the proclamation, whereby James both sanctions and dissociates himself from his tokens simultaneously. By authorizing tokens, he claims, he is "Not intending neverthelesse thereby to make them Moneyes, or Coyne"; what's more, no one will "be forced to receive them in payments, otherwise then with their owne good liking." The tokens are concurrently money and not-money, whose worth is legitimized by the sovereign only for those who choose to recognize that legitimation.

As much as the growing phenomena of counterfeit and token currencies highlighted the conundrum of what made money "truthful," these ontological doubts were in many ways initiated by sovereigns themselves. Even if most princes of this time balked at issuing token money, they often had fewer qualms about debasing their own good currency. Debasing could happen in several ways: the value of current coins in use could be "cried up" by monarchical sanction, so that their extrinsic value suddenly increased without any physical changes; the weight of coins could be reduced while keeping the same face value; or the metallic content of coins could be "adulterated" (usually with copper or bronze) without affecting their official purchasing power. All three of these methods had long been deployed before the sixteenth century, and when changes were minor and infrequent concern remained fairly low. What tended to provoke both anxiety and philosophical introspection were the more extreme instances of these techniques, especially adulteration. When the extrinsic

FIGURE 7.4: GLO-160256 James I farthing. Photographed by Bristol City Council, Kurt Adams, courtesy of The Portable Antiquities Scheme/The Trustees of the British Museum, via Wikimedia Commons.

("face") value of a coin remained constant while its intrinsic, metallic properties diminished, it could feel very much like sovereigns were beginning to counterfeit their own currency.

Medieval coins in Europe had undergone a variety of adulterations, a practice that increased as trade expanded. Minting authorities engaged in routine and competitive devaluation of currencies in the hope of advantage, and between the ninth and thirteenth centuries, silver coinage in France and Milan eventually depreciated to one-fifth of its original value; equivalent coins in Venice dropped to one-twentieth of their initial purity (Davies 2002: 171). Monetary theory seemed to follow in the wake of such trends on the continent. The Italian jurist Girolamo Butigella was among the first intellectuals who began speculating about the possibility of fiat currency, based on his controversial interpretations of Roman law.[5] In the sixteenth century, French thinkers such as Charles Dumoulin and François Hotman developed a tentative "nominalist" theory of money that would later become influential in England, proposing that the value of money was rooted in its use as "account," or tale, rather than in its intrinsic qualities. Nevertheless, as long as the specter of Aristotle fell over most discussions of numismatics, the radical implications of nominalism would be largely absent in the Renaissance prior to the seventeenth century. Dumoulin, for instance, despite his progressiveness, nevertheless maintained that currency values should never fluctuate too far from intrinsic metallic worth, and he condemned debasement for the purposes of monarchical profit. Jean Bodin's "quantity theory" of money would similarly foster a relatively conservative understanding of money's correlation to physical metals.

In examining the connections between economic change and larger theoretical development, England offers an especially fascinating case study due to its combination of monetary conservatism and radical experimentation in the sixteenth century. What made England (with Wales) unique as the century opened was its eschewal of most kinds of debasement throughout the Middle Ages, maintaining a relatively high-value penny in relation to continental currencies. This discrepancy was a point of pride on the British Isle, to be sure, although economic stability and development did not naturally follow from an insistence on numismatic purity. On the contrary, despite—and in many ways because of—such a reluctance to manipulate currencies, England suffered from considerable economic inflexibility and underdevelopment. Coins were notoriously scarce at times, and their value was often too large for small transactions. As Davies summarizes, a solid gaze at English history tends to "inhibit the ... false, damaging and insidious convention that intrinsically good money is necessarily good for the economy." In fact, he continues, "one should at least raise the question of whether medieval England was crucified on a cross of undebased silver" (2002: 172). During the Middle Ages, contrary to what one might expect, it was the countries that experienced the greatest debasement that also tended to excel in economic development.

The identification of England with quality sterling also became a key factor in the identity crisis that its coinage would undergo in the sixteenth century. As other countries began to consolidate and nationalize currencies, and as Spain began importing gold from the Americas, England increasingly found itself desperate for cash—exacerbated, no less, by an ongoing war with France. Under these circumstances, Henry VIII would initiate an infamous experiment with coinage—the so-called "Great Debasement"—that would have far-reaching philosophical and emotional ramifications on the English populace for well beyond the next century. Although minor forms of debasement had been routinely implemented in England, everything changed in the mid-1540s when adulteration turned into a fiscal policy of enriching the Crown; Challis notes that the first ten months of debasement alone resulted in a £36,000 gross profit for the government (1978: 88). What also made the debasement of this period so significant was the state's attempt to conceal the very process of doing so. Not only were the new coins released to an unsuspecting public, but after 1546—when adulteration was becoming readily visible—new coins were given a thin silver coating to keep up false appearances (see Figure 7.5). In other words, the Henrician government began using the very technique of (bad) counterfeiters in order to defraud the public.

From a governmental perspective, although this project of debasement certainly did result in an influx of cash, it was also a game of diminishing returns. Having so long become accustomed to a predictable equivalence between the external and internal value of coins, the sudden disruption of numismatic signification caused enormous insecurity once the scheme of adulteration became discovered. A vicious cycle developed, whereby the government had to raise the price it was willing to pay for bullion so as to bring in the raw materials for coins; payment for that bullion was made in newly-

FIGURE 7.5: Post-medieval coin, groat of Henry VIII, 3rd coinage. Photographed by West Yorkshire Archaeology Service, Amy Downes, courtesy of The Portable Antiquities Scheme/The Trustees of the British Museum, via Wikimedia Commons.

debased money; people became increasingly reluctant to bring in any more bullion; so, the price of bullion was augmented to attract more raw materials (Challis 1978: 92–3). And thus the pattern continued, at an ever more desperate pace, until confidence was nearly exhausted. Within a period of just six years, the English silver coinage had dropped from 92.5 percent pure to 25 percent pure. Under Henry's successor, Edward VI, it would descend even lower to 17 percent (Mayhew 1999: 46). There was a growing unwillingness to accept such coin in transactions, forcing a confrontation between philosophies of intrinsic and extrinsic values. When faced with a transaction, where was one's faith to be placed: in the metallic content of the coins or the king's proclamation of their face value? Ultimately, of course, the government itself had a stake in this controversy; as Stephen Deng summarizes, "Once the debasement was publicly known, the English state literally had to force subjects to use its coins" (Deng 2011: 91).

At a time when European commerce was vaulting several currencies into a new era of large-scale borrowing, investment, and money markets, England suddenly found itself losing its one major emblem of monetary respect even as it became alienated from the continent religiously as well. As such reconfigurations heightened the "identity politics" of currency and coinage for everyone involved, it is hardly surprising that a new introspection would develop around how value is connected to money. Not only did authorized currency, in the minds of many, begin to pass itself off as something it was not, but some of it even employed the same techniques of the most vulgar counterfeiters. "Thy Silver is drosse," pronounced Bishop Latimer in response to the 1549 debasement, echoing the prophet Isaiah, "it is not fyne, it is counterfayte" (Tawney and Power 1924:

181). Rice Vaughan, an early monetary theorist writing in the 1620s (although published decades later), would state the matter even more explicitly in retrospect: "what can be more dishonourable," he asks, "than to have the Image of the Prince, or the Mark of the Publick Attestation impressed upon false and counterfeited stuff . . .? And if there be gain made of it, it is a manifest breach of the publick Faith" (Vaughan 1675: D3r). What does it mean, then, for counterfeit money to be sanctioned by the sovereign? In a sense, this question is simply another version of the dilemma surrounding token money: that is, if fake money is accepted as "current," to what extent can it really be considered specious at all?

The wider ontological implications of the Henrician debasement were raised almost immediately by English subjects. Perhaps the most articulate (and widely referenced) of these debates emerged in a treatise called *A Discourse of the Commonweal of This Realm of England*. Written in 1549 and attributed to Sir Thomas Smith, the *Discourse* remained relevant enough among English intellectuals to become a successful publication thirty-two years later with only minor alterations. The book, structured as a conversation between Englishmen of various stations and moderated by a learned Doctor, concerns itself broadly with many issues pertaining to the "decay of this Commonweal" (1969 [1581]: 11); in doing so, however, it circles incessantly around dilemmas of coinage. The character of the Knight, in particular, is eager to downplay the necessity of "intrinsic value" as a necessary property of money. "What makes that the matter what sort of coin we have among ourselves," he asks, "so it be current from one hand to another, yea, if it were made of leather?" (1969 [1581]: 34). The Knight thus introduces an early token—or "chartal"—theory of money, where "moneyness" has nothing inherently to do with the medium of exchange and everything to do with the perceptual assumptions of its users. From this perspective, the role of the sovereign is merely to stabilize and enforce a set of values that are socially vital but ultimately arbitrary. In fact, what the Knight describes here is a version of the Henrician coinage experiment, where the "current" value of coin is determined simply by the imagination of the king.

By this same logic, as the Knight wonders later, the need for sovereign authority seems to diminish the more one posits an "intrinsic" value of coinage that can be objectively measured. The Knight asks it in this way:

Why do kings and princes strike these metals and other with a coin but because they would have that coin, of what value soever it be, to bear the state that the coin pretends; which they did in vain if they could make the metal that bears that to be neither better nor worse in estimation? Then I had as lever have small gads or plates of silver and gold without any coin at all to go abroad from man to man for exchange.

—1969 [1581]: 75

In other words, why would one need "heads" on a coin at all if its metallic content were good enough to provide a secure tale? The Doctor, however, is quick to step in and correct this unorthodox rationale; the purpose of the monarch's face, he clarifies, is not to impose a value that isn't actually "there" in the coin, but to guarantee the value that *is* there. It would certainly be inconvenient if every monetary transaction required an assaying of metallic value in the medium of exchange; the monarch, by this light, facilitates monetary circulation by "assur[ing] the receiver" that his or her coins is "no less than the weight it pretended" (1969 [1581]: 76). At least, such a correspondence is how things *should* work; according to the Doctor, the debasement of coinage fundamentally disrupts the significance of the coin's face, no longer guaranteeing anything. From this perspective, royally minted token money—rather than making the monarch essential as a determiner of value—does the opposite: it invalidates the whole point of a monarch in the first place.

And yet, as the Doctor of *The Discourse* explains his rationale, a curious paradox unfolds within his numismatics. Although he aims to dichotomize coinage into categories of objective (intrinsic value) versus subjective (extrinsic value), real versus imaginary, his description of the Henrician experiment reveals a significant blurring of these options. In matters of coinage, he explains, the growing untrustworthiness of "princes" necessitated an interpretive shift:

> princes' credit was then such among their subjects as they doubted nothing therein. As soon as they attempted to do otherwise, that is to mark the half pound with the mark of the pound and the half ounce with the mark of the ounce, awhile their credit made those coins current . . .; but as soon as it was espied, the two pieces of half pound went no further than the one piece of a whole pound went before.
>
> —1969 [1581]: 76

A troubling question arises: what if the populace had never actually found out that their currency had been adulterated? As the Doctor notes in the passage above, such currency actually did work so long as the monarch's face was given "credit." Not until the ruse was "espied" did it actually change the moneyness of the medium of exchange. A marginal note beside this passage in the 1581 edition provides it with a telling synopsis: "*What loss comes of loss of credence.*" Indeed, even in the Doctor's defense of "true" currency, "credence" cannot help but become the fulcrum on which this obsession with verity hinges.

MONETARY IMAGINATION AND THE LIMITS OF SOVEREIGN AUTHORITY

Henry VIII's manipulation of coin was in some ways a test of monarchical authority itself, an experiment concerning the limits of sovereign power in defining value. His dubious success in forcing copper to act like "real" money, merely by demanding it to, would arguably initiate a chain of speculation that began to consider the radical potential of just what else the imagination could do—with or without a monarch's fiat. Almost immediately upon gaining the throne, Elizabeth announced a recoinage back to pre-Henrician ratios, due in large part to the confusion surrounding rampant counterfeiting: "nothing is so grevous, ne lykely to disturbe and decaye the state and good order of this Realme," she proclaimed in 1560, "as the suffraunce of the base monies," adding that "by reason of these sayde base monyes, great quantitie of forged and counterfaites have ben and be dayley made and brought from beyonde the seas" (Tawney and Power 1924: 196). Shifting the purity of silver back to 92.5 percent involved vast bureaucratic dexterity on Elizabeth's part, and she was praised to the day of her death (and beyond) for her efforts—even if she herself indulged in occasional debasements toward the end of her reign. And yet, while from one perspective Elizabeth seemed to be setting things "back to normal," it is important to stress just how deep—and irreversible—the rifts in the ontology of money had become by the end of the sixteenth century, partly as a result of earlier monarchical interventions.

By the turn of the seventeenth century, the working of even the purest coinage had gained an aura of mystery and even occultism about it—or at least, such mystery was now being much more openly discussed. Gerard de Malynes, an assay master of the mint under James I, once noted that even his fellow minting authorities had very little understanding of how metals attained specific, exchangeable values. Describing a typical encounter with another assay master, Malynes posits the following scenario:

> What say you to finenesse of Gold and Silver? I do aske him first, What he taketh finenesse to be? he doth answere me, That it is a Mysterie, and that the studie of it is as intricate, as the Transubstantiation of the Papists Sacrament, as you may perceiue (saith he) by the controversie betweene the Warden of the Mint, and the Mint-master, concerning the Standards of the sterling moneys.
>
> —1622: sig. Bb2v

Coming from Protestant England, the association of money-making with Eucharistic transubstantiation clearly registered the threat of superstitious mysticism even towards coins that were supposedly reliable. As can be seen here, an attachment to standards of intrinsic value was troubled by the sheer complexity of calculating it—even though Malynes later does his best to reassure readers that things are not so difficult as they seem. Values of gold and silver were vitally tied together in a bimetallic ratio, but few people presumed to understand how this ratio was maintained or even where it came from. The ideal relationship between metals was often given an alchemical explanation, where proportional equivalence was grounded in astronomical ratios. Vaughan documents that gold is considered twelve times more valuable than silver because the "motions" of the (silver) moon in relation to the (golden) sun are at a ratio of 12:1 (1675: sig. E1v). It made a kind of intuitive sense, although attempting to delineate and enforce its practical application within the politically charged realms of coinage was not an envied task. After all, the bimetallic ratio almost never actually coincided with this ideal in Renaissance economies, and it was typical to explain deviations by blaming the manipulation of other countries. Well into the seventeenth century, mercantilist writers were arguing about the extent to which such exchange fluctuations could actually be controlled.[6]

The early modern reality of alchemy, however, itself raised several puzzling questions about the relation between sovereignty and money, all of which seemed to come to a head in the seventeenth century. Given the perpetual shortage of coin, for instance, English theorists could not help speculating whether alchemy might provide a remedy for this problem. But what would it mean for currency to be supplied by transmutation? In a 1622 treatise, Malynes praises alchemy as science "very pleasant, and full of expectation"—especially since it stands to turn "a small charge to a very great profit" (1622: sig. Z2v); the Hartlib Circle, meanwhile, actively pursued alchemical intervention to cure monetary shortages. In one sense, such proposals were not as radical as they may appear. Indeed, the royal mint—itself a laboratory of sorts where metals were mysteriously mixed and transformed into currency—had long been associated with alchemical sciences. It was also no secret that monarchs routinely employed alchemists to assist with their mints;[7] even as late as 1696, Isaac Newton's involvement with alchemy made him a good candidate for Warden of the Mint under William III. The possibility of harnessing transmutation for monetary production was only a dangerous one if it could happen independently of the Crown. After all, the practice of alchemy had been a felony in England since the reign of Henry IV not because it was a spurious science, but precisely because it wasn't: any ability to produce precious metal without governmental supervision constituted a potential threat to the sovereign prerogative of monetary control. For this reason, most economic theorists were careful to show deference to monarchical authority when suggesting alchemical improvements to the state.[8]

On the other hand, the government's very involvement in manipulating coinage left a lingering association between alchemy and debasement. Robert Cotton, in a 1626 speech before Parliament, condemns the monetary adulterations committed by previous monarchs by linking such manipulations to transmutation: "Thus we see it was with *Henry* VI. who, after he had begun with abating the Measure, he after fell to abasing the Matter; and granted Commissions to *Missenden* and others to practise *Alchimy* to serve his Mint." When Henry VIII tried the same thing, Cotton goes on, he "suffered Shipwreck of all Rock" (1856: 126). This association of alchemy with numismatic imagination had popular traction as well, as evidenced in the Jacobean drama *Eastward Ho!* (1973 [1605]). Co-written by Ben Jonson, this play features a goldsmith's apprentice named Quicksilver who explains his craft of counterfeiting by deploying an elaborately alchemical rhetoric:

> I'll tell you how yourself shall blanch copper [to look like silver coin] thus cunningly. Take arsenic, otherwise called realgar (which, indeed, is plain ratsbane); sublime 'em three or four times, then take the sublimate of this realgar, and put 'em into a glass, into *chymia*, and let 'em have a convenient decoction natural, four-and-twenty hours, and he will become perfectly fixed; then take this fixed powder, and project him upon well-purged copper, *et habebis magisterium* [and you will have the philosopher's stone].
> —1973 [1605]: 4.1.208–15

Given that Quicksilver here is describing a blanching process similar to that used by the minters of Henry VIII during the Great Debasement, there was clearly a fine line between, on the one hand, the magical dissemination of currency promised by both debasement and alchemy, and, on the other hand, the mere propagation of counterfeits.

Yet, in a manner of speaking, there was one more kind of monetary alchemy that gained momentum during this time, one that seemed to epitomize the deepening curiosities surrounding numismatic ontology: this was the alchemy of credit. The marginalia of *A Discourse of the Commonweal of This Realm of England*, it will be recalled, summarized the Henrician paradox of gilded base coin as fundamentally a dilemma of "credence": that is, it seemed to work just fine only so long as everyone believed that there was nothing different about it. As it happened, the problem of credence also became central to the burgeoning credit economies ever encroaching on the domain of coinage. Of course, the words "credit" and "credence" both have the same Latin meaning of "trust" or "belief," and economic anthropologists have documented the centrality of credit economies even to the most primitive forms of communal cohesion.[9] Once again, though, what's notable about Renaissance finance is not the emergence of borrowing and lending cultures per se, but rather their transformation into large-scale networks of fragile interdependence, with newly global implications.

Although most individuals during this time had no thought of abandoning a notion of money ultimately grounded in the "real" worth of precious metals, monetary practices nevertheless became increasingly decoupled from metallic physicality. Merchants, of course, had long been the vanguard in a trend to prefer bills obligatory over coin when conducting overseas transactions. But even among land-bound citizens, the evolution of usury laws was making it ever easier (which is not to say less problematic) to do business through debt and credit networks. Practices of investment and emergent venture capitalism, likewise, were seemingly able to multiply money out of nothing; the very belief in one's financial viability had the power to create the reality of it.[10] As Carl Wennerlind documents, certain men within the Hartlib Circle—a group that had already attempted to transform English currency by exploiting the transmutation of metals—even had plans to propagate credit systems for their similarly alchemical potential. According to these theorists, credit money *could* work like alchemy due to its ability to create an endless supply of value out of base materials—even paper. "In addition to offering solutions to the same problems," comments Wennerlind, "metallic transmutation and credit money shared the same underlying idea of using an expansion in the money stock to launch a process of continuous economic change, improvement, and growth" (2011: 68). They also shared the same capacity to undermine the need for sovereign governance when it came to monetary regulation.

William Potter was one of the earliest of these thinkers to propose the widespread use of credit money throughout England. In a 1650 treatise, he maintained that because currency shortages were the primary impediment to trade and commerce, a nationally accepted credit money could greatly boost economic circulation by facilitating fast exchange. In an assertion ahead of its time, Potter claimed that "besides *Money* there is nothing except *Credit*, upon which men can frequently & conveniently sell their *Commodities*." Furthermore, since "all the worth of money it selfe, consists in being as it were a *token* or *Ticket* for obtaining goods at pleasure," a currency that consists entirely of promissory notices should work just as well as "real" money (1650: sigs. L1v, M1r). As he goes on to explain:

> Seeing for that we cannot increase money at pleasure to any quantity needfull; we have no feasible means whereby to quicken Trade, (as I said before) but by multiplying a firme and knowne credit amongst Tradesmen, fit to transmit from hand to hand.
> —1650: sig. M1r

Potter drew his inspiration from large-scale credit institutions already in place in Europe, especially the Bank of Amsterdam. This bank, founded in 1609, in turn drew on Italian models of public deposit banking where credit could be monetized—that is, where debts between individuals became payable by means of bank credit itself, and thus where the transferring of funds could happen abstractly in an account register rather than in cash. As expressed by Henry

Robinson, another theorist backed by the Hartlibians, a bank able to induce such a credit currency would be "capable of multiplying the stock of the Nation, for as much as concernes trading *in Infinitum*: In briefe, it is the *Elixir or Philosophers Stone*" (quoted in Wennerlind 2011: 69–70).

The reason such imaginative economies were so threatening, however, was not just because they were deemed "false," but more importantly because they risked becoming uncoupled from sovereign authority. It should come as no surprise that just as unregulated alchemy was forbidden in its literal form, so were the multitude of figurative alchemies suspect from a governmental perspective. The seventeenth century abounds with monarchical attempts to intervene in merchant credit economies, as well as large-scale deposit banking systems.[11] In fact, creating value through imaginary abstraction could be even more unsettling than doing so through alchemy, although the two techniques were clearly related in people's minds. Even while openly endorsing the monetizing of merchant's bills and showing sympathy for alchemical experimentation, Malynes was one who, nevertheless, cringed at the thought of initiating wide-scale credit and banking economies. What concerned him was not so much the practices of lending or taking interest, but rather the vast amounts of mutual good faith necessary to sustain such an ephemeral medium of exchange. The bankers consolidate all of the real money, while their clients must subsist on illusory relations. "What is this credit?" he scoffs, "or what are the payments of the Bankes: but almost or rather altogether imaginative or figurative?" Economic transactions in this situation become merely an elaborate transfer of debt, where "*John* doth pay unto *William*, and *William* unto others, without that any mony is touched, but remaineth still in the Bankers hands" (1601b: sigs. C3v–C4v).

In his 1609 treatise called *A Mirrour for Merchants*, Robert Mason likewise moves directly from a discussion about transmutation—a reasonable science pursuing the "course of natures for incorporating and increasing"—to one about multiplying money through credit (1609: sig. F5v). Here, in a passage worth quoting at length, Mason is criticizing the way that money can be created through interest on loans: "Ther is great difference," he explains,

> between matter of bare imagination and conceipt, and matters of substance and truth: betweene words and actions: for a man by contemplation may behold many thousand places in a moment, and set down a thousand proportions in his mind in shorte time: conceive a journey of ten thousand miles by Sea, with all the bowings and turnings: But come to action, and you shall finde another worke and labour to performe it. A man may by conceipt and in figures, set down ten thousand millions, to be devided betweene a hundreth thousand men: but hee that shall come to action, must have mony in his purse: words will buy no meate in the market.
>
> —1609: sig. F6v

In this remarkable elaboration, Mason demonstrates an eagerness to protect monetary dealings from any kind of imaginative corruption. This, for him, is just what separates credit (especially as affiliated with usury) from alchemy: with the latter, practitioners actually work with the "substance" of metal rather than with its mere "conceipt." In doing so, he even seems to be associating imaginary money with fictional narrative: "It belongeth to Art . . . to create or raise benefite by fantasie, imagination, or any new sought devise, which wil deceive like dreames" (1609: F7r). Like credit, he asserts, stories exist merely as shadow, unable to cross the ontological boundary into substance.

CREDITING TALES: THE PROFITS OF FICTION

Despite Mason's insistence that imaginary money can never truly be reified, overwhelming instances to the contrary opened an arena of curiosity regarding just what artistic "fantasie" *could* do. I wish to suggest, in fact, that the identity crises of sixteenth-century currency discussed above might also be described as a phenomenon of money *becoming literary*. That is, money suddenly had to justify its existence as something (at least partly) fictional—something that had meaning as merely a "tale." It seems little coincidence, along these lines, that just as monetary circumstances of the sixteenth century brought new attention to the subjective forces of perception in determining value, a new fascination with the human imagination began to emerge in the form of what we now call literary theory. As with monetary innovation, debates over the social value of imaginative writing—or "poesy," as it was sometimes called—began in Italy and worked their way westward to England. And while poesy and coinage may not seem to share much common ground, they were, in fact, very much part of the same discussion; fundamentally, both were grappling with the dilemma of how to capitalize on the potentials of human imagination without losing touch with truth. Thanks in part to the debasement experiments of the sovereigns, the role of mutual crediting—that is, of collective belief—in the economic process was becoming ever more explicit in conceptualizations of currency; the problem of how the shadow of belief could inflect the substance of real value was just the knot that literary theory set out to untie.

The conundrum posed by Renaissance literary theory was at heart an ontological one, namely the problem of how something counterfeiting the truth could be taken on credit *as if* it were real. Just as with Thomas Smith's attributed *Discourse*, the dilemma is rooted in the working of "credence": that is, can something debased or artificial function as good currency so long as everyone treats it that way? Stephen Gosson was typical of many sixteenth-century English writers in his wariness of imaginative writing because of its deceptive ability to pass itself off as something real. The metaphors he uses to warn of these dangers, moreover, are often monetary ones: throughout his treatise, *The*

Schoole of Abuse (1579), bad art is consistently linked to unsound fiscal practices. "Good sentences" in frivolous fiction, for instance, tend to be used merely "as ornamentes" so that writers might "sette their trumperie to sale without suspect." Poets are associated with crimes of counterfeiting, "defacing olde stampes, forging new printes, and coining strange precepts." Most of all, the artists that Gosson excoriates are guilty of ruining good "credite" by selling shadows to gullible buyers (1579: sigs. A2r–v, B2v).

Just as Robert Mason describes specious forms of money in terms of fictional poetry or storytelling, one does not have to look far to find that denunciations of imaginative writing often went hand in hand with monetary concerns. These admonishments were generally of two kinds. On a practical level, moralists were worried that naive citizens would simply be defrauded: readers and playgoers are promised something with value, and in return for their money they are given worthless ephemera. By the time William Prynne contributes to the conversation in 1633, one finds financial offences occupying a central place in criticisms of the stage. "God himselfe inhibits Christians," Prynne declares, "to follow after vaine things which will not profit, because they are but vaine. Christians must not lay out their money for that which is not bread, and their labour for that which satisfieth not" (1633: sig. R4v). Not only is the tangibility of money here contrasted with the shadow-like void of imaginative representations, but one can see words like "profit" beginning to conflate ethical and financial imperatives. Stage-players themselves, within such rhetoric, become "crafty shifting companions, who purchase money, not by their generositie, but by their tongues and impudency; they being wise to dissemble, apt to counterfeit." In short, "they cosen and mocke us with vaine words, and we pay them good money" (1633: sigs. S3r, T3v). For Prynne, purveyors of literary fiction have become comparable not just to counterfeiters, but to usurers or bankers who exchange solid coin for mere promises.

At the same time, an even more intriguing fear developed alongside this first one, namely that the boundaries between reality and representation—between substance and shadow—would themselves begin to lose coherence. The true danger of stage plays (and other poesy), it seemed, was not so much that they could trick their viewers, but that mere imitation could become indistinguishable from what was being feigned. Gosson, for one, doubts "whether any corruption can be greater, then the which is daily bred by plaies, because the expressing of vice by imitation, brings us by the shadow, to the substance of the same" (1582: sig. G4r–v). And Prynne, once again following Gosson's lead, makes explicit the link between monetary fraud and the ontological threat of the theater. The anxieties are essentially Platonic, but they become overlaid with a contemporary economic urgency:

> the very end why Players act their Enterludes, is onely to cheate mens money out of their purses by dishonest meanes, not giving quid pro quo, . . . [for]

the mere acting of the persons, parts, gestures, offices, actions, passions . . . be it in sport, in representation onely, is hypocrisie. . . . Now this counterfeiting of persons, affections, manners, vices, sexes, and the like, which is inseparably incident to the acting of Playes; as it transformes the Actors into what they are not; so it infuseth falshood into every part of soule and body, as all hypocrisie doth; in causing them to seeme that in outward appearance which they are not in truth.

—1633: sigs. X3r–X4r

At heart in this objection is not just that the "quid pro quo" in the transaction between artist and consumer is missing, but that no one seems to mind exchanging truth for "falshood" in the first place.

Those imaginative writers who responded to such accusations were in a delicate position, being charged with an offense initiated (supposedly) by no less an authority than Plato himself. How was fiction to be vindicated on terms such as these? One line of rebuttal simply went right to the source, attempting to demonstrate—rather dubiously, perhaps—that good poetry was, in fact, more closely aligned with Platonism than even Plato himself realized. Imaginative writing at its best, by this argument, did not mislead at all but rather created a kind of ideal truth that surpassed our banal, shadowy realities. In the words of Philip Sidney—himself drawing on a rich Italian tradition of poetic theory—"onely the Poet . . . lifted up with the vigor of his owne invention, dooth growe in effect [into] another nature, in making things either better then Nature bringeth forth, or quite a newe formes such as never were in Nature." The "final end" of imaginative writing, by this logic, is "to lead & draw us to as high a perfection, as our degenerate soules made worse by theyr clayey lodgings, can be capable of" (1595: sigs. C1v, C4v).

As rousing as this argument may have been to some, however, it ultimately became secondary to a concomitant line of thought somewhat in tension with Platonism, though much more significant to the financial context I have been examining here. This second approach relied on Horace rather than Plato, and began with the premise that "enjoyment" and "instruction" could function as two sides of the same coin. Once again, Sidney—reveling in the theoretical frictions he was creating—took this premise so far as to imply that literary imagination relayed a kind of truth precisely by way of its subjective *usefulness* rather than its objective veracity. Although philosophers and historians may, indeed, pursue a kind of truth, he admits, theirs is a truth that is all but worthless: that is, while the philosopher is lost in "mistie" abstractions, the historian is overwhelmed with facts that have no higher meaning. Only the poet gives meaning to truth by prioritizing its *currency* among readers or listeners—i.e., valuing what they do with it. "[M]ooving is of a higher degree then teaching," Sidney concludes, "for who will be taught, if hee bee not mooved with desire to be taught? ... [I]t is not *Gnosis*, but *Praxis* must be the fruit" (1595: sig. E3v). The human imagination, from this perspective, is not necessarily something that contrasts with "reality" (as if it can make nothing but "castles in the air"); rather, it is something necessary for *creating* reality, for linking together the shards of factual perception in a way that can actually be profitable (1595: sig. C2r).[12] A few years after Sidney wrote his treatise, his admirer, George Puttenham, would follow through on his predecessor's implications. In *The Arte of English Poesie* (1589), Puttenham dissociates value from truth-content almost entirely: "A fained matter or altogether fabulous, besides that it maketh more mirth than any other, works no lesse good conclusions for example then the most true and veritable: but often times more" (1589: sig. F4v). We have come full circle back to Bacon's paradox, where the "mixture of falsehood," like "allay in coin of gold and silver," debases the substance even while strengthening the currency.

This is, in fact, the paradox of the "tale" itself, the tally, the story—that which tells, reckons, and calls to account. The literary and monetary significations of the word appropriately share the same root; by the same measure, they also share an uneasy proximity to the claims of the "heads." The heads, those symbols of sovereign power, insist that they are needed in order to understand the tales being told in the first place: can the products of the human imagination truly be tallied, with any meaningfulness, without a legitimizing authority? Imaginative writing, in this way, also shares the ambivalence of alchemy. As so many Renaissance theorists explicitly acknowledged, the poet conducts a kind of alchemy in transmuting nature through the refining process of the imagination: poetic "arte," claimed Puttenham, "is not only an aide and coadjutor to nature in all her actions, but an alterer of them, and in some sort a surmounter of her skill. ... So also the Alchimist counterfeits gold, silver, and all other mettals." Crucially, what alchemy and poesy have in common is their ability to enhance value by means that are explicitly *un*natural: like artists, Puttenham continues, alchemists "also be praised for their craft, and their credit is nothing empayred, to say that their conclusions and effects are very artificiall" (1589: sigs. Ll1v–Ll2r). Also like the alchemist, the poet's work could be deeply troubling if conducted beyond the purview of the sovereign. It suggested an incursion of uncontrolled imaginative production bypassing the legitimizing powers of the state, bringing social chaos and moral confusion in its wake.[13]

But was there really so much to fear? To the fascination of monetary and literary theorists alike, it was increasingly being acknowledged that "praxis" (to use Sidney's term) was, indeed, not necessarily aligned with truth—at least, not the kind of "truth" that had the stable, intrinsic qualities for which so many pined. The process by which money was becoming a kind of literary artifact was the same one that helped to complicate ingrained dichotomies of the real and the false, essence and performativity. Reflections on the phenomenon of collective "crediting" revealed a kind of *productive* belief—fragile though it might have been—that could exist in an ontological middle-ground where shadows might in fact function as substance. The great irony of the monarchical experiments with quasi-fiat currencies, designed to bolster sovereign authority, was their contribution to weakening the very "heads" that supposedly legitimized such currencies in the first place.[14] If the sovereignty of those heads could not serve as a guarantor of "intrinsic" value, were they really needed at all? Or could it be that the accounts told by currencies gained their legitimacy from a much more complex network of mutual trust? In other words, perhaps the moneyness of money lay simply in the believability of its tales, the stories it tells about debt and obligation. Bacon, once again, perfectly emblemizes the ambivalence stemming from this literary junction in Renaissance England and Europe. On the one hand, like most others of his era, he longed desperately to move truth beyond the capricious subjectivity of language; yet, on the other hand, he acknowledged that "words and writings"—despite their insubstantiality—are still our best access to "the Mint of knowledge." For "wordes," he continues, "are the tokens currant and accepted for conceits, as Moneys are for values, [and] it is fit men be not ignorant, that Moneys may bee of another kind, than gold and silver" (1605: sig. Pp4r). If not gold and silver, what then? At least in this moment, the tales have it.

NOTES

Introduction

1. Scholars of the period in question have recently begun to use the term "early modern" rather than "Renaissance" to connote the inception of many characteristics that define our "modern" world, such as the emergence of capitalism and globalization. The concept of the "Renaissance" also tends to be more Eurocentric, focusing especially on the accomplishments, first in Italy, and then throughout the rest of Europe. Despite the Eurocentric connotation of the term, we have set out in this volume to expand the analysis of money beyond Europe to include Asia, Africa, and the Americas as well.
2. Paper money had been used earlier in Ming China. See, for example, Davies (2002: 181–4) and the discussion below.
3. In his chapter, Cook mentions some examples of coins issued by non-state entities: the Vatican's "papal money"; medieval Italian communal coinage based on civic badges; dynastic-issued coinage; "cityscape" coinage by the Dutch; and the Dutch East India Company's production of local coinage in the company's name. See also Chapter 1 by Arturo Giráldez here, which discusses the decision by Ming China authorities in 1524 to allow private coinage to circulate. "The state" is, of course, a category subject to debate. For a discussion of various approaches to state formation in the early modern period, see my chapter "Dimensions of State Formation" in *Coinage and State Formation in Early Modern English Literature* (2011).
4. Another solution to the problem of "small change" was to cut coins from more precious metals in half or quarters. See, for example, Stephanie Wynne-Jones's discussion of the practice on the Swahili Coast in her chapter in this volume. Giráldez discusses other commodities used as money in the period, such as the important cowrie shells, circulating especially in Asia and Africa, the latter for the slave trade, as well as cacao beans, mate tea, and tobacco in the Americas. Some Chinese emperors used silver ingots stamped by merchants instead of coins.

5. Changes in supplies of one of the metals would affect its relative price ("the bimetallic ratio") and therefore provide incentive to focus more on one or the other metal. For example, as Giráldez notes in his chapter, when African and American gold flowed into Europe, its relative price dropped, making silver more desirable and leading to increased production from silver mines in Central Europe and Japan. Wynne-Jones discusses the importance of copper in Eastern Africa as a metal that was "linked to concepts of power and kingly authority."
6. Despite popular resentment about debasement, throughout Europe we see long-term trends in coinage devaluation between 1440 and 1760, as Giráldez notes in his chapter.
7. In his chapter, David Baker cites Diana Wood's discussion of these theories as the "metallist theory" (intrinsic) vs. the "sign theory" (extrinsic).
8. For more on this reference, see Deng (2011: 94).
9. Cook points to the interesting case of an intersection between political and religious concerns by the Qutb Shahi sultans of Golconda, who included a threat in Persian on their coins: "God curse anyone who changes the king's coin." See Deng (2011: 3–9) for examples of how the visual properties of coins have been employed for political acts of colonial appropriation and rebellion against state authority.
10. As Wynne-Jones notes, Islam in the region was a "key marker of their status" for coastal elites and differentiator from "the pagans of the hinterland." The ties of coinage to Islamic trade, therefore, contributed to its adoption as a concept and practice.
11. The importance of the balance of trade as an economic factor was not new to Mun's time; it can be traced back at least to the Middle Ages. Moreover, it was Mun's peer, Edward Misselden, who was the first writer to use the term "balance of trade" in print (1622: sig. B7r). Nevertheless, it was Mun's singlemindedness, his insistence that the balance of trade was *the only* essential factor, which made his writings influential.
12. Although there are some references to their use by Arabs in the eighth century and by Jews in the tenth (Davies 2002: 156).
13. See Wennerlind (2011) and Brian Sheerin's chapter in this volume on the Hartlib Circle, a group that was involved in alchemy and saw related potential in credit systems. As Wennerlind writes, "metallic transmutation and credit money shared the same underlying idea of using an expansion in the money stock to launch a process of continuous economic change, improvement, and growth" (2011: 68).
14. One of the earliest institutional banks that directly competed with individual usurers was the Monte di Pietá. This "bank" was set up by the Church primarily for charitable purposes to lend money to the poor at much lower interest rates than usurers charged. As Giráldez notes in his chapter, the first such Monte di Pietá was set up in Perugia in 1462. See also Giráldez's discussion of various forms of deposit banking, moneylending, and commodity-trade financing along Mediterranean and Indian Sea trade routes as well as in the Americas.
15. Richard Hildreth identifies the "first banking institution" in Venice in the twelfth century, when the Chamber of Loans was established to manage forced loans for the purpose of financing war and subsequently purchased and sold bills of exchange that bore its name. Some of its excess funds on hand were loaned out using discounting

with mercantile paper, some of the Venetian merchants would deposit their money in the Chamber, and all merchants were eventually required to have an account and clear their bills of exchange there, a rudimentary form of issuing circulating notes. These three elements constitute the three primary principles of the modern bank (1840: 8–9). Similar banks in other cities—Genoa and Barcelona—were not formed until the fifteenth century (1840: 9).
16. See Sheerin's discussion of the circulation of "bills obligatory" among merchants, which "became transferrable to third parties in a way that directly anticipated bank-issued paper money." See also Sheerin's discussion of William Potter's 1650 proposal for a national credit money.
17. See Giráldez's discussion of the late seventeenth-century Portuguese discovery of gold in Brazil and the subsequent benefits of a gold boom for Britain, where the City of London "became the center of a new political economy regulated by the legal possibility of converting the pound to gold."

Chapter One

1. The term "price revolution" was coined by Earl J. Hamilton in his 1934 book *American Treasure and the Price Revolution in Spain, 1501–1650*.
2. This is my translation of Cipolla.

Chapter Two

1. Modern English translations usually render *diorthotikon dikaion* either as "rectificatory justice" or "corrective justices." I use "commutative justice" because it is the translation favored by mercantile writers, who were influenced by Aquinas.
2. I have modernized spelling and punctuation for clarity.

Chapter Three

1. On this stamping metaphor's extension to other media such as writing and printing, see de Grazia (1996: 74–94).
2. All Shakespeare citations are from *The Riverside Shakespeare* (1997).
3. The citations from the parable (which are specified by chapter and verse) are from Hultgren (2000: 271–2).
4. This, of course, seems ironic from our own point of view, since credit default swaps are in large part the reason for our recent financial collapse, though the value of the money lent in that period would not see the wild fluctuations in value such as in our current real estate market, or the sheer level of risk exposure because of the size of the market.
5. Martin Luther found in Eck an intellectual enemy, and his views on usury were no exception. Luther proclaimed that all charging of interest—with the exception of lending to support orphans, widows, students, and ministers—should be construed as usurious and therefore sinful (Jones 1989: 15).
6. Calvin was not the first to comment on the different terms. The fourth-century Babylonian Talmudic scholar Rava interpreted no difference between the terms, but

other scholars did. A common interpretation was that the *neschech* represented the loan from the borrower's perspective, while *tarbit* represented it from the lender's (see Buckley 2000: 21).

7. Thomas Bell refutes such attempts to differentiate increase that does no harm from increase that does:

> the gaine of the borrower, cannot make vsurie without biting: the reason is manifest, because biting is included in the formal cause thereof: for as it is alreadie proued, in things consumptible with the vse, the dominion thereof is translated by the loane, & to exact surplussage for the vse of a mans owne, is mere iniustice and flat extortion.
>
> —1596: sig. D3r

8. See Jones (1989: 19–22) and Nelson (1949: 70–1).
9. Roger Fenton described the position of those supporting legalized interest as imagining the possibility of putting a "muzzle" on usury:

> This biting or gnawing, because it is not alwaies sensible, much lesse mortall ... therefore some subtill wits have deuised a new distinction to please the world. As if there were some toothelesse and harmlesse vsurie without the compasse of the word *Neschec*, and without the meaning of the law of God: as if God had neuer meant to condemne Vsurers, but onely to muzzle them for biting. So as, if lender and borrower be both gainers, who hath cause to complaine? and why may not Christians then practise so harmelesse and innocent a trade? and for that vsurie which is condemned by the name of *Neschec*, if these men had the christning of it, they would haue called it by the name of *Morsura*, not *Vsura*.
>
> —1611: sig. C4v

Chapter Four

1. This chapter was written during a period of time spent as a Pro Futura Scientia Fellow at the Swedish Collegium for Advanced Study, Uppsala, and an Affiliated Researcher at the Department of Archaeology and Ancient History, Uppsala University.

   Fieldwork at Songo Mnara was supported by the National Science Foundation (USA) under BCS 1123091; the Arts and Humanities Research Council (UK) under AH/J502716/1; and the Society of Antiquaries. The Songo Mnara Urban Landscape Project is carried out in collaboration with the Antiquities Division, Ministry of Natural Resources and Tourism, Tanzania. Thanks are due to Dr John Perkins for analysis of the Songo Mnara coins.

Chapter Five

1. For a recent survey of Ming coins, see Hartill (2005).
2. For coins of the Qing period, see Hartill (2003) and Sandrock (1995).
3. For comments on Safavid coins, see Rabino di Borgomale (1945) and Matthee, Fllor, and Clawson (2013: 33).

NOTES 175

4. Timurid coinage is not well served in the literature. See Album (2001: xiii–xv).
5. Lashari (2009) is a well-illustrated catalogue.
6. Most of the Persian couplets on Akbar's coinage relate to the coinage itself (Liddle 2005: 89).
7. For an overview, see Bank al-Maghrib (2006: 168–73, 182–91).
8. For a survey, see Weschke and Hagen-Jahnke (1983: R1–30).
9. For the only significant discussion, see Farquhar (1910). Schwoerer (1989) does not mention the coinage at all.
10. The only survey is Haczewska (2000), the catalogue of an exhibition in Cracow.

Chapter Seven

1. For the articulation of this distinction, I am drawing primarily on Valenze (2006: 51–2), but see also Hart (1986: 638). Whereas Valenze focuses on the phenomenology of money within an eighteenth-century English social context, Hart is interested in the way that tensions between defining money via "heads" or "tails" have tended to characterize the history of modern economic theory (and its discontents).
2. See Landreth (2012: 129) and Deng (2011: 110–1).
3. Quoted in Challis (1978: 205–6). Local use of unofficial tokens, Challis indicates, was by no means limited to the western regions of England.
4. In the late 1570s, the Privy Council became interested in Bristol's abundant use of token currencies; an arrangement was made whereby Bristol was allowed to implement one general stamp for its tokens, thus (theoretically) reducing confusion. See Challis (1978: 208–9).
5. For the following overview of Continental monetary theorists, I am drawing primarily on Sargent and Velde (2001: 104–7).
6. Gerard de Malynes, for instance, insisted that the king institute and enforce a universal *par*, or exchange ratio, between metals in order to hamper a money market where metals could be sold off against each other when ratios varied; other mercantilists such as Edward Misselden mocked the *par* as an artificial interference in values that were determined by the "plenty or scarcity of monies." Each side, however, was equally convinced that a strong monetary economy meant finding ways to keep precious metals from leaving the country. See Misselden (1623: sig. K3r).
7. In England, the enlistment of alchemists by monarchs can be traced back to Edward IV, and practitioners were heavily consulted by both the Tudor and Stuart dynasties (Wennerlind 2011: 47–8). Bruce Moran notes that alchemists were particularly requisite in assisting with monetary debasements that involved new metallic combinations (2005: 33).
8. Gerard de Malynes, for instance, in his treatise praising alchemy and suggesting economic reforms, opens with a dedication to James I that blatantly duplicates the king's own authoritarian rhetoric: "Kings are not only Gods Lieutenants upon earth, and sit upon his throne," Malynes asserts, "but also are called Gods, by God himselfe, in regard of their *Transcendent Preheminences* and *Prerogatives*" (1622: sig. A3r).
9. Contributions to economic anthropology are making a resurgence in the twenty-first century, although some of the most groundbreaking work was done in the early

twentieth century by Marcel Mauss: the gift-economy underlying many tribal cultures, claimed Mauss, "necessarily entails the notion of credit. The evolution in economic law has not been from barter to sale, and from cash sale to credit sale. . . . [B]arter has arisen through a system of presents given and reciprocated according to a time limit, . . . [and] buying and selling arose in the same way" (1990: 36).

10. William Fleetwood, Bishop of Ely, tellingly wondered how "Men will *appear* much Richer than they are, by all the outward Marks of Wealth . . . in order to obtain such Credit as may enable them (they think) to *be* indeed as Rich as they *appear*. And this sometimes succeeds; the Reputation of Wealth has sometimes been the Means of getting Wealth, the Shadow has drawn the Substance" (quoted in Sherman 1997: 335).

11. Since the fifteenth century, for example, English monarchs expressed open hostility to merchant practices of "dry exchange"—where business was conducted in forms of credit rather than in coin; the bill of exchange became suspect for governments not only because it was believed to mitigate the influx of precious metals into the country, but because it stood to bypass the royal prerogative of controlling exchange rates and cash flows. See Munro (1979: 198–9).

12. The affective (or "reader-response") dimensions of speaking and writing had been prioritized in the classical rhetorical traditions of Cicero and Quintilian, and had been given theoretical treatment in Aristotle's *Poetics*. It was the *Ars Poetica* of Horace, however, that most famously proclaimed the true aim of poetry *aut prodesse . . . aut delectare*—that is, to profit and to delight. Sidney, in turn, augmented the ontological dimension of "delighting" as expressed by Horace. See Cronk (1999: 199–204).

13. In some sense, the very term "author" already hints at the possible conflicts of "authority" involved in acts of writing. Indeed, certain parallel tensions as I have been describing with coinage later appear in speculations of how texts relate to their writers: to what extent, for instance, does an author stand as a kind of guarantor of the text's value (whether intrinsic or extrinsic), or to what extent is that text's worth simply created by those who utilize it? This line of inquiry, however, while philosophically interesting from a modern (or postmodern) perspective, is somewhat removed from Renaissance literary theory. Rather, early modern writers were more immediately invested in how imaginative production attained social value (or not) outside of governmental sanction. Thomas Dekker offers a representative example of traditional priorities at the end of his drama *Old Fortunatus* (1599), when the character Virtue breaks the fourth wall and turns to Queen Elizabeth for legitimation, announcing that: "I am a counterfeit, you are the true, / I am a Shaddow, at your feete I fall, / Begging for these, and these, my selfe and all. / . . . [D]red Nymph, it lyes / In you to make us substances" (1953: 5.2.358–66). Of course, a contrary impulse toward the necessity of governmental authorization was increasing at this time as well, the articulation of which culminated in John Milton's *Areopagitica* (1644).

14. Perhaps an equal irony lay in the fact that many of the Puritans responsible for ending the monarchy also rejected the very kind of imaginative literatures that arguably made such an ideological overturning possible.

BIBLIOGRAPHY

Abbott, Edwin A. (2014), *The Fourfold Gospel*, Vol. 5: *The Founding of the New Kingdom or Life Reached Through Death*, Cambridge: Cambridge University Press.

Adams, Nicholas (1978), "New Information about the Screw Press as a Device for Minting Coins: Bramante, Cellini and Baldassare Peruzzi," *Museum Notes (American Numismatic Society)*, 23: 201–6.

Agnew, Jean-Christophe (1986), *Worlds Apart: The Market and the Theater in Anglo-American Thought, 1550–1750*, Cambridge: Cambridge University Press.

Agricola, Georgius (1950 [1556]), *De Re Metallica*, New York: Dover Publications.

Album, Stephen (1999), *Sylloge of Islamic Coins in the Ashmolean: Arabia and East Africa*, Oxford: Ashmolean Museum.

Album, Stephen (2001), *Sylloge of Islamic Coins in the Ashmolean 9: Iran after the Mongol Invasion*, Oxford: Ashmolean Museum.

Allan, John (1912), "The Coinage of the Maldive Islands, with Some Notes on the Cowrie and Larin," *Numismatic Chronicle*, 4th Series, 12: 313–32.

Allen, J.D.V. (1979), "The Swahili House: Cultural and Ritual Concepts Underlying its Plan and Structure," in J.D.V. Allen and T.H. Wilson (eds.), *Swahili Houses and Tombs of the Coast of Kenya*, 1–32, London: Art and Archaeology Research Papers (AARP).

Alonso Barba, Alvaro (1817), *Arte de los Metales*, Lima: Real Tribunal de Minería.

Alves, André Azevedo and José Manuel Moreira (2010), *The Salamanca School*, London: Continuum Books.

Amussen, Susan D. (2012), "Political Economy and Imperial Practice," *William and Mary Quarterly*, 69 (1): 47–50.

Aquinas, St. Thomas (1947), *Summa Theologica*, 2 vols, trans. Fathers of the English Dominican Province, New York: Benziger Brothers.

Aristotle (1953), *Generation of Animals*, trans. A.L. Peck, Cambridge: Harvard University Press.

Aristotle (2009), *The Nicomachean Ethics*, trans. David Rose, revd Lesley Brown, Oxford: Oxford University Press.

Attwood, Philip (2003), *Italian Medals c. 1530–1600 in British Public Collections*, London: British Museum.

Attwood, Philip (2004), "Cellini's Coins and Medals," in Margaret A. Gallucci and Paolo L. Rossi (eds.), *Benvenuto Cellini: Sculptor, Goldsmith, Writer*, 97–121, Cambridge University Press.

Azpilcueta, Martín de (2007 [1556]), *Commentary on the Resolution of Money*, trans. Jeannine Emery, in Stephen J. Grabill (ed.), *Sourcebook in Late-Scholastic Monetary Theory: The Contributions of Martín de Axpilcueta, Luis de Molina, S.J., and Jaun de Mariana, S.J.*, 21–108, New York: Lexington Books.

Bacon, Francis (1605), *The Twoo Bookes of Francis Bacon: Of the Proficience and Advancement of Learning, Divine and Humane*, London.

Bacon, Francis (1625), *The Essayes, or Counsels, Civill and Morall*, London.

Bacon, Francis (2002), "Of Usury," in *Francis Bacon: The Major Works*, ed. Brian Vickers, 421–3, Oxford: Oxford University Press.

Baker, David J. (2009), *On Demand: Writing for the Market in Early Modern England*, Stanford, CA: Stanford University Press.

Baker, Donald C. (1961), "Gold Coins in Medieval English Literature," *Speculum*, 36: 282–7.

Bakewell, Peter (1984), "Mining in Colonial Spanish America," in Leslie Bethel (ed.), *The Cambridge History of Latin America*, Vol. 2: *Colonial Latin America*, 105–52, Cambridge: Cambridge University Press.

Bank al-Magrib (2006), *Les Trésors du Musée de la Monnai*, Rabat: Bank al-Magrib.

Bargalló, Modesto (1955), *La minería y la metalurgia en la América española durante la época colonial*, Mexico City: Fondo de Cultura Económica.

Barr, James (2013), *Bible and Interpretation: The Collected Essays of James Barr*, Vol. 1, ed. John Barton, Oxford: Oxford University Press.

Barret, Ward (1990), "World Bullion Flows, 1450–1800," in James D. Tracy (ed.), *The Rise of Merchant Empires: Long-Distance Trade in the Early Modern World, 1350–1750*, 224–54, Cambridge: Cambridge University Press.

Barrett, William L.S. (1988), *Brunei and Nusantara: History in Coinage*, Bandar Seri Begawan: Brunei History Centre.

Barth, Jonathan (2016), "Reconstructing Mercantilism: Consensus and Conflict in British Imperial Economy in the Seventeenth and Eighteenth Centuries," *William and Mary Quarterly*, 73 (2): 257–90.

Bateson, J.D. (1997), *Coinage in Scotland*, London: Spink & Son.

Bell, Thomas (1596), *The Speculation of Vsurie*, London.

Bergwerk und Probierbüchlein (1949), New York: American Institute of Mining.

Bernal, Antonio M. (1999), "Remesas de Indias: de 'dinero político' al servicio del Imperio a indicador monetario," in Antonio M. Bernal (ed.), *Dinero moneda y crédito en la Monarquía Hispánica*, 353–84, Madrid: Marcial Pons Ediciones de Historia, Fundación ICO.

Biringuccio, Vanoccio (1540), *De la Pirotechnia*, Venice.

Blair, Ann (1997), *The Theater of Nature: Jean Bodin and Renaissance Science*, Princeton, NJ: Princeton University Press.

Bodin, Jean (1962 [1576]), *The Six Bookes of Commonweale: A Facsimile Reprint of the English Translation of 1606, Corrected and Supplemented in the Light of a New Comparison with the French and Latin Texts*, ed. Kenneth Douglas McRae, Cambridge: Harvard University Press.

Bodin, Jean (1992), *On Sovereignty: Four Chapters from* The Six Books of the Commonwealth, ed. and trans. Julian H. Franklin, Cambridge: Cambridge University Press.

Bodin, Jean (1997 [1568]), *Response to the Paradoxes of Malestroit*, trans. and ed. Henry Tudor and R. W. Dyson, Bristol: Thoemmes Press.

Boomgaard, Peter (2008), "Early Globalization: Cowries as Currency, 600 BCE—1900," in Peter Boomgard, Dick Kooiman, and Henk Schulte Nordholt (eds.), *Linking Destinies: Trade, Towns and Kin in Asian History*, 13–28, Leiden: KITLV Press.

Boxer, Charles R. (1970), "Plata es Sangre: Sidelights on the Drain of Spanish American Silver in the Far East, 1550–1700," *Philippine Studies*, 18: 457–78.

Braudel, Fernand (1981), *Civilization & Capitalism 15th–18th Century*. Vol 1: *The Structures of Everyday Life*. New York: Harper & Row.

Braudel, Fernand (1982), *Civilization & Capitalism 15th–18th Century*, Vol. 2: *The Wheels of Commerce*, New York: Harper & Row.

Broome, Michael (1980), "Islam and the Near East," in Martin Jessop Price (ed.), *Coins: An Illustrated Survey 650 BC to the Present Day*, 259–85, New York: Methuen.

Broome, M. (1985), *A Handbook of Islamic Coins*, London: Seaby.

Brown, H.W. (1991), "Three Kilwa Gold Coins," *Azania*, 26: 1–4.

Brown, H.W. (1992), "Early Muslim Coinage in East Africa: The Evidence from Shanga," *Numismatic Chronicle*, 152: 83–7.

Brown, H.W. (1993), "Coins of East Africa: An Introductory Survey," *Yarmouk Numismatics*, 5: 9–16.

Brown, H.W. (1996), "The Coins," in M.C. Horton (ed.), *Shanga: The Archaeology of a Muslim Trading Community on the Coast of East Africa*, 368–75, London and Nairobi: British Institute in Eastern Africa.

Buckley, Susan (2000), *Teachings on Usury in Judaism, Christianity and Islam*, Lewiston, NY: Edwin Mellen Press.

Burzio, Humberto F. (1945), *La Ceca de la villa imperial de Potosí y la moneda colonial*, Buenos Aires: Peuser.

Caesar, Philipp (1578), *A General Discourse against the Damnable Sect of Vsurers*, London.

Calvin, Jean (1583), *The Sermons of M. Iohn Caluin vpon the Fifth Booke of Moses Called Deuteronomie*, London.

Calvin, Jean (1616), "An Epistle of that Reverend and Judicious Diuine, Master Iohn Calvine, Touching Vsurie: Faithfullie Translated out of Latine," in James Spottiswood, *The Execution of Neschech and the Confyning of His Kinsman Tarbith. Or A Short Discourse, Shewing the Difference Betwixt Damned Usurie, and That Which is Lawfull*, Sig. F3r–G3r, Edinburgh.

Carande, Ramón (1990), *Carlos V y sus banqueros. 1. La vida económica en Castilla*, Barcelona: Editorial Crítica.

Céspedes del Castillo, G. (1972), "Las Indias Durante los Siglos XVI y XVII," in J. Vicens Vives (ed.), *Historia de España y América Social y Económica*, Vol. 3: *Los Austrias. El Imperio Español en América*, 321–536, Barcelona: Vicens-Vives.

Challis, C.E. (1978), *The Tudor Coinage*, Manchester: Manchester University Press.

Chaudhuri, K.N. (1978) *The Trading World of Asia and the English East India Company, 1660–1760*, Cambridge: Cambridge University Press.

Chaudhuri, K.N. (1986), "World Silver Flows and Monetary Factors as a Force of International Economic Integration 1658–1758," in W. Fischer, R. W. McInnis, and J. Schneider (eds.), *The Emergence of a World Economy 1500–1914*, vol. 1, 61–82, Stuttgart: Franz Steiner.

Chittick, H.N. (1961), *Kisimani Mafia: Excavations at an Islamic Settlement on the East African Coast*, Dar es Salaam: Antiquities Division.

Chittick, H.N. (1965), "The 'Shirazi' Colonization of East Africa," *Journal of African History*, 6 (3): 275–94.
Chittick, H.N. (1973), "On the Chronology and Coinage of the Sultans of Kilwa," *Numismatic Chronicle*, 13: 193–200.
Chittick, H.N. (1974) *Kilwa: An Islamic Trading City on the East African Coast*, Nairobi and London: British Institute in Eastern Africa.
Chown, John (1994) *A History of Money: From AD 800*. London: Routledge.
Chuan, Hang-sheng (1969), "The Inflow of American Silver into China from the Late Ming to the Mid-Ching Period," *Journal of the Institute of Chinese Studies of the Chinese University of Hong-Kong*, 2: 61–75.
Cipolla, Carlo M. (1993), *Before the Industrial Revolution: European Society and Economy 1000–1700*, 3rd edn, New York: W.W. Norton.
Cipolla, Carlo M. (1996), *Conquistadores, pirati, mercantati: La saga dell'argento spagnuolo*, Bologna: il Mulino.
Cook, Barrie (1995), "Showpieces: Medallic Coins in Early Modern Europe," *The Medal*, 26: 3–25.
Cook, Barrie (1998), "The Early European Coinages for Sri Lanka," in O. Bopearachchi and D.P.M. Weerakkody (eds.), *Origin, Evolution and Circulation of Foreign Coins in the Indian Ocean*, 241–54, New Delhi: Manohar Publishers.
Cook, Barrie (2017), "*Like Philip and Mary on a Shilling*: The Literary Legacy of a Tudor Coin," *Numismatic Chronicle*, 177: 399–411.
Cook, Barrie (2019), "*Stampt with your own Image*: The Numismatic Dimension of Two Stuart Successions," in Paulina Kewes and Andrew McRae (eds.), *Stuart Succession Literature: Moments and Transformations*, 309–18, Oxford: Oxford University Press.
Cotton, Robert (1651 [1626]), 1856. *A Speech . . . Touching the Alteration of Coin*, London. Reprinted in *A Select Collection of Scarce and Valuable Tracts on Money*, ed. John Ramsay McCulloch. London.
Craig, John (1953), *The Mint: A History of the London Mint from A.D. 287 to 1948*, Cambridge: Cambridge University Press.
Cribb, Joe (1980), "The Far East," in Martin Jessop Price (ed.), *Coins: An Illustrated Survey 650 BC to the Present Day*, 294–311, New York: Methuen.
Cribb, Joe (2009), "Money as Metaphor 4: Power," *Numismatic Chronicle*, 169: 461–529.
Crippa, Carlo (1990), *Le monete di Milano durante la dominazione spagnola dal 1535 al 1706*, Milan: Carlo Crippa.
Cronk, Nicholas (1999), "Aristotle, Horace, and Longinus: The Conception of Reader Response," in Glyn P. Norton (ed.), *The Cambridge History of Literary Criticism*, Vol. 3: *The Renaissance*, 199–204, Cambridge: Cambridge University Press.
Cross, Harry E. (1983), "South American Bullion Production and Export, 1550–1750," in John F. Richards (ed.), *Precious Metals in the Later Medieval and Early Modern Worlds*, 397–424, Durham: Carolina Academic Press.
Crusafont, Miguel, Anna Balaguer, and Philip Grierson (2013), *Medieval European Coinage 6: The Iberian Peninsula*, Cambridge: Cambridge University Press.
Cuelbis, Diego (2002), *Andalucía en 1599 vista por Diego Cuelbis*, ed Salvador Raya Retamero, Benalmádena (Málaga): Caligrama.
D'Ewes, Sir Simonds (1682), *The Journals of All the Parliaments During the Reign of Queen Elizabeth*, London.
Dasí, Tomás (1950), *Estudio de los reales de a ocho. También llamados pesos, dólares, piastras, patacones o duros españoles*, 5 vols, Valencia: Sucesores de Vives Mora.

Davies, Glyn (2002), *History of Money: From Ancient Times to the Present Day*, Cardiff: University of Wales Press.
de Grazia, Margreta (1996), "Imprints: Shakespeare, Gutenberg and Descartes," in Terence Hawkes (ed.), *Alternative Shakespeares*, vol. 2, 63–94, London: Routledge.
de Morga, Antonio (1971), *Sucesos de las Islas Filipinas*, Cambridge: Cambridge University Press.
De Roover, Raymond (1974), *Business, Banking, and Economic Thought in Late Medieval and Early Modern Europe*, ed. Julius Kirshner, Chicago, IL: University of Chicago Press.
Dekker, Thomas (1953), *The Dramatic Works of Thomas Dekker*, vol 2, ed. Fredson Bowers. Cambridge: Cambridge University Press.
Dekker, Thomas (1990), *The Shoemaker's Holiday*, ed. Anthony Parr, London: A & C Black.
Deloney, Thomas (1961), *The Novels of Thomas Deloney*, ed. Merritt E. Lawless, Bloomington, IN: Indiana University Press.
Deng, Stephen (2009), "'So Pale, So Lame, So Lean, So Ruinous': The Circulation of Foreign Coins in Early Modern England," in Jyotsna G. Singh (ed.), *A Companion to the Global Renaissance: English Literature and Culture in the Era of Expansion*, 262–78, Chichester: Wiley-Blackwell.
Deng, Stephen (2011), *Coinage and State Formation in Early Modern English Literature*, New York: Palgrave Macmillan.
Dhopate, Sashikant G. (2002), "Some Coins Assignable to Vijayanagara Rulers," *Studies in South Indian Coins*, 12: 55–8.
Disney, A.R. (2009), *A History of Portugal and the Portuguese Empire: From Beginnings to 1807*, vol. 1, Cambridge: Cambridge University Press.
Domínguez Ortíz, Antonio (1971), *The Golden Age of Spain: 1516–1659*, New York: Basic Books.
Donne, John (1953–62), *The Sermons of John Donne*, ed. Evelyn M. Simpson and George R. Potter, Berkeley, CA: University of California Press.
Drappier, Jean (1978), "Iconographie des rois de France: le porte de la barbe aux XVIe et XVIIe siècles," in *La monnaie: miroir des rois*, 295–306, Paris: L'Hôtel.
Eggert, Katherine (2015), *Disknowledge: Literature, Alchemy, and the End of Humanism in Renaissance England*, Philadelphia, PA: University of Pennsylvania Press.
Ehrenberg, Richard (1963), *Capital & Finance in the Age of the Renaissance*, New York: Reprints of Economic Classics.
Eiji, Izawa (2013), "Developments in Japanese Copper Metallurgy for Coinage and Foreign Trade in the Early Edo Period," in Nanny Kim and Keiko Nagase-Reimer (eds.), *Mining, Monies and Culture in Early Modern Society*, 13–24, Leiden and Boston, MA: Brill.
Fairbank, John King and Merle Goldman (1998), *China: A New History*, Cambridge, MA: Harvard University Press.
Farquhar, Helen (1907), "Portraits of our Tudor Monarchs on their Coins and Medals," *British Numismatic Journal*, 4: 49–143.
Farquhar, Helen (1910), "Portraits of our Stuart Monarchs on their Coins and Medals Part 3: William and Mary," *British Numismatic Journal*, 10: 199–267.
Fenton, Roger (1611), *A Treatise of Vsurie*, London.
Fernández de Oviedo, G. (1944), *Historia General y natural de las Indias*, vol. 2, Asunción: Editorial Guaraní.

Finkelstein, Andrea (2000), *Harmony and the Balance: An Intellectual History of Seventeenth-Century English Economic Thought*, Ann Arbor, MI: University of Michigan Press.

Fitton, T. and S. Wynne-Jones (2017), "Understanding the Layout of Early Coastal Settlement at Unguja Ukuu, Zanzibar," *Antiquity*, 91 (359): 1268–84.

Fleisher, J.B. and S. Wynne-Jones (2010), "Kilwa-type Coins from Songo Mnara, Tanzania: New Finds and Chronological Implications," *Numismatic Chronicle*, 170: 494–506.

Fleisher, J.B. and S. Wynne-Jones (2013), "Archaeological Investigations at Songo Mnara, Tanzania," June–July 2011, Report submitted to Antiquities Division, Tanzania.

Flood, F. (2009), *Objects of Translation: Material Culture and Medieval "Hindu-Muslim" Encounters*, Princeton, NJ: Princeton University Press.

Foxe, John (1583), *Actes and Monuments of Matters Most Speciall and Memorable, Happenyng in the Church with an Vniuersall History of the Same*, London.

Franklin, Julian H. (1963), *Jean Bodin and the Sixteenth-Century Revolution in the Methodology of Law and History*, New York: Columbia University Press.

Franklin, Julian H. (1973), *Jean Bodin and the Rise of Absolutist Theory*, Cambridge: Cambridge University Press.

Freeman-Grenville, G.S.P. (1957), "Coinage in East Africa before Portuguese Times," *Numismatic Chronicle*, 17: 151–79.

Freeman-Grenville, G.S.P. (1958), "The Chronology of the Sultans of Kilwa," *Tanganyika Notes and Records*, 50: 85–93.

Freeman-Grenville, G.S.P. (1962) *The East African Coast: Select Documents from the First to the Earlier Nineteenth Centuries*, London: Clarendon Press.

Freeman-Grenville, G.S.P. (1971), "Coin Finds and Their Significance for Eastern African Chronology," *Numismatic Chronicle*, 11: 284–301.

García Guerra, E. (2000), "Las decisiones monetarias de la Monarquía castellana del siglo XVII y su incidencia en el funcionamiento del crédito privado," in Antonio M. Bernal (ed.), *Dinero moneda y crédito en la Monarquía Hispánica*, , 575–92, Madrid: Marcial Pons Ediciones Historia, Fundación ICO.

Garlake, P.S. (1966), *The Early Islamic Architecture of the East African Coast*, London: Oxford University Press.

Geiss, J.P. (1979), "Peking under the Ming, 1368–1644," PhD thesis, Princeton University, NJ.

Gil Farrés, Octavio (1959), *Historia de la moneda española*, Madrid: Diana.

Glamann, Kristof (1977), "European Trade 1500–1750," in Carlo M. Cipolla (ed.), *The Fontana Economic History of Europe*, Vol. 2: *The Sixteenth and Seventeenth Centuries*, 427–526, New York: Harvester Press/Barnes & Noble.

Gosson, Stephen (1579), *The Schoole of Abuse*, London.

Gosson, Stephen (1582), *Playes Confuted in Five Actions*, London.

Grice-Hutchinson, Marjorie (1952), *The School of Salamanca: Readings in Spanish Monetary Theory*, Oxford: Clarendon Press.

Grice-Hutchinson, Marjorie (1978), *Early Economic Thought in Spain 1177–1740*, London: George Allen & Unwin.

Grierson, P. (1960), "The Monetary Reforms of 'Abd al-Malik: Their Metrological Basis and their Financial Repercussions," *Journal of Economic and Social History of the Orient*, 3 (3): 241–64.

Grierson, Philip (1964), "The Origin of the English Sovereign and the Symbolism of the Closed Crown," *British Numismatic Journal*, 33: 118–34.

Grierson, Philip (1971), "The Monetary Pattern of Sixteenth-Century Coinage," *Transactions of the Royal Historical Society*, 5th Series, 21: 45–60; reprinted in Philip Grierson (1979), *Later Medieval Numismatics*, London: Variorum.
Grierson, Philip (1972), "Notes on Early Tudor Coinage," *British Numismatic Journal*, 41: 80–94.
Grierson, Philip (1975), *Numismatics*, London: Oxford University Press.
Grierson, Philip (1991), *Coins of Medieval Europe*, London: B.A. Seaby Ltd.
Haczewska, Bogumila (2000), *Portrety Miast* [City Portraits], Cracow: Muzeum Narodowe w Krakowie.
Haider, Najaf (1996), "Precious Metal Flows and Currency Circulation in the Mughal Empire," *Journal of the Economic and Social History of the Orient*, 39 (3): 299–364.
Hamashita, Takeshi (1994), "The Tribute System of Modern Asia," in A.J.H. Latham and Heita Kawakatsu (eds.), *Japanese Industrialization and the Asian Economy*, 91–107, London: Routledge.
Hamilton, Earl J. (1934), *American Treasure and the Price Revolution in Spain, 1501–1650*, Cambridge, MA: Harvard University Press.
Haring, Clarence H. (1964), *Trade and Navigation between Spain and the Indies in Times of the Hapsburgs*, Gloucester: Peter Smith.
Harris, Jonathan Gil (2003), *Sick Economies: Drama, Mercantilism, and Disease in Shakespeare's England*, Philadelphia, PA: University of Pennsylvania Press.
Hart, Keith (1986), "Heads or Tails? Two Sides of the Coin," *Man*, New Series, 21: 637–56.
Hartill, David (2003), *Qing Cash*, Special Publication, 37, London: Royal Nunismatic Society.
Hartill, David (2005), *Cast Chinese Coins: A Historical Catalogue*, Victoria: Trafford Publishing.
Hawkes, David (2001), *Idols of the Marketplace: Idolatry and Commodity Fetishism in English Literature, 1580–1680*, New York: Palgrave.
Hawkes, David (2010), *The Culture of Usury in Renaissance England*, New York: Palgrave Macmillan.
Hawkes, J. and S. Wynne-Jones (2015), "India in Africa: Trade Goods and Connections of the Late First Millennium," *Afriques: Débats, Méthodes et Terrains d'Histoire*, 6. Available at: https://afriques.revues.org/1752 (accessed September 17, 2016).
Herbert, E.W. (1984), *Red Gold of Africa: Copper in Precolonial History and Culture*, Madison, WI: University of Wisconsin Press.
Hildreth, Richard (1840), *Banks, Banking, and Paper Currencies*, Boston, MA: Whipple & Damrell.
Hill, George (1930), *A Corpus of Italian Medals of the Renaissance*, London: British Museum.
Hipkiss, Edwin J. (1937), "A Florentine Coin of the Sixteenth Century," *Bulletin of the Museum of Fine Arts*, 33: 11.
Horton, M.C. (1987), "The Swahili Corridor," *Scientific American*, 257 (3): 86–93.
Horton, M.C. (1991), "Primitive Islam and Architecture in East Africa," *Muqarnas*, 8: 103–16.
Horton, M.C. (1996), *Shanga: The Archaeology of a Muslim Trading Community on the Coast of East Africa*, Nairobi: British Institute in Eastern Africa.
Horton, M.C. and J. Middleton (2000), *The Swahili: The Social Landscape of a Mercantile Society*, Oxford: Blackwell.

Horton, M.C., W.A. Oddy, and H.W. Brown (1986), "The Mtambwe Hoard," *Azania*, 21: 115–23.
Huffman, T.N. (1972), "An Arab Coin from Zimbabwe," *Arnoldia*, 5: 1–7.
Hultgren, Arland J. (2000), *The Parables of Jesus: A Commentary*, Grand Rapids, MI: William B. Eerdmans Publishing Company.
Hunt, Edwin S. and James M. Murray (1999), *A History of Business in Medieval Europe, 1200–1550*, Cambridge: Cambridge University Press.
Inalcik, Halil (1995), *The Ottoman Empire: The Classical Age 1300–1600*, London: Phoenix, Orion Books.
Innes, Robert LeRoy (1980), "The Door Ajar: Japan's Foreign Trade in the Seventeenth Century," vol 1, PhD dissertation, University of Michigan, Ann Arbor, MI.
James I (1613), "A Proclamation for Farthing Tokens," London.
Jessop Price, Martin (ed.) (1980), *Coins: An Illustrated Survey 650 BC to the Present Day*, New York: Methuen.
Johnson, Marion (1997), "The Cowrie Currencies of West Africa," in Dennis O. Flynn and Arturo Giráldez (eds.), *Metals and Monies in an Emerging Global Economy*, 193–248, Aldershot: Variorum.
Jones, Norman (1989), *God and the Moneylenders: Usury and the Law in Early Modern England*, Oxford: Blackwell.
Jonson, Ben, George Chapman, and John Marston (1973 [1605]), *Eastward Ho!*, ed. C.G. Petter, New York: W.W. Norton.
Keynes, John Maynard (1950), *A Treatise on Money*, 2 vols, London: Macmillan.
Killick, D.J. (2009), "Agency, Dependency, and Long-Distance Trade: East Africa and the Islamic World, *ca*. 700–1500 CE," in S.E. Falconer and C.L. Redman (eds.), *Polities and Power: Archaeological Perspectives on the Landscapes of Early States*, 179–207, Tucson, AZ: University of Arizona Press.
Kimbro, Devori (2015), "'A Cardinalles Red-Hat, and a Kings Golden Crown': Pamphlet Anti-Catholicism and Fabricated Authority in Thomas Milles's *The Misterie of Iniquite* (1611)," *Prose Studies*, 37 (3): 181–99.
Kitch, Aaron (2009), *Political Economy and the States of Literature in Early Modern England*, Burlington: Ashgate.
Krisadaolarn, Ronachai and Vasilijs Mihailovs (2012), *Siamese Coins: From Funan to the Fifth Reign*, Bangkok: River Books.
Krmnicek, S. (2012), "Coins in Walls, Floor and Foundations: A Contextual Approach. The Case of the Magdalensberg, Austria," in G. Pardini (ed.), *Preatti del I Workshop Internazionale di Numismatica. Numismatica e Archeologia. Monete, Stratigrafie e Contesti*, 249–50, Roma: Dipart. di Scienze dell'Ant.
Kus, S.M. and V. Raharijaona (2008), "'Desires of the Heart' and Laws of the Marketplace: Money and Poetics, Past and Present, in Highland Madagascar," in E.C. Wells and P.A. McAnany (eds.), *Dimensions of Ritual Economy*, Research in Economic Anthropology 27, 149–87, . Bingley: Emerald Group Publishing.
Kusimba, C.M. (1999), *The Rise and Fall of Swahili States*, Walnut Creek, CA: AltaMira Press.
Lambek, M. (2001), "The Value of Coins in a Sakalava Polity: Money, Death, and Historicity in Mahajanga, Madagascar," *Comparative Studies in Society and History*, 43 (4): 735–62.
Lampe, G.W.H. (1951), *The Seal of the Spirit: A Study in the Doctrine of Baptism and Confirmation in the New Testament and the Fathers*, London: Longman.

Landreth, David (2012), *The Face of Mammon: The Matter of Money in English Renaissance Literature*, Oxford: Oxford University Press.
Langholm, Odd (1983), *Wealth and Money in the Aristotelian Tradition: A Study in Scholastic Economic Sources*, Bergen: Universitetsforlaget.
Langholm, Odd (1992), *Economics in the Medieval Schools: Wealth, Value, Money and Usury according to the Paris Theological Tradition 1200–1350*, Leiden: Brill.
Langholm, Odd (1998), *The Legacy of Scholasticism in Economic Thought: Antecedents of Choice and Power*, Cambridge: Cambridge University Press.
Lashari, Ali (2009), *Coins of the Mughal Emperors in the State Bank Museum*, Sindh: State Bank of Pakistan.
Leinwand, Theodor B. (1999), *Theatre, Finance and Society in Early Modern England*, Cambridge: Cambridge University Press.
Leydi, Silvio (2012), "Leone Leoni *scultore delle stampe della Cecca di Milano* (1542–90)," in Stephan F. Schröder (ed.), *Leone & Pompeo Leoni: actas del congreso internacional, Museo Nacional del Prado, Madrid octubre de 2011*, 19–32, Madrid: Museo del Prado.
Liddle, Andrew (2005), *The Coinage of Akbar: The Connoisseur's Choice*, New Delhi: Kapoori Devi Charitable Trust.
Liddle, Andrew (2013), *Coins of Jahangir: Creations of a Numismatist*, New Delhi: Manohar.
Lowick, N.M. (1985), *Siraf XV: The Coins and Monumental Inscriptions*, London: British Institute of Persian Studies.
Lowick, N.M. (1990), *Coinage and History of the Islamic World*, Aldershot: Variorum.
Macarius (1921), *Fifty Spiritual Homilies of St. Macarius the Egyptian*, ed. A.J. Mason, D.D., New York: Macmillan.
Magalhães Godinho, Vitorino (1984), *Os Descobrimentos e a Economia Mundial*, 2nd edn, 4 vols, Lisboa: Editorial Presença.
Magnusson, Lars (1994), *Mercantilism: The Shaping of an Economic Language*, London: Routledge.
Magnusson, Lars (2015), *The Political Economy of Mercantilism*, New York: Routledge.
Malynes, Gerard de (1601a), *Saint George for England, Allegorically Described*, London.
Malynes, Gerard de (1601b), *A Treatise of the Canker of Englands Common Wealth*, London.
Malynes, Gerard de (1603), *England's View in the Unmasking of Two Paradoxes*, London.
Malynes, Gerard de (1622) *Consuetudo, vel lex mercatoria, or The Ancient Law-Merchant*, London.
Manca, Joseph (1989), "The Presentation of a Renaissance Lord: Portraiture of Ercole I d'Este, Duke of Ferrara (1471–1505)," *Zeitschrift für Kunstgeschichte*, 52: 522–38.
Marx, Karl (1906), *Capital: A Critique of Political Economy*, trans. Samuel Moore and Edward Aveling, New York: Modern Library.
Mason, Robert (1609), *Mirrour for Merchants*, London.
Matson, Cathy (2012), "Imperial Political Economy: An Ideological Debate and Shifting Practices," *William and Mary Quarterly*, 69 (1): 35–40.
Matthee, Rudi, Willem Floor, and Patrick Clawson (2013), *The Monetary History of Iran from the Safavids to the Qajars*, London: I B Tauris

Maurer, B. (2005), "Does Money Matter? Abstraction and Substitution in Alternative Financial Forms," in D. Miller (ed.), *Materiality*, 140–64, Durham, NC: Duke University Press.
Mauss, Marcel (1990), *The Gift: The Form and Reason for Exchange in Archaic Societies*, trans. W.D. Halls, New York: Norton.
Mayhew, Nicholas (1999), *Sterling: The Rise and Fall of a Currency*, London: Allen Lane.
Mayhew, N.J. (2013), "Prices in England, 1170–1750," *Past and Present*, 219 (1): 3–39.
Melanchthon, Philipp (1548), *The Iustification of Man by Faith Only*, London.
Middleton, Henry (1603), *The Last East-Indian Voyage*, London.
Middleton, J. (2003), "Merchants: An Essay in Historiographical Ethnography," *Journal of the Royal Anthropological Institute*, 9: 509–26.
Milles, Thomas (1608), *The Custumers Alphabet and Primer*, London: William Jaggard.
Milton, John (1644), *Areopagitica*, London.
Misselden, Edward (1622), *Free Trade, or, The Meanes to Make Trade Florish*, London.
Misselden, Edward (1623), *The Circle of Commerce, or The Balance of Trade*, London.
Mitchiner, M. (1977), *Oriental Coins and their Values: The World of Islam*, vol. 1, London: Hawkins Publications.
Montaigne, Michel de (1603), *The Essayes or Morall, Politike and Millitarie Discourses*, trans. John Florio, London.
Montchrétien, Antoyne de (1970 [1615]), *Traicté de l'œconomie politique*, Geneva: Slatkine Reprints.
Monter, William (2013), "Gendered Sovereignty: Numismatics and Female Monarchs in Europe, 1300–1800," *Journal of Interdisciplinary History*, 41: 533–64.
Moran, Bruce T. (2005), *Distilling Knowledge: Alchemy, Chemistry, and the Scientific Revolution*, Cambridge, MA: Harvard University Press.
Moser, H. and H. Tursky (1977), *Die Münzstätte Hall in Tirol*, i. 1477–1665, Innsbruck: Dr. Rudolf Erhard.
Mossman, Philip L. (1993), *Money of the American Colonies and Confederation*, Numismatic Studies 29. New York: American Numismatic Society.
Mote, F.W. (1999), *Imperial China 900–1800*, Cambridge, MA: Harvard University Press.
Muldrew, Craig (1998), *The Economy of Obligation: The Culture of Credit and Social Relations in Early Modern England*, Basingstoke: Palgrave.
Mun, Thomas (1621), *A Discourse of Trade from England unto the East-Indies*, London.
Mun, Thomas (1664), *England's Treasure by Forraign Trade*, London.
Munro, John H. (1979), "Bullionism and the Bill of Exchange in England, 1272–1663: A Study in Monetary Management and Popular Prejudice," in *The Dawn of Modern Banking*, 169–239, New Haven, CT: Yale University Press.
Munro, John H. (2012), "The Technology and Economics of Coinage Debasements in Medieval and Early Modern Europe: With Special Reference to the Low Countries and England," in John H. Munro (ed.), *Money in the Pre-Industrial World*, 15–32, London: Pickering & Chatto.
Muntoni, Francesco (1972–3), *Le monete dei papi degli Stati Pontifici*, Rome: P. & P. Santamaria.
Murthy, A.V. Narasimha (2002), "Four Sarasvati Type Copper Coins of Vijayanagrara," *Studies in South Indian Coins*, 12: 59–64.

Nef, John U. (1997), "Silver Production in Central Europe," in Dennis O. Flynn and Arturo Giráldez (eds.), *Metals and Monies in an Emerging Global Economy*, 1–17, Aldershot: Variorum.

Nelson, Benjamin N. (1949), *The Idea of Usury: From Tribal Brotherhood to Universal Otherhood*, Princeton, NJ: Princeton University Press.

Newell, Margaret Ellen (2012), "Putting the 'Political' Back in Political Economy (This Is Not Your Parents' Mercantilism)," *William and Mary Quarterly*, 69 (1): 57–62

Nicholl, Charles (1992), *The Reckoning: The Murder of Christopher Marlowe*, New York: Harcourt Brace.

Oresme, Nicholas (1956), *The De Moneta of Nicholas Oresme and English Mint Documents*, trans. Charles Johnson, London: Thomas Nelson.

Pallaver, K. (2009), "'A Recognized Currency in Beads': Glass Beads as Money in 19th-century East Africa: The Central Caravan Road," in C. Eagleton, H. Fuller, and M.J. Perkins (eds.), *Money in Africa*, 20–9, London: British Museum Press.

Parker, Geoffrey (1997) "The Emergence of Modern Finance in Europe, 1500–1730," in Carlo M. Cipolla (ed.), *The Fontana Economic History of Europe*, Vol. 2: *The Sixteenth and Seventeenth Centuries*, 527–89, New York: Harvester Press/Barnes & Noble.

Pepys, Samuel (1971), *The Diary of Samuel Pepys*, vol. 4, ed. Robert Latham and William Matthews, London: Bell and Hyman Ltd.

Pérez Sindreu, Francisco de Paula (1991), *La Casa de la Moneda de Sevilla: su historia*, Sevilla: Publicaciones de la Universidad de Sevilla/Fundación Fondo de Cultura de Sevilla.

Perkins, M.J. (2013), "The Coins of the Swahili Coast c. 800–1500," PhD thesis, University of Bristol.

Perkins, M.J., J.B. Fleisher, and S. Wynne-Jones (2014), "A Deposit of Kilwa-type Coins from Songo Mnara, Tanzania," *Azania: Archaeological Research in Africa*, 49 (1): 102–16.

Pieper, Renate (1999), "Consideraciones acerca del uso de los metales preciosos Americanos en la Europa de los Austrias," in Antonio M. Bernal (ed.), *Dinero moneda y crédito en la Monarquía Hispánica*, 425–38, Madrid: Marcial Pons Ediciones Historia, Fundación ICO.

Pincus, Steve (2012), "Rethinking Mercantilism: Political Economy, the British Empire, and the Atlantic World in the Seventeenth and Eighteenth Centuries," *William and Mary Quarterly*, 69 (1): 3–34.

Porteous, John (1969), *Coins in History*, New York: G.P. Putnam's Sons.

Potter, William (1650), *The Key of Wealth or, A New Way, for Improving of Trade*, London.

Prestholdt, J. (1998), *As Artistry Permits and Custom May Ordain: The Social Fabric of Material Consumption in the Swahili World, circa 1450 to 1600*, Evanston, IL: Northwestern University Press.

Probert, Alan (1969), "Bartolomé de Medina: The Patio Process and the Sixteenth Century Silver Crisis," *Journal of the West*, 8 (1): 90–124.

Prynne, William (1633), *Histrio-mastix: The Players Scourge, or, Actors Tragædie*, London.

Puttenham, George (1589), *The Arte of English Poesie*, London.

Qin, D. and D. Yu (2018), "Mambrui and Malindi," in S. Wynne-Jones and A. LaViolette (eds.), *The Swahili World*, London: Routledge.

Rabino di Borgomale, H.L. (1945), *Coins, Medals and Seals of the Shahs of Iran, 1500–1941*, Caxton Hill: Stephen Austin and Sons.

Rhodes, N.G., K. Gabrisch, and C. Valdettaro Pontecorvo della Rocchetta (1989), *The Coinage of Nepal from the Earliest Times until 1911*, London: Royal Numismatic Society Special Publication 21.

Ryner, Bradley D. (2014), *Performing Economic Thought: English Drama and Mercantile Writing, 1600–1642*, Edinburgh: University of Edinburgh Press.

Salmon, Christopher J. (2010), *The Silver Coins of Massachusetts*, New York: American Numismatic Society.

Sandrock, John E. (1995), *Copper Cash and Silver Taels: The Story of Manchu China*, Baltimore, MD: Gateway Press Inc.

Sanz, Eufemio Lorenzo (1979), *Comercio de España con América en la época de Felipe II*, 2 vols, Valladolid: Servicio de publicaciones de la Diputación Provincial de Valladolid.

Sargent, Thomas J. and François R. Velde (2001), *The Big Problem of Small Change*, Princeton, NJ: Princeton University Press.

Schindel, N. (2010) "The Balkh 93AH Fulus Revisited," in B. Calleghre and A. D'Ottone (eds.), *The 2nd Simone Assemani Symposium on Islamic Coins*, 70–89, Trieste: University of Trieste.

Schleiner, Winfried (1970), *The Imagery of John Donne's Sermons*, Providence, RI: Brown University Press.

Schwoerer, Lois G. (1989), "Images of Queen Mary II, 1689–1695," *Renaissance Quarterly*, 42: 717–48.

Sellwood, David (1986), "The Trial of Nicholas Briot," *British Numismatic Journal*, 56: 108–23.

Shakespeare, William (1997), *The Riverside Shakespeare*, 2nd edn, ed. G. Blakemore Evans and J.J.M. Tobin, Boston, MA: Houghton Mifflin.

Sherman, Sandra (1997), "Promises Promises: Credit as Contested Metaphor in Early Capitalist Discourse," *Modern Philology*, 94 (3): 327–49.

Sidney, Philip (1595) *An Apologie for Poetrie*, London.

Silver, Harry (2008), *Marketing Maximilian: The Visual Ideology of a Holy Roman Emperor*, Princeton, NJ: Princeton University Press.

Sinclair, Paul and N. Thomas Håkansson (2000), "The Swahili City-State Culture," in M.H. Hansen (ed.), *A Comparative Study of Thirty City-State Cultures*, 463–82, Copenhagen: Royal Danish Academy of Sciences and Letters.

Sinclair, Paul, Anneli Ekblom, and Marilee Wood (2012), "Trade and Society on the South-East African Coast in the Later First Millennium AD: The Case of Chibuene," *Antiquity*, 86 (333): 723–37.

Smith, Adam (1937), *The Wealth of Nations*, New York: Modern Library.

Smith, Henry (1591), *The Examination of Vsury*, London.

Smith, Thomas (attr.) (1969 [1581]), *A Discourse of the Commonweal of this Realm of England*, ed. Mary Dewar, Charlottesville, VA: University Press of Virginia.

Spooner, Frank C. (1972), *The International Economy and Monetary Movements in France, 1493–1725*, Cambridge, MA: Harvard University Press.

Stahl, Alan M. (1990), "Coinage in the Name of Medieval Women," in Joel T. Rosenthal (ed.), *Medieval Women and the Sources of Medieval History*, 321–41, Athens, GA: University of Georgia Press.

Stahl, Alan M. (2001), "Numismatic Portraiture in Renaissance Venice," *Numismatica e Antichità Classiche*, 30: 305–12.

Stahl, Alan (2012), "The Making of a Gold Standard: The Ducat and its Offspring, 1284–2001," in John H. Munro (ed.), *Money in the Pre-Industrial World*, 45–62, London: Pickering & Chatto.

Stern, Philip J. and Carl Wennerlind (ed.) (2013), *Mercantilism Reimagined Political Economy in Early Modern Britain and Its Empire*, Oxford: Oxford University Press.

Sultan, Jem (1977), *Coins of the Ottoman Empire and the Turkish Republic*, Thousand Oaks, CA: B & R Publishers.

Sutton, J.E.G. (1993), "The Southern Swahili Harbour and Town on Kilwa Island, 800–1800 AD: A Chronology of Booms and Slumps," in P.J.J. Sinclair (ed.), *The Development of Urbanism from a Global Perpective*, Uppsala: Department of Archaeology and Ancient History, Uppsala Universitet.

Sutton, J.E.G. (1997), "The African Lords of the Intercontinental Gold Trade before the Black Death: Al-Hasan bin Sulaiman of Kilwa and Mansa Musa of Mali," *Antiquaries Journal*, 77: 221–42.

Symonds, Henry (1910), "The Mint of Queen Elizabeth and those Who Worked There," *Numismatic Chronicle*, 7: 61–105.

Tawney, R.H. and Eileen Power (eds.) (1924), *Tudor Economic Documents*, vol. 2, London: Longmans, Green.

Usher, Abbot Payson (1959), *A History of Mechanical Inventions*, Boston, MA: Beacon Press.

Valenze, Deborah (2006), *The Social Life of Money in the English Past*, Cambridge: Cambridge University Press.

Van der Wee, Herman (1977), "Monetary Credit and Banking Systems," in E.E. Rich and C. H. Wilson (eds.), The *Cambridge Economic History of Europe*, Vol. 5: *The Economic Organization of Early Modern Europe*, 290–329, Cambridge: Cambridge University Press.

Van der Wee, Herman (2012), "The Amsterdam Wisselbank's Innovations in the Monetary Sphere: the Role of 'Bank Money,'" in John H. Munro (ed.), *Money in the Pre-Industrial World*, 87–96, London: Pickering & Chatto.

van Gelder, H. Enno, and Marcel Hoc (1960), *Les monnaies pay-bas bourguignons et espagnols, 1434–1713*, Amsterdam: J Schulman.

Vaughan, Rice (1675), *A Discourse of Coin and Coinage*, London.

Vilar, Pierre (1974), *Oro y moneda en la historia. 1450–1920*, 3rd edn, Barcelona: Editorial Ariel.

Vilches, Elvira (2010), *New World Gold: Cultural Anxiety and Monetary Disorder in Early Modern Spain*, Chicago, IL: Chicago University Press.

von Glahn, Richard (1996), *Fountain of Fortune: Money and Monetary Policy in China 1000–1700*, Berkeley, CA: University of California Press.

Walker, J. (1936), "The History and Coinage of the Sultans of Kilwa," *Numismatic Chronicle*, 16: 43–81.

Walker, J. (1939), "Some New Coins from Kilwa," *Numismatic Chronicle*, 19: 223–7.

Walker, J. and G.S.P. Freeman-Grenville (1956), "The History and Coinage of the Sultans of Kilwa," *Tanganyika Notes and Records*, 45: 33–65.

Ward, Richard (1640), *Theologicall Questions, Dogmaticall Observations, and Evangelicall Essays, vpon the Gospel of Jesus Christ, according to St. Matthew*, London.

Wasserstein, David J. (1993), "Coins as Agents of Cultural Definition in Islam," *Poetics Today*, 14: 303–22.

Wennerlind, Carl (2011), *Casualties of Credit: The English Financial Revolution, 1620–1720*, Cambridge: Cambridge University Press.

Wernham, R.B. (1968), "Introduction," in R.B. Wernham (ed.), *The New Cambridge Modern History*, Vol. 3: *The Counter-Reformation and Price Revolution 1559–1610*, 1–13, Cambridge: Cambridge University Press.

Weschke, Joachim and Uesula Hagen-Jahnke (1983), *Gold Coins of the Middle Ages*, Frankfurt am Main: Deutsche Bundesbank.
Willet, Andrew (1633), *Hexapla in Genesin & Exodum*, London.
Wilson, Thomas (1572), *A Discourse Vppon Vsurye*, London.
Wodak, E. and F. Pridmore (1957), "The Trade Coinage of Queen Elizabeth I," *Spink's Numismatic Circular*, 65: 302–5.
Wood, Diana (2002), *Medieval Economic Thought*, Cambridge: Cambridge University Press.
Wood, M. (2000), "Making Connections: Relationships between International Trade and Glass Beads from the Shashe-Limpopo Area," *Goodwin Series*, 8: 78–90.
Wood, M. (2011), *Interconnections: Glass Beads and Trade in Southern and Eastern Africa and the Indian Ocean—7th to 16th Centuries AD*, Uppsala: Uppsala Universitet.
Wright, H.T. (1993), "Trade and Politics on the Eastern Littoral of Africa, AD 800–1300," in T. Shaw, P.J.J. Sinclair, B. Andah, and A. Okpoko (eds.), *The Archaeology of Africa: Food, Metals and Towns*, 658–72, London: Routledge.
Wrightson, Keith (2000), *Earthly Necessities: Economic Lives in Early Modern Britain*, New Haven, CT: Yale University Press.
Wynne-Jones, S. (2013), "The Public Life of the Swahili Stonehouse," *Journal of Anthropological Archaeology*, 32: 759–73.
Wynne-Jones, S. (2016), *A Material Culture: Consumption and Materiality on the Coast of Precolonial East Africa*, Oxford: Oxford University Press.
Wynne-Jones, S. and J.B. Fleisher (2010), "Archaeological Investigations at Songo Mnara, Tanzania, 2009," *Nyame Akuma*, 73: 2–8.
Wynne-Jones, S. and J.B. Fleisher (2011), "Archaeological Investigations at Songo Mnara, Tanzania, 2011," *Nyame Akuma*, 76: 3–8.
Wynne-Jones, S. and J.B. Fleisher (2012), "Coins in Context: Local Economy, Value and Practice on the East African Swahili Coast," *Cambridge Archaeological Journal*, 22 (1): 19–36.
Wynne-Jones, S. and J.B. Fleisher (2015), "Coins and Other Currencies on the Swahili Coast," in C. Haselgrove and S. Krmnicek (eds.), *Archaeology of Money*, 115–36, Leicester: Leicester University Press.
Wynne-Jones, S. and J.B. Fleisher (2016), "The Multiple Territories of Swahili Urban Landscapes," *World Archaeology*, 48 (3): 349–62.
Yang, Bing (2004), "Horses, Silver and Cowries, Yunnan in a Global Perspective," *Journal of World History*, 15 (3): 281–322.
Yang, Lien-sheng (1952), *Money and Credit in China*, Cambridge, MA: Harvard University Press.

INDEX

Italic numbers are used for illustrations. **Bold** numbers are used for tables.

abassi (Iran) 29
adornment, coins used for 94
adulteration of coinage. *See* debasement of coinage
adultery, likened to counterfeit coins 64–5
Afghanistan 105
African gold 17–18
Agnew, Jean-Christophe 133, 144
Agricola, Georgius, *De Re Metallica* 19, *20*
Ahmad al-Mansur, Sa'adi Sharif 109
Akbar, Mughal Emperor 108
alchemy 161–2, 168
Algeria 106
Ali ibn al-Hasan, Sultan of Kilwa 83, **84**, 85, 86, 91
almonds 35
Alonso Barba, Alvaro, *Arte de los Metales* 23
Americas
  coins 123, *124*, 125
  gold 18, 38
  mines 18, 22, 23
angel (England) 6, 114
Ankor, Kampuchea 112
aqche (Ottoman) 28
Aquinas, Thomas 70
  Summa Theologica 41–2
Arguin 17
Aristotle 8–9, 64, 69–70
  Nicomachean Ethics 40, 41

art and representation 99–125
  the Americas 123, *124*, 125
  Asia 110, *111*, 112–13
  China and its neighbors 101–4, *102*
  Europe, late medieval 113–15
  European cities 119–21, *120*
  European Princes 115–18, *116*
  European Queens 118–19, *118*
  Islamic world 104–10, *106*, *108–9*, *111*
  Renaissance legacy 121–3
Augustine of Hippo 64
Azpilcueta, Martín de, *Commentary on the Resolution of Money* 42–5

Bacon, Francis 76–7, 150, 169
Bakewell, Peter 23
balance of trade 7, 55–6
Bank of Amsterdam 38, 163
banking systems 1, 10–12, 37–8
banknotes 11–12
Barr, James 60
Barret, Ward 6, 23
Barros, João de 35
beneficio de cajones 23
beneficio de patio 22–3
Bermuda 123, *124*
Bernal, Antonio-Miguel 23, 26
Besley, Edward 20
bills obligatory 152

bills of exchange 7–8, 12, 37
bimetallic ratios 18, 25, 29, 161
Biringuccio, Vanoccio, *De la Pirotechnia* 21–2, *22*
black money 1, 32
blanks 16, 30
Bodin, Jean 155
   Response to the Paradoxes of Malestroit 45–7
   Six Books of the Republic 47–8
Bohemia 21, *21*, 117
Bolivia 123
Bramante, Donato 30
brassage 4, 17
Braudel, Fernand 1, 15, 32, 36, 37
Brazil 18, 38
Brown, H.W. 87
Brunei 110
Bucer, Martin 74, 75
bullet coins 112
bullion 27–8, 31, 115, 156–7
bullion purity 16–17
bullionists 51
Burma 113
Butigella, Girolamo 155

cacao beans 35
Caesar, Philipp 74
Cairo mint 96, 106
Calvin, Jean 61, 68–9, 71, 72–5, *72*, 76, 77
Cambodia 112
capitalism 16
cavallo (Naples) 32
Cellini, Benvenuto 30, 116, 117
Challis, C.E. 151, 156
Charles I, King of Spain 17
Charles V, Holy Roman Emperor 30, 36, 116, *116*
Chaudhuri, Kirti 28
checks 12
China
   coin designs 101–3, *102*, 104
   copper coinage 25, 33–4
   and Eastern Africa 82
   paper money used in 11, 25, 102
   silver, demand for 24–6
cho-gin (Japan) 24
Cipolla, Carlo 26, 28
cities, coinage of 119–21, *120*

Clement VII, Pope 117
clipping of coins 2, 32, 129, *129*, *147*
coinage 1–2
colonial coins 29, 35, 123, *124*
   See also pieces of eight
commodity fetishism 136, 137
commodity, money as a 43–5, 52
common stock 36
commutative justice 40, 48, 49, 51, 52–3, 55
cooperative loan societies 37
copper added to coinage 16
copper coinage 32–4
   Chinese 25, 101–2
   Eastern African 83, 86, 89, 93–4
   Indian 29
   Islamic 96, 106
corn banks 36
Cotton, Robert 161–2
counterfeit coins
   in China 34
   in England 129, 151–2, *151*
   religious imagery of 64–5, 66
counterfeiting 2
cowrie shells 34–5, *35*, 94
credit 9–10, 36–7, 129–31, 162–5
credit default swaps 70
credit fetishism 137–9, 140–1, 143
cruzado (Lisbon) 17, *18*
Cuelbis, Diego 27

dam (India) 29
Dasí, Tomás 31
Davies, Glyn 38, 152, 156
de Morga, Antonio 34
De Roover, Raymond 10, 11
debasement of coinage 2, 4–5, 128, 154–5, 156–9, 161–2
Dekker, Thomas, *The Shoemaker's Holiday* 132, 133–5, 138, 141–4, *142*
Deloney, Thomas
   The Gentle Craft, Part I 132–3, 138, 139–41
   Thomas of Reading 146–7
Deng, Stephen 6, 129, 134, 157
designs of coins 99–125
   the Americas 123, *124*, 125
   Asia 101–4, *102*, 110, *111*, 112–13
   European cities 119–21, *120*

INDEX 193

European Princes 115–18, *116*
European Queens 118–19, *118*
Islamic world 104–10, *106*, *108–9*
late medieval Europe 113–15
the Renaissance legacy 121–3
See also iconography of coinage
devaluation of coinage 155
dinar (Islamic) 96
dirham (Islamic) 28, 96
disknowledge 145
Disney, A.R. 38
distributive justice 40, 48, 49, 51–2, 53
Domínguez Ortíz, Antonio 26
Donne, John 65–6
Du Moulin, Charles 155
   Tractatus commerciorum et usurarum 71
ducats 18, *19*
Dutch East India Company 37, 125

East India Company 29, 55–6
Eastern African Coast, everyday money on the 79–98
   background 80, *81*, 82
   context and archaeology 85–6
   international standards and the tri-metallic system 86–7
   the Islamic world 95–8
   mints and rulers 82–5, *83*, *84*
   routes to value 91, *92*
   Swahili coins 91, 93–5
   use of coins 88–9, *88*, *89*, 91
Eck, Johann, *Tractatus contractu quinque* 71
Edward VI, King of England 157
Eggert, Katherine 145–6
electronic money 12–13
Elizabeth I, Queen of England 31, 119, 128, 153, 160
empires, rise of 16
England
   coin designs 114, 119, 121, 122
   coinage 19, 32
   credit and commodity fetishism 136–9
   credit used in 129–31, *130*, 163
   debasement of coinage 128, 156–9, 161–2
   economic awareness 143–5
   foreign coins in circulation 129, 134
   gold coinage 38
   interpretation of money, examples from literature 132–5, 138–44, 146–7
   milling machines 31
   paper money 128, 152
   shortage of money 127–8, 151, 156
   token money 152–4, *153–5*
   usury in 74–6
   value of money 128
English Civil War 11–12
English mercantile writers 50–7
European coinage
   cities on 119–21, *120*
   late medieval 113–15
   Princes on 115–18, *116*
   Queens on 118–19, *118*
excelente (Spain) 18, 20, 118, *118*
exchange rates 7, 37, 43, 44, 46, 47, 52–5
extrinsic theory of monetary value 2–4, 12

fairs 37
fals (Islamic) 96
fanam (India) 29
farthing (England) 32
farthing token (England) 153, *155*
Ferdinand II, King of Aragon 118, *118*
Fernández de Oviedo, Gonzalo 35
Fernández de Velasco, Pedro 23
fiat currency 4, 12, 155
fineness 16–17
Fiorentino, Adriano 117
Florence 28, 116
foreign exchange 2–3, 6–8
Foxe, John, *Acts and Monuments* 61–2
France
   coin designs 114, 121–2
   coin technology 16, *17*, 32
   prices in 46
Francis I, King of France 121
fraud, financial and literary 165–9
Freeman-Grenville, G.S.P. 91, 93
Fuggers, bankers 19, 22

Gede, Kenya 94
Geiss, J.P. 25
Germany 19, 20–1, 22, 31, 32
global market for coins 15–16
Goa 29, 125
goats 35

God's stamp 60, 61–9, 67
gold
   Brazilian 38
   cycle of (1443–1560) 17–23, *18–22*
   Spanish, quality of 27–8
gold coinage 16–18, *17–18*, 24, *24*, 29, 38, 86
gold standard 12, 38
goldsmith bankers 11–12, 37
Gosson, Stephen, *The Schoole of Abuse* 165–6
Great Debasement 4–5, 128, 156–9
Gresham, Sir Thomas 31
Grierson, Philip 21, 23, 30, 31
Guldiner (Tyrol) 20, 117

Habsburg coinage 21, *21*, 117
haifuki cupellation process 23
Halbguldiner (Tyrol, 1477) 20–1
half-pound of Castile 16, 18
halfpenny (England) 32
Hall, Tyrol, mint 117
Hamashita, Takeshi 25–6
hammered coinage 1, 16–17, *17*, 32
Haring, Clarence H. 27
harmonic justice 48–50
Hartlib Circle 161, 163
al-Hasan ibn Sulaiman, Sultan of Kilwa **84**, 85, 86, 91
hedging of exchange rates 37
Henry V, King of England 114
Henry VII, King of England 19, 121
Henry VIII, King of England 4, 121, 128, 156
heraldic devices 114
Holy Roman Empire 18, 120, 122
Horace 167
horseshoes 35–6
Horton, M.C. 87, 91
Hultgren, Arland 68
humans as coins 61

iconography of coinage 5, 19–21
   See also designs of coins
ideas of money 39–57
   economic justice 50–7
   harmonic justice 45–50
   money as measure and commodity 40–5
illegitimate production 64–5

image and text tradition of coin design 110–25
   the Americas 123, *124*, 125
   Asia 110, *111*, 112–13
   European cities 119–21, *120*
   European, late medieval 113–15
   European Princes 115–18, *116*
   European Queens 118–19, *118*
   Renaissance legacy 121–3
imaginative writing 165–9
improvement funds 36
India 29, 107–9, *108*, 112, 125
Indonesia 104
inflation 15, 28, 33, 44, 47
inland bills 12
Innes, Robert LeRoy 25
interest 70–1, 75, 76–7, 164
international exchange. *See* exchange rates
interpretation of money in England 127–47
   credit and commodity fetishism 136–9
   credit used in 129–31, *130*
   economic awareness 143–5
   examples from literature 132–5, 138–44, 146–7
   shortage of money 127–8
intrinsic theory of monetary value 2–4, 12, 17, 155, 158
Iran 11, 29, 107
Isabella I, Queen of Castile 118, *118*
Islam in Eastern Africa 82, 94, 95
Islamic coinage 95–6, 104–10, *106*, *109*
issues of the age 149–69
   coinage and credence 150–9, *151*, *153–5*, *157*
   profits of fiction 165–9
   sovereign authority 160–5
Italy 115–16
   See also Milan; Venice

Jahangir, Mughal Emperor 108, *108*
James I, King of England 100, *100*, 153–4
Japan 6, 23–4, *24*, 34, 103
Java 104
Joachimsthaler (Bohemia) 21, *21*, 117
Johnson, Ben, *Eastward Ho!* 156
Johore 110
Jones, Norman 70, 72, 74, 75

jugate portraits 119
Julius II, Pope 116

kalima (Word or Logos) 104, 105, 107
Kan'ei ts h (Japan) 34
kashu (Goa) 29
Keynes, John Maynard 16
Kilwa Kisiwani, Tanzania *81*, 83, 85, 87, 94
Kilwa-type coins 84–6, **84**, 88–9, *88*, **90**, 91, **92**, 94, *95*, 97
koban (Japan) 24
Korea 103

Lampe, G.W.H. 63–4, 66
land banks 36
Landreth, David 62–3, 131, 150
larins 29, 110, *111*
late medieval European coinage 113–15
Latimer, Hugh, Bishop 157
lead coinage 96
lead and silver refining 23
Leo X, Pope 116–17
Leonardo da Vinci 30
Leoni, Leone 30, 116, *116*
lira Tron (Venice) 19, 115
literary theory 165–9
loan contracts 70–1, 72–3, 74
loan societies 37
loans. *See* credit; usury
Louis XIV, King of France 122
Low Countries 32, 36, 114, 129
  See also Netherlands

Macarius of Egypt 66
Magalhães Godinho, Vitorino 24–5
Malacca 110, 123, 125
Malaysia 110
Maldives 110
Malestroit, Jean Cherruies, Lord, *Paradoxes* 45
Mali 17
Malynes, Gerard de 7, 50, 51, 52, 160–1, 164
  Lex Mercatoria 51
  Treatise of Saint George for England 53–4
  Treatise of the Canker of Englands Common Wealth 52
marc (*marco*) 16, 18

market forces 49–50
Marlowe, Christopher 151
Marx, Karl 136
Mason, Robert, *A Mirrour for Merchants* 164–5
Massachusetts 123
mate tea 35
Matthew
  22:15–21 59–60, 61–4, 66, 78
  25:14–30 61, 66–8, 67
Maximilian I, Holy Roman Emperor 117
Medici, Alessandro de 116
Medici, Giovanni de 116–17
Medina, Bartolomé de, *Medina Codex* 22–3
Mehmed I, Ottoman Sultan 105
Melanchthon, Philipp 62
mercantile writers 50–7
mercantilism 6–7
merchandizing exchange 52
mercury and silver refining 21–3
Mestrel, Eloi 31
metals, sources of. *See* mines
Mexico 22–3, 123
Middleton, Sir Henry 99
Middleton, John 87, 91, 93
Milan 19, 20, 115, 116, *116*
Milles, Thomas 50, 51
  Custumers Alphabet and Primer 51–2
milling machines 30–2
mines
  African 17–18
  American 18, 22, 23
  European 19, 22, 23
  Japanese 23–4
  refining technologies 20, 21–2
Misselden, Edward 50, 51
  Circle of Commerce 55
monarchs, role of 7, 45, 47–8, 51, 55, 56–7, 63
monetary sovereignty. *See* sovereign authority
money as a measure 40–5
moneys of account 36
Mongolia 11
Monomotapa Kingdom 29
Montaigne, Michel de 149
monti di pietá 36
Morocco 109, *109*
Mote, F.W. 25

Muldrew, Craig 9, 10, 127, 129–30, 131, 136, 138, 144
Mun, Thomas 7, 50, 51
   Discourse of Trade 55–6
   England's Treasure by Forraign Trade 56–7
Muzaffar Shah, Sultan of Malacca 110

Nelson, Benjamin 71
Nepal 112–13
neschech (biting usary) 9, 61, 68–9, 73, 74, 75, 76, 77–8
Netherlands 20, 26, 32, 35, 120
Newton, Isaac 38, 161
nominalist theory of monetary value 3, 155
non-exchange uses of coinage 5–6

oban (Japan) 24, *24*
Olivier, Aubin 30
ontological status of money 149
opportunity cost 70
Oresme, Nicholas, *De moneta* 63
Orfini, Emiliano 116
Ottoman Empire 28, 105–7, *106*

pan amalgamation extraction method 23
paper money
   Chinese 25, 102–3
   English 128
   extrinsic value of 4
   Japanese 24
   origins of 1, 11–12, 152
Parable of the Talents 61, 66–8, *67*
pawnbrokers 36, 37
Pepys, Samuel 115
Persia. *See* Iran
Peru 22, 23, 27–8
Philippines 125
piece of eight (Spain) 26–8, *27*, 33, 125
Pieper, Renate 32
plate money 33
plåtmynt (Sweden) 33
Plato 167
poesy 165–9
political economics 39
popes, coinage of 116–17
Porteous, John 30
portraits on coins 19, 115–19, *116*, *118*, 122

Portugal
   African trade 87
   coinage 17–18, *18*, 32, 123
   gold trade 38
   India, influence on 29, 125
Potter, William 163
Price Revolution 13, 15, 28, 38
profits from trade 41–2, 43–4
propaganda coins 122
Prynne, William 166
purity of coins 16–17
Puttenham, George, *The Arte of English Poesie* 168

qian (China) 101–2
quantity theory of money 42, 43, 45, 155

Raizer, Cristobal 22
refining technologies *20*, 21–2
render unto Caesar. *See* Matthew 22:15–21
Rennaisance
   definition of 1, 171n1
   influence on coin design 115, 121–2
republics, coinage of 119–21, *120*
rings of silver 110, *111*, 112
ritual and religion 59–78
   God's stamp 61–9, *67*
   usury 69–78, *69*
Robinson, Henry 163–4
rupee (India) 29

Safavid coinage 107
saotomé (Goa) 29
Scotland 114
scrofula 6
seigniorage 4, 17
Sforza, Francesco, Duke of Milan 115
Shakespeare, William
   Cymbeline 64–5
   Merchant of Venice 70
Shanga, Kenya 82–3
shilling (England, 1503–4) 19
shortage of money 156
Sidney, Philip 167–8
Sidney, Robert 151–2
Sigismund of Tyrol 20, 117
silver
   demand for in China 24–6
   price of 13, 15, 28, 38
   quality of Peruvian 27–8

INDEX

refining technologies 21–4
rings of 110, *111*, 112
sources of 19, 21, 22–3
silver coinage 19–21, *19*, *21*, 27, 86
  See also pieces of eight
Sixtus IV, Pope 116
Smith, Adam 38
Smith, Henry 73
Smith, Sir Thomas, *A Discourse of the Commonweal of This Realm of England* 158–9, 162
Songo Mnara, Tanzania 85–6, 89, 90, 91, *92*
sources of metals. *See* mines
sovereign (England) 121
sovereign authority 47–8, 128–9, 158, 160–5
Spain
  coin designs 121
  coinage 18, 20, 118, *118*
  copper coinage 32–3
  gold and silver, quality of 27–8
  milling machines 31
  mines 23
Sri Lanka 112, 125
Stahl, Alan 18
stamp of God 60, 61–9, 67
stamps, coin 3–5
stock markets 37
Suleiman I, Ottoman Sultan 105, *106*
Sumatra 104
Summenhart, Conrad 70–1
Swahili coins 79–98
  background 80, *81*, 82
  context and archaeology 85–6
  international standards and the tri-metallic system 86–7
  the Islamic world 95–8
  mints and rulers 82–5, *83*, *84*
  routes to value 91, *92*
  Swahili coins 91, 93–5
  use of coins 88–9, *88*, *89*, 91
Sweden 33

tael ingots (China) 26
tarbit (increasing usury) 9, 61, 68–9, 73–4, 77–8
technologies 15–38
  copper coinage 32–4
  credit and banking 36–8

Eastern empires 28–9
global market for coins 15–16
gold, cycle of (1443–1560) 17–23, *18–22*
golden years, end of 38
hammered coinage 16–17, *17*
pieces of eight 26–8, *27*
silver, supply and demand 23–6, *24*
small change and moneys of account 34–6, *35*
uniform coinage, production of 30–2, 115
teston (Milan) 19, 30, 117
text tradition of coin design 101–10
  China and its neighbors 101–4, *102*
  Islamic world 104–10, *106*, *108–9*
Thailand 110, *111*, 112
Thaler (Bohemia) 21, *21*
theories of money. *See* extrinsic theory; intrinsic theory; nominalist theory; quantity theory
Thomas Aquinas 70
  Summa Theologica 41–2
Timbuktu 17
Timurid coinage 105
tin coins 110, 123, 125
tobacco leaves 35
token money 130, 152–4, *153–5*
Tokugawa Ieyasu 24
tongqian (China) 101–2
towns in Eastern Africa 80, *81*, 82
tri-metallic system of the East African Coast 86–7, 93
triple contracts 70–1
Tron, Nicolò 19, 115
Tunisia 107
Turkestan 105
Tyrol 19, 20–1, *21*, 117

uniform coinage, technology for 30–2
Ursentaler, Ulrich, the Elder 117
Usher, Payson, Abbot 30
usury 69–78, *69*
  Aristotle on 69–70
  biblical prohibition of 69
  contrast with trade 42
  and exchange rates 53
  and Parable of the Talents 66, 68
  practice of 8–9
  types of 61

value of goods 41–2
value of money 2–5, 45, 51, 53–4
Van der Wee, Herman 9, 36
Vaughan, Rice 158, 161
Vellerino de Villalobos, Baltasar 31
vellón (Spain) 32
Venice 18, 19, 115–16
Vietnam 103
visual properties of coinage 5–6
Vivero y Velasco, Rodrigo de 24
von Glahn, Richard 33

Ward, Richard 62
Welsers, bankers 22

wen (China) 101–2
Wennerlind, Carl 136, 137, 163
Willet, Andrew 77
Wilson, Thomas 9
wire coins 110, *111*
Wisselbank (Amsterdam) 38, 163
Wolley, Sir John 75
world markets 6–7
Wrightson, Keith 145

Yang, Bing 34
Yang, Lien-sheng 25
Yemen 106
Young, John 74